WITHDRAWN
UTSA Libraries

Economic Valuation of River Systems

NEW HORIZONS IN ENVIRONMENTAL ECONOMICS

Series Editors: Wallace E. Oates, *Professor of Economics, University of Maryland, College Park and University Fellow, Resources for the Future, USA and* Henk Folmer, *Professor of Research Methodology, Groningen University and Professor of General Economics, Wageningen University, The Netherlands*

This important series is designed to make a significant contribution to the development of the principles and practices of environmental economics. It includes both theoretical and empirical work. International in scope, it addresses issues of current and future concern in both East and West and in developed and developing countries.

The main purpose of the series is to create a forum for the publication of high quality work and to show how economic analysis can make a contribution to understanding and resolving the environmental problems confronting the world in the twenty-first century.

Recent titles in the series include:

Climate Change and the Economics of the World's Fisheries
Examples of Small Pelagic Stocks
Edited by Rögnvaldur Hannesson, Manuel Barange and Samuel F. Herrick Jr

The Theory and Practice of Environmental and Resource Economics
Essays in Honour of Karl-Gustaf Löfgren
Edited by Thomas Aronsson, Roger Axelsson and Runar Brännlund

The International Yearbook of Environmental and Resource Economics 2006/2007
A Survey of Current Issues
Edited by Tom Tietenberg and Henk Folmer

Choice Modelling and the Transfer of Environmental Values
Edited by John Rolfe and Jeff Bennett

The Impact of Climate Change on Regional Systems
A Comprehensive Analysis of California
Edited by Joel Smith and Robert Mendelsohn

Explorations in Environmental and Natural Resource Economics
Essays in Honor of Gardner M. Brown, Jr.
Edited by Robert Halvorsen and David Layton

Using Experimental Methods in Environmental and Resource Economics
Edited by John A. List

Economic Modelling of Climate Change and Energy Policies
Carlos de Miguel, Xavier Labandeira and Baltasar Manzano

The Economics of Global Environmental Change
International Cooperation for Sustainability
Edited by Mario Cogoy and Karl W. Steininger

Redesigning Environmental Valuation
Mixing Methods within Stated Preference Techniques
Neil A. Powe

Economic Valuation of River Systems
Edited by Fred J. Hitzhusen

Economic Valuation of River Systems

Edited by

Fred J. Hitzhusen

Professor of Environmental and Natural Resource Economics, The Ohio State University, USA

NEW HORIZONS IN ENVIRONMENTAL ECONOMICS

Edward Elgar

Cheltenham, UK • Northampton, MA, USA

© Fred J. Hitzhusen, 2007

Published by
Edward Elgar Publishing Limited
Glensanda House
Montpellier Parade
Cheltenham
Glos GL50 1UA
UK

Edward Elgar Publishing, Inc.
William Pratt House
9 Dewey Court
Northampton
Massachusetts 01060
USA

A catalogue record for this book
is available from the British Library

Library of Congress Cataloguing in Publication Data

Economic valuation of river systems/Fred J. Hitzhusen ... [et al.].
    p. cm. — (New horizons in environmental economics)
    Includes bibliographical references and index.
    1. Stream restoration—Economic aspects—Great Lakes Region (North America)—Case studies. 2. Watershed management—Economic aspects—Great Lakes Region (North America)—Case studies. 3. Rivers—Economic aspects—Great Lakes Region (North America)—Case studies. 4. Sustainable development—Great Lakes Region (North America)—Case studies. 5. Contingent valuation—Great Lakes Region (North America)—Case studies.
I. Hitzhusen, Fredrick J.
QH76.5.G72E26   2007
333.91'62153—dc22

                                                          2007025565

ISBN 978 1 84542 634 7

Printed and bound in Great Britain by MPG Books Ltd, Bodmin, Cornwall

Contents

Contributors

Ashraf Abdul-Mohsen is a Post-doctoral Fellow at the US Environmental Protection Agency, Washington, DC, USA. Ashraf Abdul-Mohsen's area of specialization is environmental and resource economics. His primary research interests focus on the valuation of river ecosystems and environmental improvements using stated preference methods such as contingent valuation. Particularly, his research covers issues related to the validity of contingent valuation and environmental justice. His current research focuses on using referenda and ballot initiatives to value water quality improvements.

Radha Ayalasomayajula majored in Economics in undergraduate studies from Andhra University, India, and received a Master's degree in Resource Economics from The Ohio State University, USA. She worked for a few years in the US with Rivers Unlimited, an environmental conservation organization, as a researcher. She now lives in India, working at the US Embassy. She also consults for the United Nations Development Program (UNDP) (India) in their Human Development Resource Centre. Her other interests include studying arts and craft through the ages, and understanding the relationship between science and spirituality.

Joana J. Ferreti-Meza obtained her BS in Economics at the Research Center "Centro de Investigacion y Docencia Economicas" (CIDE) in Mexico City and her MS in Agricultural, Environmental, and Development Economics at The Ohio State University (OSU) in the USA. She joined the multidisciplinary research center "Centro Regional de Investigaciones Multidisciplinarias-Universidad Autonoma de Mexico" (CRIM-UNAM) in Cuernavaca, Mexico, for a few years and specialized in the Economics of Water. She is currently working at the Ohio Department of Natural Resources (ODNR) on the Economic Assessment of Ohio's Natural Resources. She has enjoyed the support of sponsors such as Fulbright-COMEXUS, CIDE, and CRIM-UNAM. Her passion is working with multidisciplinary teams on behalf of the environment and people. She loves spending her free afternoons dancing or admiring art.

D. Lynn Forster is a professor in the Department of Agricultural, Environmental, and Development Economics at The Ohio State University.

His research focuses on issues relating to farms, agribusinesses, and the environment. Courses taught regularly include principles of food and resource economics, principles of agribusiness finance, and a PhD seminar. He serves as the department's undergraduate program leader and is a member of a regional research committee investigating agricultural finance issues.

Timothy C. Granata is a research scientist at The Ohio State University, specializing in eco-hydraulics and ecological engineering. He has over 18 years of experience in coastal zone and coastal watershed research. He is a licensed engineer and a registered senior ecologist.

Tim Haab is a professor in the Department of Agricultural, Environmental, and Development Economics at The Ohio State University. Dr Haab has over ten years' experience in the valuation of environmental amenities. He has published over 30 journal articles on valuation techniques, many appearing in the top environmental economics and economics journals. His 2002 book, *Valuing Environmental and Natural Resources: The Econometrics of Non-Market Valuation*, co-authored with Kenneth E. McConnell, has become a standard reference for nonmarket valuation researchers and practitioners.

Fred J. Hitzhusen is a Professor of Environmental and Natural Resource Economics in the Department of Agricultural, Environmental, and Development Economics and a Professor in the Environmental Science Graduate Program at The Ohio State University. Professor Hitzhusen has over 30 years of experience in doing research and teaching related to valuation of a wide range of natural resource and environmental systems in the US, Europe, and several developing countries. He has over 150 publications, has been Principal Investigator on $2 million+ in research grants, and has been a consultant to numerous organizations and served on several commissions concerned with the management of natural resources and the environment.

Marc Hnytka received his BSBA in Marketing from The Ohio State University. He is pursuing a graduate program at The Ohio State University in AED Economics. He plans to finish a master's degree and pursue a PhD, and is interested in studying the social, political, and economic components of human sustainability. Primary interests are peak oil, natural and energy efficient building practices, sustainable and organic agriculture, and renewable energy resources.

Stephen Irvin has over six years' experience in the field of environmental economics focusing mostly on renewable and alternative energy. Starting in 1999, Stephen began working as an economist for Rivers Unlimited to protect miles of rivers and streams throughout the Midwestern USA from industrial pollution and ecological degradation. He was awarded a National

Science Foundation Fellowship in 2002 at the University of California in Santa Barbara to study renewable energy in developing countries. This led him to Nepal in 2003, where he worked with the Nepali government providing subsidies for solar PV home systems, biogas digesters, and micro-hydro power plants. After leaving Nepal, he returned to the university to research the use of solar PV and biogas to reduce indoor air pollution in villages throughout Southeast Asia. Mr Irvin holds an MA in Economics from the University of California and an MS in Environmental Economics from The Ohio State University.

P. Wilner Jeanty is a PhD candidate in the Department of Agricultural, Environmental, and Development Economics at The Ohio State University. His research areas include environmental and development economics. Mr Jeanty has been working on estimating nonmarket economic benefits of using biodiesel fuel in Ohio, and assessing Ohio's biomass energy potential using geographic information system (GIS). His recent studies have focused on determining the effects of local development pressure on land prices, estimating nonmarket economic benefits of river restoration, and analyzing the impacts of civil wars and conflicts on food security in developing countries using instrumental variable panel data models. He has strong interests in applied econometric methods of nonmarket valuation, spatial econometrics and GIS, discrete choice analysis, and panel data modeling.

Sarah A. Kruse received her PhD from The Ohio State University in environmental and natural resource economics. She currently serves as the staff economist at Ecotrust, a nonprofit think-tank in Portland, Oregon, where she conducts research to identify and analyze linkages between economic, environmental, and social systems. Before graduate school, she also spent time as a Peace Corps Volunteer in Paraguay after completing a BS in Economics from the College of Wooster.

Sarah Lowder received her PhD in AED Economics from The Ohio State University in 2004, where she worked as instructor, teaching and research associate in various courses and projects on sustainable development (including the restoration of Muskingum River). She has held consultancies (with the World Food Program [WFP], OXFAM America, and Food and Agriculture Organization [FAO]) doing research on food aid, which was the topic of her dissertation. She is currently based in Bangkok, working as an economist for the Environment and Sustainable Development Division of the United Nations Economic and Social Commission for Asia and the Pacific. In her spare time she enjoys studying foreign languages; she is currently learning Thai, has studied Swahili in Tanzania, and is fluent in French.

Chris Murray holds a BA in Economics from Wittenburg College and an MS in AED Economics at The Ohio State University, and has more than six years' experience in economic and policy analysis in a broad range of issues including the environment and health care. Currently, Chris is employed by The Ohio Academy of Nursing Homes as the Director of Economic and Policy Analysis, where he performs analysis and research on issues in long-term care. Chris also teaches Economics at Capital University in Columbus, Ohio. Chris is the proud father of twin baby girls, Maya and Keira, and spends his free time doting on them.

Brent Sohngen is a professor in the Department of Agricultural, Environmental, and Development Economics at The Ohio State University. His research focuses on the economics of climate change and water quality issues. He leads a research-based outreach educational program on benefit cost analysis of conservation programs and water quality trading.

Allan Sommer is a watershed economist for the United States Department of Agriculture – Natural Resources Conservation Service, where he conducts benefit cost analyses for watershed protection and improvement projects. Allan has over six years of experience in environmental economics and policy analysis on topics ranging from greenhouse gas emissions to national park visitation. Allan holds a BS in resource management and an MS in environmental economics, both from The Ohio State University.

David Warren is Research Analyst at the Brookings Institution's Metropolitan Policy Program in Washington, DC, where he conducts research on urban sprawl, demographic change, and geographic disparities. David holds a master's degree in environmental economics from The Ohio State University and a bachelor's degree in economics and environmental policy from the University of Wisconsin-Green Bay. If he is not at his desk toiling with SAS or ArcGIS, there is a decent chance you will find him at RFK Stadium catching a Nationals game.

Ulrike Zika received an ScD from the Swiss Federal Institute of Technology in Zurich, Switzerland. Dr Zika is an aquatic ecologist/environmental scientist with expertise in ecological engineering, stream restoration, stream classification, and habitat evaluations in fluvial and coastal systems. She assessed woody debris, deflectors and dam removal as stream restoration tools in Ohio and in watersheds in Switzerland, and settlement processes and habitat requirements of a littoral marine fish in Spain. She currently works for Oxbow River & Stream Restoration, Inc. in Ohio.

Preface

This book reports on a large, eight-year research program at The Ohio State University to develop estimates of the benefits and costs of various water quality, infrastructure, scenic and historic river corridor impacts and improvements as a guide to economic analysis and public policy on river and related watershed restoration. The research is focused on evaluation of rivers in the Great Lakes region of the United States and involves a team of environmental economists, an ecological engineer and an aquatic biologist. When the various corridor impact or improvement benefits or values broadly conceived are expressed in a common economic metric and compared to their full economic costs, one has a basis for assessing river corridors in an economic development, welfare economic and public policy context.

Rivers have the potential to play an important role in the development of an economically depressed region by providing water supply, transportation, waste assimilation, and a wide array of recreation and tourism activities. The earliest civilizations were developed along rivers for the rich farmland along their banks and easy transportation. Irrigation of farm lands and water-powered industry were followed by large dams and locks for irrigation, residential and industrial water supply, recreation boating and fishing, hydroelectric power and barge transportation of products. Rivers as a source of waste disposal are increasingly in conflict with water supply, recreation and tourism, and major intra- and inter-country conflicts exist over the use rights to large river systems. Thus, the river corridor system or basin appears to be an important, but relatively underutilized focus for economic analysis and public policy.

Treatment costs, hedonic pricing, contingent valuation, benefit transfer and capture estimation, aquatic biology, and hydrodynamic-ecologic simulation models and methods are developed to value river corridor impacts. Impacts include household waste, pesticides, industrial toxics, gravel mining and agricultural run-off as well as improvements such as household waste treatment, dredging of toxics, zoning, greenways, dam removals, dam and lock upgrades, bike trails, towpaths, ramps and other recreational infrastructure. Some important innovations are introduced for codification of river supply and demand factors, testing for scope, context, and sequence effects in contingent valuation method (CVM) mail surveys, combining revealed and stated preference techniques, utilizing structured elicitation groups for assessing constructed vs static preferences, benefit transfer including recalibrated transfer functions, benefit capture including the linking of first-stage hedonic pricing and property tax/revenue models, distribution impacts and equity weighting for contaminated river segments, and integration of economic, ecologic, and aquatic models for assessing dam removal.

Finally, using codification, and benefit transfer techniques, the authors classify rivers particularly in the Great Lakes region of the US into major types and attempt to generalize some of the key findings from these research efforts to those prototype rivers. This should provide an analytical and public policy assist for both professional and citizen groups concerned about methods for valuing river systems, degradation, and the restoration of rivers, particularly as catalysts for economic development. The methods and results should have important implications for river systems in the Great Lakes region of the US as well as for Europe and other temperate, developed regions of the world.

Acknowledgments

My team of co-authors and collaborators represents the fields of environmental economics, ecological engineering, and aquatic biology as well as academic, governmental, non-governmental, and private consulting organizations. It has been rewarding to work for almost ten years with these talented professionals on evaluation of important water quality and infrastructure aspects of temperate climate river systems. Mike Fremont, President Emeritus of Rivers Unlimited, has been a constant source of inspiration and support and it is a great pleasure to dedicate this book to him. John Wells, the former president of the Morgan County, Ohio Chamber of Commerce and current mayor of McConnelsville, Ohio, was critical to the evolution of our first study in the Muskingum River corridor. Numerous other federal, state, and local government officials and private citizens have played crucial roles as well.

Financial support has come from a wide range of sources including: Rivers Unlimited, The Great Lakes Protection Fund, the George Gund Foundation, the US Fish and Wildlife Service, the Joyce Foundation, the Ohio and US Environmental Protection Agencies, The Cleveland Foundation, and numerous individual contributors. Data provided by the Northern Ohio Data and Information Service at Cleveland State University, as well as from numerous county auditor offices, made it possible to conduct several hedonic pricing analyses relating river water quality and infrastructure to river corridor residential property values. The editorial staff members at Edward Elgar Publishing have been very responsive and professional in all our dealings. Finally, my colleagues and staff members in AED Economics at OSU, Joan Weber and Judy Luke, have been outstanding in helping with all the fiscal, logistical, and editorial details of getting from field research to rough drafts to a final product.

To all of the above and others not mentioned specifically a big Thank You!

F.J. Hitzhusen

Dedication

Mike Fremont, President Emeritus of Rivers Unlimited, has been the inspiration and advocate for the series of studies presented in this book. He also continues to "carry the torch" for additional resource economic analysis of river corridors and systems. His admonition has been that "we should determine if cleaner, more inviting rivers make economic sense and, if they do, people are more likely to protect and restore them."

Mike is 85 years young, a graduate of Yale, a marathon runner, a canoe racer, and an effective environmental advocate. Rivers Unlimited is the nation's oldest statewide river protection and restoration organization. It has operated in Ohio since 1972 and has worked on over 180 projects to improve river corridor scenic beauty and water quality on behalf of citizen groups. Mike and his wife, Marilyn Wall, continue to be highly active and respected voices for river restoration and a wide range of other environmental and human dietary causes.

1. The role of biology and ecological engineering in watershed and river restoration

Timothy C. Granata and Ulrike Zika

INTRODUCTION

This chapter examines the role of biology and ecological engineering in watershed and river restoration by combining concepts of ecosystem theory into environmental design. The chapter is organized in the following way: first, a brief introduction to the biology of rivers and streams, second a review of different classification systems of streams, followed by the presentation of some accepted ecological concepts in riverine systems. Next, the use of classification systems and ecological theories is discussed in the context of the emerging field of ecological engineering. Some general restoration concepts for riverine ecosystems then are presented. Finally, the idea of sustainability is introduced followed by a discussion of how ecology, economic, and engineering principles go together to make a sustainable design.

BIOLOGY OF RIVERS AND STREAMS

In lotic (that is, flowing) systems, primary production is usually dependent on light intensity, and nutrients are supplied by the flow. In smaller streams in wooded areas with high shading, primary production is very low. This is also true for large "murky" rivers, where a large part of the light is absorbed in the turbid water column and cannot penetrate to the bottom. However, slow-flowing areas in large streams can have a high level of planktonic production, similar to lentic (lake and reservoir) systems. In contrast to other ecosystems (forests, lakes), rivers are not autonomous regarding their energy supply. They depend on surrounding ecosystem for energy input. In a small stream, Fisher and Likens (1973) found that less than 1 percent of the total energy input came from primary production within (autochtone

1

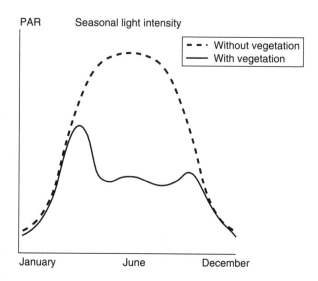

Note: PAR stands for Photosynthetically Active Radiation.

Figure 1.1   *The seasonal light intensity usually follows a sinus wave in open areas (dashed line), but vegetation cover in summer (solid line) can modify the pattern*

production), resulting in a one-sided energy flux from leaf litter from sur-rounding trees.

The primary producers in a stream are divided into two major groups: the attached community ("Aufwuchs") and macrophytes. Environmental factors such as water temperature, light availability, and flow are the most important factors determining the distribution and composition of the attached communities. Substrate type is mostly important for stability and different substrates with similar stability often show similar community structures. Water temperature and light intensity are difficult to separate because, during the coldest time of the year, light intensity is also the lowest. It is commonly known that in altered (channelized) streams where vegetation is missing and the stream bed is consequently exposed to full sunlight, algal growth can be extreme, reducing the hydraulic discharge abilities of the channel. Algae show seasonal cycles, given by the two factors light and temperature. Air temperature and light follow roughly a sinusoidal curve, with the light intensity peaking in June–July, dipping in December (Figure 1.1). This is the case in open areas, however vegetation, for example a forest canopy, can drastically change this pattern through shading (Figure 1.1).

In lotic systems, flow patterns, light intensity, and temperature changes occur on small spatial scales, resulting in a spatial zonation of algae, comparable to seasonal succession. Even on small spatial scales the availability of light and the influence of flow results in different community structures. For example, even relatively small rocks can be covered by different communities: upstream sections (with direct exposure to flow) are inhabited by flow tolerant species, downstream section with less tolerant species, and bottoms with low light tolerant species.

Higher order plants (macrophytes) are mainly influenced by the same factors (light intensity, temperature, and flow). It has been suggested that macrophytes "clean" the river by absorbing nutrients and therefore lower nutrient loads. Unfortunately, these plants only take up small amounts of nutrients themselves. However, their large surface area provides habitat for microorganisms (epiphytic "Aufwuchs"), which do play an important role in nutrient uptake. Additionally, the nutrient spiraling concept (Newbold, 1992) shows that N moves downstream, cycling from organic N retained in biomass to inorganic N dissolved in the water column, but it does not permanently remove nitrogen from the system. Denitrification is the microbially mediated process where, under low oxygen and anaerobic conditions, NO_3 is reduced to N_2. This biologically mediated process is irreversible, and therefore a sink for N.

Flow velocity is the most important characteristic of the lotic habitat. When water flows over objects, its velocity is increased resulting in pressure drag and skin friction drag. This shear stress, sediment transport, and temporal fluctuations of other important parameters (short-term high fluctuations of temperature, discharge, chemistry, and so on), make rivers a rather hostile habitat. Morphologic, physiologic, and behavioral adaptations made it possible for some species to inhabit stream habitats. Less than 4 percent of European insect species are found in lotic systems (Illies, 1978) and only one-third of all aquatic animals live in streams. The mechanical effect of flow, temperature, and food supply are the most important parameters determining which invertebrate species from a potential pool are found in any stream segment. For species adapted to these conditions, the stream habitat provides some advantages: (1) the constant movement of the water ensures a consistent gas exchange, facilitating respiration; (2) the permanent transport of nutrients and food (particular organic matter); and (3) specialized organisms avoid competitive pressure, resulting in localized high densities.

One morphological adaptation is how bodies are shaped. The force of the flow on bodies is proportional to the frontal area (pressure drag), the body surface (skin friction drag), and the viscosity of the medium. Therefore, for small animals, minimizing the hydraulic force by reducing the body surface (sphere or hemisphere) is most beneficial, while larger animals tend to reduce the size of the frontal area (streamlined body). Further, retention mechanisms such as suction cups or suction cup-like structures (for example, snails), threads to tie themselves to the substrate, or ballast to increase their body weight (sand and small gravel), are used to withstand the force of the flow. In addition to morphologic adaptations, physiologic adaptations (metabolism) and behavioral adaptations make life in flowing water possible. For example, filter feeders using nets to catch food particles use different mesh sizes depending on water velocities. Larger mesh sizes withstand higher velocities and the smaller surface area of the net is compensated with the larger volume filtered. Another important factor is drift and drift compensation. During events of high flow or poor water quality (low oxygen levels, pollution) animals can be transported against their will (catastrophic drift) but drift can also be used to willingly change position (behavioral drift) to get to areas with higher food supply or to avoid predators. Nevertheless, drift would eventually lead to deserted habitat areas. Therefore, drift needs to be compensated either through upstream migration of larvae against the water flow or compensation flights during their terrestrial adult stages.

Within the life span of an animal, different habitats are needed. In the aquatic system this is true for macro-invertebrates and fish. Most fish are large compared to macro-invertebrates and able to swim longer distances. Migration patterns are categorized as ozeanodromous (within an ocean, for example, herring), littoral (along coast lines), katadromous (spawning in salt water, adult stages in fresh water, for example, eels), and anadromous (spawning in fresh water, adult stages in salt water, for example, salmon). Habitat needs have to be put in perspective of life-history and life-cycle stages (Figure 1.2) and can encompass large spatial scales. Different habitat compartments are, for example, spawning sites, egg incubation areas, hunting grounds, nursery grounds, over-wintering sites, and so on. Migration connects the different habitat compartments. Northcote (1987) differentiates four types of migration: (1) optimization of the food supply, (2) avoidance of unfavorable conditions, (3) optimization of reproductive success, and (4) colonization of new areas. To ensure the survival of a population, all habitat requirements of all stages need to be filled.

The functional relationships between physical and biological factors influencing life stages of migratory fishes will be discussed for walleye (*Sander vitreum*). The walleye is a very important commercial and recreational fish species in Lake Erie (Leach and Nepszy, 1976). Figure 1.2 outlines the life stages of walleye in the river and lake. Adult walleye migrate from Lake Erie upstream to the spawning grounds in its tributaries, most importantly the Maumee and Sandusky Rivers in Ohio (USA). The

Walleye life cycle

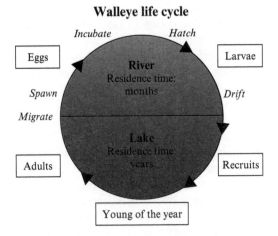

Note: River stages encompass several months, lake stages years.

Figure 1.2   Life cycle of migratory walleye: each life stage (eggs, larvae, recruits, young of the year, adults) is in need of different microhabitats within its macrohabitat (river and lake)

suitability of the spawning grounds is dependent on substrate type, water velocity, and depth. Eggs need favorable water temperatures, water quality (dissolved oxygen, pH, and ammonia), and water velocities to hatch. Larval walleye then drift back to nursery grounds in the Lake, their survival dependent on predators, water velocity, temperature, and the distance from the spawning grounds to the Lake. In the Sandusky River, mean velocities greater than $0.3~ms^{-1}$ reduced walleye survival presumably as a result of turbulence (Mion et al., 1998). Additionally, it was reported that longer distance between the spawning grounds and the lake may increase mortality as a result of starvation (Iguchi and Mizuno, 1999). If the mean river velocity is less than $0.3~ms^{-1}$, transport could potentially be slower than yolk absorption, causing fry to die. The juveniles that survive the drift will then spend several years in the lake until reaching maturity, when the river born fish are believed to return to their native rivers to spawn and complete the life cycle. These concepts are applied in case studies on dam removal and improved fish habitat in Chapters 4 and 5.

During migration, fish find many natural (water falls, debris dams) and man-made (dams, pipes) obstacles. Alterations of a river, such as channelization and straightening, are usually done to increase its hydraulic capacity, or conveyance. Instream vegetation, riparian vegetation, organic debris (for example, woody debris), and meanders are removed to decrease the roughness and facilitate flow. The most important negative influences of river regulation for fish habitats (see Swales, 1989) are: reduction of stream length (straightening), habitat diversity and environmental stability; removal of fish refuge sites within the channel; loss of pool-riffle sequence and aquatic vegetation; removal of riparian vegetation; changes in substrate composition, discharge regime, water quality and temperature; reduction of prey. Additionally, as fish-rearing habitat becomes limited, protection for fish from velocities during bankfull conditions is reduced, and banks become seriously eroded (Nunnally, 1978). Recently, there has been increasing emphasis on river restructuring to improve habitat conditions and water quality. One successful and economical method of reconstructing channelized streams to improve salmonid habitat is the introduction of large woody debris (Zika and Peter, 2002). Brown trout (*Salmo trutta*) and rainbow trout (*Oncorhynchus mykiss*) populations and stream morphology were monitored before and after the introduction of woody debris and compared to a control section lacking woody debris. Abundance and biomass of both brown and rainbow trout increased in the treatment section compared to the control, which was most pronounced during the winter months. Brown and rainbow trouts sought the woody debris structures for cover. Mean water velocities decreased and number and volume of pools increased in treatment sections, decreasing stream monotony.

To compare research results and advance our understanding of lotic systems, it is necessary to classify streams and rivers by common characteristic parameters. The following paragraphs summarize different classification approaches and discuss the use of the classification systems and ecological theories in the context of the emerging field of ecological engineering, general restoration concepts, and how ecology, economic, and engineering principles go together to make a sustainable design.

CLASSIFICATION OF STREAMS

Fluvial systems are very complex because running water changes over time and space. Flow, defined by the variables velocity and depth, is the most important ecological factor for plant and animal species in fluvial systems. Rivers and streams differ based on local climate, geology, and hydrology. Additionally, each stream is characterized by different factors such as morphology, communities, productivity, and so on, which change in response to climate, hydrology, or disturbances. Researchers and managers would like to compare different stream systems for restoration and conservation purposes. However, in order to conduct meaningful comparisons, a classification

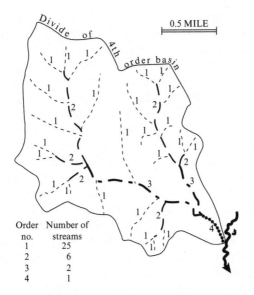

Note: The smallest tributary is given Order 1, when two Order 1 streams join, they form an Order 2 stream, when two Order 2 streams join they form an Order 3 stream and so forth.

Source: © 1957, American Geophysical Union. Reproduced by permission of the American Geophysical Union.

Figure 1.3   Stream Order classification modified from Horton (1945), in Strahler (1957)

scheme that integrates biological and physical aspects is necessary. Historically, several classification systems have been proposed and used. The most important ones will be summarized. For additional and more in-depth information, many more references exist that discuss different classification schemes but cannot be included in this short summary.

In a review by Strahler (1957), a variety of approaches to describe drainage basins systematically are presented. All of these approaches are based on river systems that developed by normal processes of water erosion. The most notable approach is the analysis based on stream order following a system slightly modified from Horton (1945). This principle allows the distinction of systematical classes of running waters with similar physiographic conditions. The smallest tributary (headwater) is given Order 1. When two Order 1 channels meet, a stream of Order 2 is formed. When two streams of Order 2 join, they form an Order 3 channel and so on (Figure 1.3). However, when a stream Order 1 joins a stream Order 2, the confluence stays Order 2.

If a sufficiently large sample is treated, order number has been found to be directly proportional to relative watershed dimensions, channel size, and stream discharge at that place in the system. So the higher the order number, the longer and larger the channel is within the river system. The smaller the order number, the higher the number of small streams but the smaller the average width, average and maximal depth, and discharge. Horton's bifurcation ratio (in Strahler, 1957) shows that on average there are 3.5 times as many streams of one order as of the next higher order. In other words, roughly four similar streams need to join to make the next higher river order.

Early typological classification is based on indicator fish or invertebrate species occurring in different zones of the river system (most notably Huet, 1949; 1954). These zones or regions follow from spring to river mouth, however, individual zones can be exchanged, overlapping, or even missing. Fish diversity usually increases with increasing river size. These classifications recognized the correlation between the biotic zones and abiotic factors such as bed slope, temperature, and water quality. Huet (1954) also incorporated a larger spatial scale, the valley form.

An important step in river classification was when Vannote et al. (1980) defined "The River Continuum Concept". This concept sees stream systems as longitudinally connected systems where downstream biological communities capitalize on upstream processing inefficiencies. This happens, for example, by way of drift and migration of organisms, or gradients of physical, chemical, and biological environmental factors. This concept is based on the energy equilibrium theory of fluvial geomorphologists and it is theorized that biological communities develop based on minimal energy loss. Although it has been mainly developed for natural, undisturbed stream systems, disturbances can be seen as mechanisms to reset the energy level. Alterations in biotic and abiotic variables result in changes in community structure and function, shifting the overall continuum response based on population time scales.

By viewing streams in a watershed context, Frissell et al. (1986) created a hierarchical framework for streams. It focuses on how streams are organized in space and change through time. First, hierarchical levels are defined, where the different levels are spatially nested within each other (see Figure 1.4). These system levels range in spatial and temporal scales from 10^3 m to 10^{-1} m and 10^6 years to 10^{-1} years. Secondly, after defining hierarchy levels, boundaries between the systems need to be delineated and differences and similarities of the systems determined. This model is intended for interpreting the natural variability in streams but not to reflect their organization.

A boundary is a zone of transition between differing ecological systems (or ecotones). They have specific chemical, physical, and biological

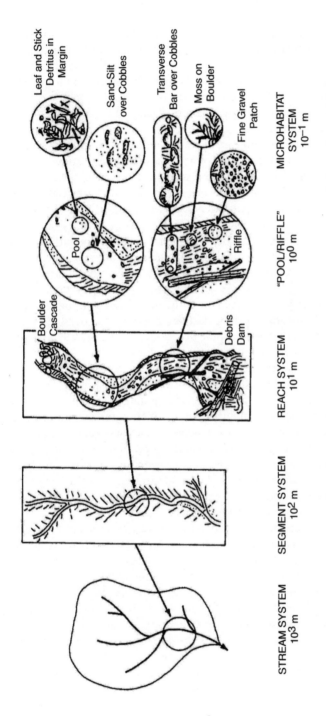

Note: Hierarchical levels are spatially nested within each other, ranging in spatial and temporal scales from 10^3 m to 10^{-1} m and 10^6 years to 10^{-1} years.

Source: Developed by Frissell et al. (1986), with kind permission of Springer Science and Business Media.

Figure 1.4 The hierarchical framework for streams

9

characteristics and interactions between such boundaries can vary in space and time, determining organization, diversity and stability of aquatic communities in streams. Naiman et al. (1988) suggest that rivers should not be seen as simple longitudinal systems where downstream and upstream ecosystems are connected by a unidirectional flow. Rather, they view river systems as a collection of resource patches separated by dynamic boundaries. The hierarchical framework approach by Frissell et al. (1986) is also applicable for boundaries, however, more specific information on boundary dynamics is needed to understand drainage basin characteristics.

Rivers and streams flow through terrestrial areas, connecting headwaters with lowland terrains. The interface between aquatic and terrestrial systems is called the riparian zone, which extends outward to the limits of flooding and upward to the canopies of streamside vegetation. Fluxes occur not only in a downstream direction, but also laterally, especially during events of high flow. Riparian zones widely determine structure and processes of the river system, for example, as sources of organic and inorganic material, and need to be seen from an ecosystem perspective (Gregory et al., 1991). According to Gregory et al. (1991) focusing on isolated components leads to an ecologically incomplete model. They present an ecosystem model based on the premise that geomorphic processes create a mosaic of stream channels and floodplains within a river valley floor.

Looking at streams from a geologic perspective, the Hierarchical River Inventory was proposed by Rosgen (1994; 1996). Its goal is to determine stream stability and to assess if a channel is changing as a result of geologic or anthropogenic processes, an important distinction for river restoration. Rosgen hypothesizes that stability is reached when the stream maintains its dimension, pattern, and profile without either aggrading or degrading sediments, thus there is a balance between erosive and depositional processes on time scales of years. The removal of riparian vegetation, among other improper management practices, leads to increasing bank and bed erosion and, ultimately, to instability of the channel.

Most recently, river character and behavior were analyzed at four interlinked scales by Briery and Fryirs (2000). Their approach is based on the hierarchical framework by Frissell et al. (1986) but for geomorphic river characterization. The four scales are: catchments, landscape units, river styles, and geomorphic units. The catchment unit encompasses the land surface area, which is defined by the watershed divide. Nested within the catchment is the landscape unit. It determines the boundaries for the river and is based on relief, morphology, and position of the river. The unit nested in the landscape is the river style, which are uniform sections, where no significant changes in discharge or sediment load occur. The last scale is the geomorphic unit, which is the fluvial landform largely determined by discharge, bed slope, and bed structure. Different geomorphic units (for example, pools and riffles) support different biotic assemblages. The type and number of geomorphic units are then used to determine connected processes along river stretches. In summary, the River Styles framework provides a geomorphic template for assessing biophysical processes within a catchment context (Brierly et al., 2002).

THE MARRIAGE OF ENGINEERING DESIGN AND ECOLOGICAL THEORY

Ecological engineering is an emerging field that combines engineering and ecological principles with the goal of developing a sustainable ecosystem design. In aquatic systems, engineers focus on hydraulics and hydrology over a range of spatial and temporal scales. Engineers see watersheds as the basic land unit in the hydrologic cycle. Watersheds intercept precipitation and deliver it to surface and ground waters. A fraction of the precipitation falling on the watershed infiltrates into the soil, while the excess water is transported in ephemeral rills down slope as runoff. Rills eventually empty into a network of surface channels. The channel network progresses from upstream to downstream starting with smaller flow or discharge rates coincident with the smaller spatial scales of streams (1 km) and creeks (10 km) to larger discharges and spatial scales for rivers (10–1000 km). In the upper watershed, the smaller channels are more numerous and are called headwaters. In the lower watershed (downstream), the channels are larger but less numerous. This surface continuum of channel size and flow regime defines the ecosystem structure (for example, habitat and species) and biogeochemical processes in the watershed.

Like most civil engineering disciplines, ecological engineering also considers human needs, but as part of a sustainable design. Rivers eventually meander to coastlines terminating the surface runoff process. Along the route from rills to rivers the surface flow transports not only water but also a solution of dissolved and suspended materials of inorganic and organic composition. Human populations are scattered over major watersheds with urban areas generally concentrated downstream of headwaters, on major rivers and in coastal zones. These large rivers provide a variety of societal services, including water supply, recreation, energy, navigation, sediment mining, and irrigation, but to name a few. For example, in the Midwest even today, headwaters are sparsely populated compared to the higher order tributaries downstream. These headwaters are in rural, agricultural areas and in many instances have been transformed into drainage ditches for the intense and productive row crops in the region. Farther downstream, the lower order tributaries give rise to villages and towns. Larger towns and cities occur as the river network develops farther downstream.

Historically, engineers have played a major role in harnessing rivers to aid in human settlement and growth in the watershed. Typical engineering solutions to flooding were to build levees and reservoirs, which disconnected the watershed, disrupting the flow of nutrients and sediments. To promote navigation, channels were dredged and locks and canals were built which destroyed habitat for keystone species and reduced biological diversity. To advance industry, mills powered by dams, and later hydroelectric dams, were built, modifying the sediment budget when particles accumulated behind the dams. Agricultural engineers laid tiles to drain agricultural fields, which increased peak discharge to river channels and carried fertilizers and pesticides along with these high flows. Environmental engineers built water treatment plants to withdraw drinking water and wastewater treatment systems to dispose of human wastes, enhancing nutrient levels in waterways.

Within the last two decades, engineers have realized that rivers are also important to biogeochemical cycles and ecosystem processes, hence the call for ecological engineering approaches to classical engineering problems (Liggett, 2002). By the 1990s, ecological engineering began gaining prominence and will probably establish itself as a field within environmental engineering within the next 20 years (Mitsch and Jorgensen, 1989).

The role of ecological engineering is in restoration of various components of the watershed. Early on, ecological engineers were concerned with constructed wetlands. More recently they have expanded into topics such as bioengineering methods in bank stabilization, dam removal, watershed restoration, alternative ecological technologies, and sustainable development. The future of water resources engineering is gradually merging with the field of applied ecology to provide benefits for humans as well as nature.

RESTORATION OF AQUATIC SYSTEMS

In ecological engineering, engineering design principles are combined with ecological aspects in the design to get past the "build it and they will come" doctrine. Although the restoration of aquatic systems usually targets river channels and adjacent floodplains, it should also encompass larger scales (for example, watersheds) and ecosystem dynamics (habitat, migrations, organisms, cycles, and so on) because of the connectivity of these scales and systems.

In restoring flowing water systems, such as streams, rivers and their riparian zones, the concept of natural channel design (NCD) promoted by Rosgen (1996) is one of the main tools used by ecological engineers during the design phase. Recently, the concepts of aquatic habitat design (AHD) proposed by Newbury (1995) have been used to enhance the NCD implementation of fish habitat (Phillips, 2005). The use of woody debris in NCD also has been investigated as a means of improving aquatic habitat through flow modification (Sheilds et al., 2001; Zika and Peter, 2002).

The Rosgen approach for NCD emphasizes stream morphology of a stable channel, where stability is defined by a net zero sediment load accumulating in the restored section or reach. Despite this definition, it is still debated whether or not sediment transport is tightly linked to morphology and geometry of the channel. One reason for the debate is that the methods for determining sediment transport give highly variable results (Clausen and Plew, 2004).

Despite the short-comings of the theory, the organized or systematic approach used in NCD has been appealing to environmental designers (Figure 1.5). Also practitioners have found that for many restored stream beds, the stream geometry does not change appreciably over time (Wilcock, 2004) unless high flows increase and modify sediment transport into the restored section.

SUSTAINABILITY OF WATERSHEDS – THE E^3 APPROACH

By combining ecology, economics, and engineering, what we call the E^3 approach, humans can provide a range of technological solutions for restorations. However, the science alone cannot always provide the best solution since social, political, and economic factors set the conditions for the restoration, which is the focus of this book. Further, restoration is not isolated in space or time within a watershed. Since river ecosystems are networks within a larger watershed, changes in one part of the watershed may affect processes in distant reaches of the network. Dams are a perfect example. Depending on the slope of the riverbed and landscape, and the height of the dam, ecological and hydraulic effects can vary upstream and downstream of a dam (Granata et al., forthcoming). For instance, a 1 m high dam (termed low-head) built on a mild sloping channel bed of 0.0001 m/m would impound water 10 kilometers upstream of the dam (1 m/0.0001 m/m), which is the same as a high-head dam of 10 m on a steeper riverbed of 0.001 m/m (10 m/0.001 m/m). Conversely, the low-head dam on the steep riverbed would create a backwater of 1 km (Figure 1.6).

Note: The restoration was based on Rosgen's natural channel design with habitat features based on Newbury's methods.

Source: Image provided by Steve Phillips, Oxbow River and Stream Restoration Inc.

Figure 1.5   Restoration of a G channel to a more stable C channel which provides riffle and pool habitat

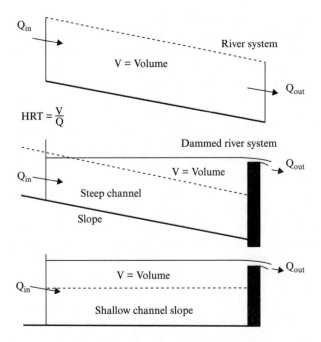

Note: A dam built on a steep channel bed will create a less extensive backwater upstream (middle) than the same dam on a mild slope.

Figure 1.6   Diagram of a free flowing river (top) where the volume of water stored is based on the flow, Q, based on the depth and velocity and the width of the channel

Thus, both dam height and watershed topography determine the volume of water stored in the channel. Another important aspect is the hydraulic retention time (HRT) of a channel, which is the time required to completely flush the impounded volume downstream. The theoretical HRT is volume/discharge. Using the example above, both dams would have roughly the same volume impounded behind the dam but they may have different HRTs depending on the flow regime. If the low-head dam were in a headwater of the watershed, and the high-head dam much farther downstream (as is the case of the Ballville Dam highlighted in Kruse et al., Chapter 4 of this book), then, except for any diversions, discharge would probably be higher for the downstream dam, and thus it would have a shorter HRT.

Because the river continuum details the ecological connections of flora and fauna upstream and downstream and in the adjacent floodplains, ecological engineers must recognize these connections in restoration designs and must plan for the whole watershed, not just a small section of the network. By planning on a watershed scale, ecological engineers can evaluate which projects are most beneficial to societal and natural interests. It makes no sense to remove a functional dam to restore only 2 kilometers of river when resources could be used to remove a non-functional, dangerous dam in a sensitive ecosystem. Here again, scientific judgment must be placed in a social, political, and economic context to provide the most effective management of the watershed. A concrete example dealing with dam removal and river restoration is water supply reservoirs. Humans will always need ample supplies of fresh drinking water. When considering storing water supplies in a watershed, ecological engineers must also consider keeping the rivers flowing. One way to accomplish both goals is to build off-line reservoirs alongside the river channel, not in it. In this way, water can be diverted into the reservoir during high flows (providing storage capacity, as well as flood control) and conditions of good water quality, to preserve the purity of the water supply, but not during base flows or spawning/incubation seasons of key species when ecosystems are most vulnerable to diversions. Another good example is the turn of the twentieth century flood control reservoirs build by A.E. Morgan for the Miami Conservancy District in southwestern Ohio. These were probably the first "ecological dams" in the country since they provided for both ecosystem and hydraulic connectivity longitudinally in the watershed, while assuring dangerous flood waves do not reach the Cities of Dayton and Cincinnati, Ohio (for more details, see Morgan, 1951).

CONCLUSIONS

Ecological engineering is still not an exact discipline and there are no design manuals for restoring streams, rivers or watersheds. Classifications of river systems, ecological theory, and design guidelines for wetlands, natural channels, and habitat are being used by restoration practitioners, but their success is varied and there is seldom a complete monitoring program to assess if restoration goals are attained. As the field of ecological engineering expands, research will provide better tools and design principles, which can be applied, tested and improved. In building these better tools, it is important to incorporate what we call the E^3 approach.

As the name ecological engineer implies, revitalizing our environment requires an interdisciplinary effort. Thus, it is absolutely necessary to not only integrate classical engineering principles with ecology, but also with economics and social sciences in order to successfully restore these complex systems in a sustainable manner.

REFERENCES

Brierly, G. and K. Fryirs (2000), "River styles, a geomorphic approach to catchment characterization: implications for river rehabilitation in Bega catchment, New South Wales, Australia," *Environmental Management*, **25**, 661–79.

Brierly, G., K. Fryirs, D. Outhet, and C. Massey (2002), "Application of the river styles framework as a basis for river management in New South Wales, Australia," *Applied Geography*, **22**, 91–122.

Clausen, B. and D. Plew (2004), "How high are bed-moving flows in New Zealand rivers?" *Journal of Hydrology (NZ)*, **43**, 19–37.

Fisher, S.G. and G.E. Likens (1973), "Energy flow in Bear Brook, New Hampshire: An interactive approach to stream ecosystem metabolism," *Ecological Monographs*, **43**, 421–39.

Frissell, C.A., W.J. Liss, C.E. Warren, and M.D. Hurley (1986), "A hierarchical framework for stream habitat classification: viewing streams in a watershed context," *Environmental Management*, **10**, 199–214.

Granata, T.C., F. Cheng, and M. Nechvatal (forthcoming), "Discharge and suspended sediment transport during deconstruction of a low-head dam," *Journal of Hydraulic Engineering* (in press).

Gregory, S.V., F.J. Swanson, W.A. McKee, and K.W. Cummins (1991), "An ecosystem perspective of riparian zones," *BioScience*, **41**, 540–51.

Horton, R.E. (1945), "Erosional development of streams and their drainage basins: hydrophysical approach to quantitative geomorphology," *Bulletin of the Geological Society of America*, **56**, 275–370.

Huet, M. (1949), "Aperçu dés relation entre la pente et les populations des eaux courantes," *Schweizerische Zeitschrift für Hydrologie*, **11**, 333–51.

Huet, M. (1954), "Biologie, profils en long et en travers des eaux courants," *Bulletin Français de Pisciculture*, **175**, 41–53.

Iguchi, K. and N. Mizuno (1999), "Early starvation limits survival in amphidromous fishes," *Journal of Fish Biology*, **54**, 705–12.

Illies, J. (ed.) (1978), *Limnofauna Europea.* Stuttgart: Fischer Verlag.

Leach, J.H. and S.J. Nepszy (1976), "The fish communities of Lake Erie," *Journal of the Fisheries Board of Canada*, **33**, 622–38.

Liggett, J.A. (2002), "What is hydraulic engineering?" *Journal of Hydraulic Engineering*, **128**, 10–19.

Mion, J.B., R.A. Stain, and E.A. Marschall (1998), "River discharge drives survival of larval walleye," *Ecological Applications*, **8**, 88–103.

Mitsch, W.J. and S.E. Jorgensen (eds) (1989), *Ecological Engineering: An Introduction to Ecotechnology*, New York: John Wiley & Sons.

Morgan, A.E. (ed.) (1951), *The Miami Conservancy District*, New York: McGraw-Hill.

Naiman, R.J., H. Décamps, J. Pastor, and C.A. Johnston (1988), "The potential importance of boundaries to fluvial ecosystems," *Journal of the North American Benthological Society*, **7**, 289–306.

Newbold, J.D. (1992), "Cycles and spirals of nutrients," in P. Calow and G.E. Petts (eds), *The Rivers Handbook*, Oxford: Blackwell Science, pp. 379–408.

Newbury, R. (1995), "Rivers and the art of stream restoration," in J.E. Costa, A.J. Miller, K.W. Potter, and P.R. Wilcock (eds), *Natural and Anthropogenic Influences in Fluvial Geomorphology*, Washington, DC: American Geophysical Union, pp. 137–49.

Northcote, T.G. (1987), "Fish in the structure and function of freshwater ecosystems: a 'top–down' view," *Canadian Journal of Fisheries and Aquatic Sciences*, **45**, 361–79.

Nunnally, N.R. (1978), "Stream renovation: an alternative to channelization," *Environmental Management*, **2**, 403–11.

Phillips, S. (2005), "Creating fish habitat in newly constructed channels: the restoration of Woodiebrook," *Ecological Engineering*, special issue.

Rosgen, D.L. (1994), "A classification of natural rivers," *Catena*, **22**, 169–99.

Rosgen, D.L. (ed.) (1996), *Applied River Morphology*, Pagosa Springs, CO: Wildland Hydrology Books.

Shields, D.F., N. Morin, and C.M.N. Cooper (2001), "Design of large woody debris structures for channel rehabilitation," paper presented at the Seventh Federal Interagency Sedimentation Conference, March.

Strahler, A.N. (1957), "Quantitative analysis of watershed geomorphology," *Transactions, American Geophysical Union*, **38**, 913–20.

Swales, S. (1989), "The use of instream habitat improvement methodology in mitigating the adverse effects of river regulation in fisheries," in J.A. Gore and G.E. Petts (eds), *Alternatives in Regulated River Management*, Boca Raton, FL: CRC Press, pp. 185–208.

Vannote, R.L., G.W. Minshall, K.W. Cummins, J.R. Sedell, and C.E. Cushing (1980), "The river continuum concept," *Canadian Journal of Fisheries and Aquatic Sciences*, **37**, 130–37.

Wilcock, P. (2004), "Coupling sediment transport and channel morphology: must we?" *Eos Transactions of the American Geophysical Union*, **85** (47), 45–55.

Zika, U. and A. Peter (2002), "The introduction of woody debris into a channelized stream: effect on trout populations and habitat," *River Research and Applications*, **18**, 355–66.

2. Codification, case studies, and methods for economic analysis of river systems

Fred J. Hitzhusen

CODIFICATION IN A SUPPLY-DEMAND CONTEXT

The preceding chapter by Granata and Zika reviews the role of biology and the evolution of various classification systems for rivers and streams over time and develops ecological engineering concepts for the restoration of riverine ecosystems. Fluvial systems are very complex and vary based on local climate, flow (velocity and depth), geology, hydrology, morphology, productivity, and so on. Comparison of different stream or river systems for restoration or conservation typically involves a classification system that integrates physical and biological aspects, such as classifying running waters with similar physiographic conditions, classification based on indicator fish or invertebrate species occurring in different zones of the river system, the river continuum concept or viewing streams in a watershed content.

Economic analysis of a river system requires classification or codification based on the principles of supply and demand. The supply side includes cost of production of various river system attributes and the demand side includes human preferences or willingness to pay (WTP) for attributes. Determining supply side factors includes identifying the hydrological, biological, and human-made infrastructure characteristics (for example, access points, parking, picnic facilities) of the river in question. On the other hand, demand-side factors require the identification of individual characteristics and demographic traits (for example, income, education, values, recreation levels) that influence the WTP of individuals for river-based amenities, that is, recreation, water quality, aesthetics, and so on.

The demand-side codification allows for an analysis of how supply-side characteristics either positively or negatively affect individuals, which issues are most important to those individuals, and how much they are willing to pay for a change in the level of a particular river related good or service. These demand-side characteristics are typically fairly consistent across sites, but the magnitude of individual characteristics such as age, income and distance from the river corridor affecting demand for the goods and services offered may vary considerably between sites.

The codification of supply-side factors allows for an assessment of the quality of the river ecosystem by examining how certain characteristics, either natural or human-made, have led to the current quality of the river or river corridor. A second aspect of supply side codification is the identification of river corridors that may serve as substitutes for the river of focus. The existence of unique supply-side characteristics such as Cuyahoga River National Park or Muskingum River, historic dams and locks may increase WTP for river-based amenities, but also make it more difficult to transfer the results to other river systems. Conversely, supply-side infrastructure characteristics such as access ramps and bike trails are more common and the resulting WTP for them may be more readily transferred to other sites facilitating policies and recommendations for a broader array of rivers from a limited number of detailed case studies. This issue is discussed in detail in Chapter 12.

CASE STUDIES

The selection of the case studies developed in Chapters 4–11 of this book was in part to reflect the variation in supply of and demand for various attributes of river systems in the Great Lakes US context. Appendix 2A.1 outlines the actual research projects/cases over the past eight years that have formed the basis for this book. They represent rural and urban river systems that have been impacted by household wastes, pesticides, industrial toxics, gravel mining in-stream, and agricultural run-off. The cases also represent actual or proposed improvements including household and municipal waste treatment, dredging of toxics, zoning, greenways, dam removals, dam and lock upgrades, bike trails, towpaths, access ramps, and other recreational infrastructure.

Detailed economic analysis in hydrologic and ecologic context of the impacts and improvements represented in each of the cases are presented in Chapters 4–11, after Chapter 3 assesses the overall WTP of Ohio residents for incremental changes in water quality in Ohio river and stream surface waters. An overview of the actual financial and economic analysis methods employed is developed in the next section of this chapter. A very large literature exists on these methods, too voluminous to fully develop here, but Chapters 3–11 will develop more methodological detail. A good survey of these methods can be found in *Revealing the Economic Value of Protecting the Great Lakes* (Cangelosi et al., 2001). Chapter 12 utilizes codification, and approaches including benefit transfer techniques to generalize these case results to other river systems.

FINANCIAL/ECONOMIC ANALYSIS METHODS

Box 2.1 summarizes a progression of river-related financial/economic values and analyses employed in the case studies and generalizations in this book. The notion of codification or classification of river systems has already been discussed in the first section of this chapter and approaches for the generalization of cost and benefit values to other river systems will be developed in Chapter 12. The remaining methods in Box 2.1 will be developed in the following section.

BOX 2.1   A PROGRESSION OF RIVER-RELATED FINANCIAL/ECONOMIC VALUES/ANALYSIS

1. Codification of river supply (for example, biotic, hydrologic, human-made infrastructure, history, culture) and demand (for example, income, education, environmental values) attributes or factors.
2. Market activity and prices generated locally and/or regionally from river-related amenities/businesses (for example, fishing, boating, hiking, biking, "birding", cooling industrial plants, shipping, mining, and so on).
3. Private and public expenditures for river-related disamenities (for example, avoidance, clean up and treatment costs).
4. Surrogate market or revealed preference measurers of river amenities gained or lost (use values):
    (a) Travel cost (TCM)
        ● willingness to incur private costs (including time and other travel related costs) to visit/use river amenities;
    (b) Hedonic pricing (HPM)
        ● amenities and disamenities capitalized into river corridor property values (primarily residential).
5. Constructed market or contingent valuation (CVM) surveys of stated preferences for river amenities or disamenities (use and nonuse values)
    ● willingness to pay or accept compensation.
6. Incidence of net economic gains and losses (unweighted and weighted) by income class, ethnicity, and so on.
7. Capture and transfer of benefits and generalization of results.

Financial vs Economic Analysis

Gittinger (1982) argues for distinguishing between financial and economic analysis, where financial analysis refers to net returns to private equity capital based on market or administered prices. Financial analysis also treats taxes as a cost and subsidies as a return; interest paid to outside suppliers of money or capital is a cost while any imputed interest on equity capital is a part of the return to equity capital. By contrast, Gittinger sees economic analysis as concerned with net economic returns to the whole society, frequently based on shadow prices to adjust for market or administered price imperfections. In economic analysis, taxes and subsidies are treated as transfer payments, that is, taxes are part of the total benefit of a project to society and subsidies are a societal cost. For purposes of this analysis, financial and economic analysis will refer to private and social concepts of economic efficiency analysis, respectively.

This financial vs economic distinction is important, but the complementarity of these analytical approaches is equally relevant. Financial analysis provides information on the profitability of a given river-related economic activity, for example, canoe rental to individual entrepreneurs or investors, and thus gives an indication of the incentive structure and potential adoption rate. Economic or social cost–benefit analysis attempts to determine profitability from a societal standpoint, taking into consideration externalities or environmental costs, pricing of underemployed or unemployed factors, currency evaluation, and so on. The appropriateness of these analytical alternatives depends on the question one is asking. Generally speaking it is relatively straightforward to assign values to the cost and benefit streams in financial analysis; market prices suffice. However, this is substantially more difficult in full social analysis.

Social costs and benefits or gains and losses from an economic perspective refer to the aggregation of individual producer and consumer measures of full willingness to accept or pay compensation. Individual preferences count in the determination of social benefits and costs and are weighed by income or more narrowly by market power. Since most policy changes involve economic gainers and losers, economists have developed the concept of potential Pareto improvement (PPI) to add up gains and losses to get net benefits. Simply stated, the concept holds that any policy change is a PPI or an increase in economic efficiency if at least one individual is better off after all losers are compensated to their original or before the policy change utility or income position. The compensation need not actually occur but must be possible (Dasgupta and Pearce, 1979).

These measures of social costs and benefits are often not fully reflected in current market prices (or in government regulated prices) as in the case of crop production in a watershed with high rates of soil erosion. This divergence results from several factors. First, government subsidies of inputs and/or outputs can lead to levels of input use and outputs which are not economically efficient or environmentally sustainable, such as in the case of agricultural chemicals and sediments. Technological externalities in agricultural production exist when external to the production and consumption of the resulting output, individuals, households or firms experience uncompensated real economic losses (or gains) from soil erosion, agricultural chemicals or other residuals. Secondly, because there are consumers willing to pay more and producers willing to sell for less than prevailing market or regulated prices, they receive what economists call consumer and producer surpluses. Finally, there may be willingness to pay to keep future economic options such as hydroelectric generation open (see Veloz et al., 1985) or WTP for existence value of aquatic species threatened by river water pollution which are not reflected in the market or government regulated prices of agricultural inputs and/or outputs.

Expenditures for River Disamenities

In some cases it is possible to get low-bound estimates of the value of various improvements to a river system by looking at reductions in private market or public expenditures as a result of the improvements. These expenditures or costs are usually referred to as replacement, restoration, clean-up or avoidance costs. For example, reduction of river pollution from either point or nonpoint sources (such as agricultural chemicals) may result in reductions in private or public water treatment (see Chapter 8) or avoidance costs. The clean-up costs of removing and safely containing toxic sediments from a river (see Chapter 9) represent a low-bound benefit or WTP estimate of not allowing toxics to build up to unsafe levels in bank and bottom sediments.

Revealed Preference Methods

Surrogate market, or revealed preference methods for measuring river amenities gained or lost include travel cost and hedonic pricing models. Surrogate markets involve actual, rather than hypothetical, behavior of producers and consumers in markets for private goods that are related to the public goods or river attributes of concern.

Travel cost models (TCMs) capture the WTP to travel to consume a public good or service. Visitors incur economic costs in time, travel, entry fees, on-site expenditures, and so on to participate in river-related recreation or sightseeing activities. These models assume weak complementarity between a desired river attribute or activity, for example, fly fishing, and the consumption expenditures related to that activity. Valuation of the opportunity costs or time is a complex issue that has received considerable discussion. Observing the number of sightseeing or recreation visits at different levels of travel and other related costs traces out a proxy demand function (see Chapter 10). This function can in turn be utilized to measure aggregate river-related recreation or sightseeing use value or the WTP for any incremental changes in one or more river attributes, for example, water quality. Count or random effects models which predict the number of trips as a function of price, income and other factors are also utilized and discussed in more detail in Chapter 7.

Hedonic pricing models (HPMs) relate vectors of environmental, community and actual property attributes to the price or assessed market value of individual property parcels (usually residential housing and accompanying lots), that is, a characteristics theory of value. The models assume that the housing market is well functioning (for example, no major problem with concessionary sales) and that buyers can perceive the relative impact of various property, community, and environmental attributes, for example, river water quality on the value of property. Differentiation of individual attributes in the hedonic price equation gives marginal implicit prices of each in terms of impacts on property values. By linking these HPMs to tax revenue functions, it is possible to show potential changes in property tax revenues for various local government services resulting from river corridor water quality or infrastructure improvements (see Chapters 6 and 10).

Stated Preference Methods

Contingent valuation models (CVMs), or constructed market survey measures of stated preferences are utilized when there are no prices or revealed preferences for the attributes of concern. These CVM surveys attempt to measure WTP or willingness to accept (WTA) directly for various attributes of a river system such as improved water quality, access ramps, bike trails, docks, and so on. Contingent valuation models provide a more inclusive measure of various use and nonuse values than the TC and HP revealed preference models. Various forms of strategic behavior of respondents and bias are a concern and many methodological innovations including referendum formats have addressed these concerns. Other techniques such as testing for scope, context and sequence effects in mail surveys and determining any effect of assuming well-defined stated vs constructed preferences have also been developed and applied. Finally, hydrodynamic simulation and aquatic models are utilized to better predict changes in stream regimes, habitat and fish populations from dam removal which makes CVM surveys more realistic. The foregoing methodological variations are discussed in more detail and applied in Chapters 3–6, and 9.

Benefit Transfer and Capture

The *benefit transfer* (BT) method allows researchers to obtain economic estimates using secondary data or previous studies for a distinct alternative application (Brookshire and Neill, 1992). For example, Desvouges et al. (1992, p. 675) describe a typical BT setup as follows: "The river where an existing study was conducted is termed the 'study site' and the river under consideration for a water quality improvement the 'policy site'. The estimated benefits are transferred from study site to policy site."

Bergstrom and De Civita (1999) state that BT methods can be divided into three major groups: fixed value transfer, expert judgment, and value estimator models. While there is no doubt that this broad classification captures most if not all the BT schemes, there remains a question as to the relation of these three sets. The authors present these groups as implicitly disjoint. However, there are examples of BT schemes which simply do not fit into a single category. For instance, the authors describe an example of a fixed value transfer where "the total benefits of fishing at the policy site may be estimated as the product of some standard value per fishing day at the study site and total fishing days at the policy site." However, in choosing an appropriate study site a researcher would need to consider the similarities shared with the policy site. Since there are no formalized rules for a policy site selection, the researcher is ultimately bound to use an expert judgment approach (see French and Hitzhusen, 2001; and see Chapters 10 and 12).

Another example that illustrates the dependence between the major types of BT is the Bayesian technique. The Bayesian technique, as described, for example, by Atkinson et al. (1992), implicitly incorporates an expert opinion in choosing a prior. On the other hand, by the Bergstrom and De Civitis classification, the inference procedure itself would fall under a value estimator model. Thus, this methodology is a combination of expert judgment and value estimator models. There are perhaps other examples that illustrate this interdependence, but the general conclusion is that a BT scheme may involve a combination of characteristics from two or more of the major types. Recognition of this fact is important for better classification of future BT studies. Figure 2.1 summarizes benefit transfer and capture approaches.

In environmental economics, including analysis of river systems, *benefit capture* generally relates to attempts by environmental economists to estimate nonmarket or extra market values for various natural resource projects

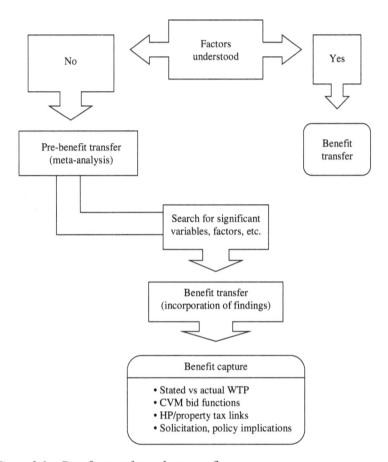

Figure 2.1   Benefit transfer and capture flow

or policy initiatives. Pearce and others have suggested that environmental economics is concerned with not just the measurement or estimation but also the capture and internalization of benefits and costs from environmental service and residual flows (Pearce and Turner, 1990). Considerable research activity over the past 20 years or more has been concerned with nonmarket valuation techniques for measuring and transferring the economic benefits including nonuse values of various environmental goods and services from an analysis site to a policy site (for example, Boyle and Bergstrom, 1992; French and Hitzhusen, 2001; Smith, 1993; Walsh *et al.* 1992). Less attention has been given to how some of these benefits could be captured and by whom in a real world policy context. Chapter 6 of this book explores two approaches for answering these questions in the context of a benefit cost analysis of several proposed upgrades to the Muskingum River corridor in southeastern Ohio.

From the statements and literature review thus far, it is evident that the concept and protocol for benefit capture is not clearly defined in the literature. For example, early research by Bishop et al. (1983) found differences between willingness to pay and willingness to sell as well as differences between hypothetical and actual WTP for goose-hunting permits in Wisconsin. Many subsequent studies have had similar findings. Actual WTP would appear relevant in assessing benefit capture if one is concerned about increasing the probability of nonmarket WTP values actually being paid.

It is also clear that benefit capture is not a homogenous phenomenon. For example, one could posit a continuum with pure private market goods at one end and pure public goods at the other. Samuelson actually set this up as a dichotomy in his classic "The pure theory of public expenditure" (1954). Randall (1981) protests the use of the concept of "public goods" and proposes in its place four categories of goods: divisible exclusive goods; divisible, nonexclusive goods; indivisible exclusive goods and indivisible, nonexclusive goods. This is helpful since a benefit-capture related continuum would appear more useful for natural resource and environmental policy than a dichotomy.

Using the river corridor example, bait shops and other private businesses on the river or related to the use of the river, as well as those in communities within a commuting pattern of the river would expect direct revenue increases and the resulting sales tax increases from more recreational use of a river with improved infrastructure and/or higher water quality. Likewise, property values may also increase. However, as soon as the assessed value of the property increases, property taxes will increase and the revenues will accrue to local governments and school districts unless millage rates are decreased. As indicated earlier, hedonic pricing can empirically establish the implicit prices of various amenities or river corridor improvements and these first-stage hedonic models can in turn be linked to tax revenue functions through the millage rates.

Attempts to estimate WTP for some preservation or nonuse values of the river corridor with contingent valuation survey methods provides additional points on the continuum. With careful CVM protocols these values can be accurately estimated, but those responsible (for example, local and state governments) for corridor improvements do not receive any immediate payments from the CVM-based WTP of bidders. The CVM aggregate WTP evidence could be used to eventually increase public support for increased taxes to upgrade corridors. In addition, carefully constructed bid functions, may identify demographic factors associated with WTP that could make efforts to increase taxes and/or fund-raising more effective.

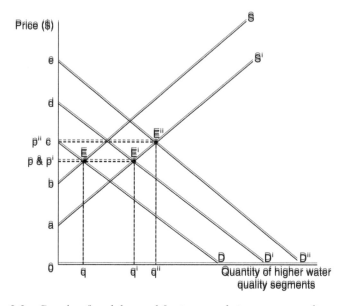

Figure 2.2   Supply of and demand for improved river water quality

It is possible to illustrate some of these points on the continuum of benefits from the river corridor example with the simple demand and supply graphic in Figure 2.2. Assume that improvement in water quality from improved household septic systems results in increased supply of clean water habitat and increased demand for fishing, boating, residential riverside properties and aquatic biodiversity. The increase in market-demand related expenditures for increased fishing and boating and the increase in prices for riverside residential properties are represented by the shift in demand to D' and the new E' equilibrium price and output, p' and q'. This results in an increase (E, E', q', q) in the expenditure rectangle which represents the market benefits that would be "captured" by bait shops, boating supply outlets, realtors, and so on.

The nonmarket estimate of WTP for increased aquatic biodiversity determined from a CVM survey is represented by the further shift in demand to D''. Since this represents stated not actual WTP, the implied increase in the expenditure rectangle is hypothetical. However, the benefit arguments so far have only included actual market expenditures not changes in producer and consumer surplus or social welfare. If the latter measures are included, the total change in economic welfare from the improved water quality is represented by the area a, e, E'' minus c, b, E, and could be considered the maximum estimate of benefit capture in this example.

The differences in the expenditure rectangles and the net changes in the economic welfare are not trivial in scope or concept. This has been the source of long-term debate between economists doing regional or input-output models and analysis and economists doing applied welfare economic, for example, nonmarket, benefit cost models and analysis. It depends, of course, on the accounting stance in space and time one takes to generate results for a particular purpose or audience, that is, benefits and costs to whom (see Gittinger, 1982; Hitzhusen, 1984; Schmid, 1989; and Appendix 2A.2). Are we speaking to fishers, boaters, businessmen including real estate agents and house builders in a river-related city or to a state or regional public agency concerned with public policy on natural resource management in river corridors? Chapter 10 develops an empirical comparison of these alternative accounting stances and measures of economic value.

Incidence of Economic Gains and Losses

The previous discussion has related to methods and measures of aggregate economic efficiency. The incidence of benefits and costs or the distribution of net benefits is also important for public policy. In fact, it may be more important to actual public decision-making than measures of aggregate economic efficiency.

There is a tendency among economists to accept the notion of trade-offs rather than any complementary relationships between equity and efficiency (for example, Okun, 1975) or between meeting basic needs and increasing economic growth. In fact, the earlier Harod-Domar growth model and the growth-weighted project evaluation procedures that followed in the 1960s assumed that income inequality was a stimulus to economic growth, that is, the rich and government recipients of project benefits were assumed to have higher "marginal propensity to save" (MPS) and thus stimulate investment and growth.

This can lead to the conclusion that poverty and inequality concerns are more subjective and normative and/or are detrimental to the desire for economic growth. However, when one looks at the assumptions of neoclassical welfare economics regarding constant marginal utility of economic gains and losses, costless transfers to compensate losers and hypothetical compensation of losers, these appear no less subjective or even speculative. Numerous polls suggest that most citizen-consumers believe that a marginal dollar to a poor person is worth more than a marginal dollar to a rich person. Transfers to compensate for income losses or to reallocate income are not likely to be costless and hypothetical compensation is unlikely to be politically feasible. It is also likely that satisfying the most basic of needs in human health and nutrition (for example, Hicks, 1980) is a complement or precondition, rather than a substitute, for economic growth. Finally, the MPS arguments can fail on two counts: MPS rates may not be much higher for the rich, and even if they are, they may not result in higher rates of investment in the poor region. Thus, efficiency analysis and pronouncements are also not free of normative judgments.

In addition to the longstanding Lorenz curve and Gini coefficient measures of income and wealth concentration, economists have proposed several alternative methods for evaluating income inequality and distribution impacts including: (1) shadow pricing under or unemployed labor, (2) the constrained maximum redistribution or setting a redistribution minimum and maximizing economic efficiency, (3) unweighted distribution of net benefits by income, region, ethnic group, and so on, (4) provision of alternative weighting functions and assessment of their distribution consequences for decision-makers, (5) explicit weighting of net benefits by income class based on past tax or expenditure decisions including switching or equity weights (Ahmed and Hitzhusen, 1988), and (6) survey techniques to directly elicit income distribution weights.

Some prior evidence existed regarding a higher proportion of low income and people of color residing in a polluted 30-mile segment of the Mahoning River in northeastern Ohio. This led to a focus on the distribution and equity weighting effects of a proposed US Corps of Engineers project to dredge and safely dispose of toxics embedded in the banks and bottom sediments which is discussed in Chapter 9.

REFERENCES

Ahmed, H. and F. Hitzhusen (1988), "Income distribution and project evaluation in LDCs: an Egyptian case," paper for International Association of Agricultural Economics meeting, Argentina, August.

Atkinson, S.E., T.D., Crocker, and J.F. Shogren (1992), "Bayesian exchangeability, benefit transfer, and research efficiency," *Water Resources Research*, **28**: 715–22.

Bergstrom, J.C. and P. De Civita (1999), "Status of benefits transfer in the United States and Canada: a review," *Canadian Journal of Agricultural Economics*, **47**: 79–87.

Bishop, R., T.A. Heberlein, and M.J. Kealy (1983), "Contingent valuation of environmental assets: comparisons with a simulated market," *Natural Resources Journal*, **33**: 619–33.

Boyle, K.J. and J.C. Bergstrom (1992), "Benefit transfer studies: myths, pragmatism and idealism," *Water Resources Research*, **28**: 657–63.

Brookshire, D.S. and H.R. Neill (1992), "Benefit transfers: conceptual and empirical issues," *Water Resources Research*, **28**: 651–5.

Cangelosi, A., R. Weiher, J. Taverna, and P. Cicero (2001), "Tools of the trade: placing a value on Great Lakes environmental benefits," *Revealing the Economic Value of Protecting the Great Lakes*, Washington, DC: Northeast-Midwest Institute and National Oceanic and Atmospheric Administration, ch. 7.

Dasgupta, A.K. and D.W. Pearce (1979), *Cost–Benefit Analysis: Theory and Practice*, London: Macmillan.

Desvouges, W.H., M.C. Naughton, and G.R. Parsons (1992), "Benefit transfer: conceptual problems in estimating water quality benefits using existing studies," *Water Resources Research*, **28**: 675–83.

French, D.D. and F.J. Hitzhusen (2001), "Status of benefit transfer in the United States and Canada-Commout," *Canadian Journal of Agricultural Economics*, **49**: 259–61.

Gittinger, J.P. (1982), *Economic Analysis of Agricultural Projects*, Baltimore, MD: Johns Hopkins University Press.

Hicks, N. (1980), "Is there a trade-off between growth and basic needs?" *Finance and Development*, June: 17–20.

Hitzhusen, F.J. (1984), "Cost benefit analysis: cornerstone or Achilles' heel of social science?" ESO 1230, Department of Agricultural Economics and Rural Society, The Ohio State University, Columbus, OH, November.

Hitzhusen, F.J. (2005), "Reader," for AEDE 807, "Economic analysis for collective choice," The Ohio State University, Columbus, OH, June.

Okun, A.M. (1975), *Equity and Efficiency: The Big Trade-Off*, Washington, DC: Brookings Institution.

Pearce, D.W. and R.K. Turner (1990), *Economics of Natural Resources and the Environment*, Hemel Hempstead: Harvester Wheatsheaf.

Randall, A. (1981), *Resource Economics: An Economic Approach to Natural Resource and Environmental Policy*, Columbus, OH: Grid Publishing.

Samuelson, P.A. (1954), "The pure theory of public expenditure," *Review of Economics and Statistics*, **36**, 387–90.

Schmid, A.A. (1989), *Benefit Cost Analysis: A Political Economy Approach*, Boulder, CO: Westview Press, pp. 157–90.

Smith, V.N. (1993), "On-market valuation of environmental resources: an interpretive appraisal," *Land Economics*, **69** (1): 1–26.

Veloz, A., D. Southgate, F.J. Hitzhusen, and R. Macgregor (1985), "The economics of erosion control in sub-tropical watersheds: a Dominican case," *Land Economics*, **61** (2): 145–55.

Walsh, R.G., D.M. Johnson, and J.R. McKean (1992), "Benefit transfer of outdoor recreation demand studies, 1968–88," *Water Resources Research*, **28**: 707–13.

APPENDIX 2A.1

Table 2A.1 The Ohio State University river economics corridor research projects

Study/ location	Pollution source	Environmental economic valuation	Study objectives	Expected benefits from study
Muskingum River valuation	Household/domestic wastes, point source from industries and households	Benefit transfer, hedonic pricing, CVM	Quantifying net benefits resulting from selected corridor improvements: dam and lock repair, sewer and septic, zoning and greenway extension	• Increasing residential property value • Increase tax base, and tax revenues to local governments and school districts of the area • Increasing recreation and therefore benefiting the local economy • Preserving historical dams and locks
Dredging/toxic removal in Mahoning	River bed sediments, heavy metal deposits from industries	Travel cost method, CVM, hedonic pricing	Determine benefits from improved water quality from dredging of toxics	• Healthier ecosystem • Lifting human health advisory • Recreational activities • Increasing residential property value • Enhancing local economy
All surface waters in Ohio	All NPDES and PTI permits to discharge	CVM	Derive demand function for available pollutant assimilative capacity (APAC)	• Fulfill requirements of the Clean Water Act by estimating benefits lost from a lowering of water quality

Case study	Source/problem	Methodology	Objective	Benefits
Pesticide study in Maumee	Non-point source agricultural runoff	Multivariate regression analysis	Determine benefits from alternate farm management	• Protocol of OEPA evaluation of discharge permits • Provide farm management practices that reduce treatment costs • Increase water quality
Dam removal study in Ohio and New York	Sediments behind the dam structure, impeding migration of sport fish to Great Lakes, disruption of natural stream habitat	Ecological-engineering-economics methodologies	Estimate benefits with and without dam removal and/or restoration	• Increased walleye population in the river and Lake Erie • Increased tourism • Restoration of natural stream habitat • Free flowing river for non-motorized boating and fishing
The Great Miami River valuation	Gravel mining, point sources from households and industries	Hedonic pricing, benefit transfer	Determine benefits from decreased/regulated gravel mining, septic improvements, increased access to the river for recreationists	• Healthier ecosystem • Increasing residential property values • Increase tax base • Increased recreation
The Cuyahoga River Valley	Sewer overflows, industry point sources	Hedonic pricing CVM Benefit transfer Codification Supply and demand factors	Determine benefits to improvements in water quality, recreation/transport infrastructure and historic legacy	• Increased recreation • Residential housing values increase • Increased visitation for historic legacy

APPENDIX 2A.2

Table 2A.2　Financial and "economic" efficiency analysis

	Financial (private) vs Economic (social cost–benefit) ◄·············· Accounting stance ··············►	
Focus:	Net returns to equity capital	Net returns to society (long and wide view)
Prices:	Market or administered (may assume that markets are perfect or that administered prices have compensated for imperfections), interest rate	May require "shadow prices" e.g., monopoly in markets e.g., external effects e.g., unemployed or underemployed factors e.g., labor e.g., overvalued currency e.g., opportunity cost of capital
Taxes:	Cost of production	Part of total societal benefits
Subsidies:	Source of revenue	Part of total societal cost
Purpose(s):	Measure of profitability to individual investors Indication of incentive to adopt or implement	Measure "profitability" or net economic returns to society Determine if government investment is justified on economic efficiency basis
Income distribution:	Can be measured re: net returns to individual factors of production such as land, labor and capital	Is not considered in economic efficiency analysis. Can be done as separate analysis or as weighted efficiency analysis

Source:　Hitzhusen (2005).

3. Estimating willingness to pay for additional protection of Ohio surface waters: contingent valuation of water quality

Stephen Irvin, Tim Haab, and Fred J. Hitzhusen

INTRODUCTION

Public good provision usually depends on governmental intervention in the form of regulations or standards. Regulations try to level the playing field in markets involving externalities like pollution. The difficulty comes in trying to find the right amount of externality to regulate. In the case of rivers, state environmental protection agencies must decide the amount of pollutant discharge to permit into the water. The rules regarding discharge consider rivers and other water bodies as surface water.[1] The amount of pollution admitted to enter surface water determines the level of public good available to all consumers. These rules are the regulations established by state governments to protect rivers and provide nonmarket benefits to the public in the form of cleaner water, recreational opportunities, scenic views, and healthy diverse ecosystems. They are usually confusing to the general public, but have value in that they facilitate the provision of a public good.

In Ohio, the regulation concerning discharge into surface waters is known as the Antidegradation Rule. The rule outlines a quality criterion for surface water, known as the minimum pollutant assimilative capacity, which states the level at which surface water cannot accept any more discharge in order to protect human health and wildlife (Ohio EPA, 2003). Any discharge beyond this point would create hazardous conditions.

Some surface waters have the ability to assimilate more pollution without violating the quality criterion. In these cases, the ambient quality of surface water is above the quality criterion and the water is said to have an available pollutant assimilative capacity. This capacity is measured by the amount of a regulated pollutant the water has the ability to assimilate without endangering human health and wildlife or disrupting the water's designated use.

To abide by the Clean Water Act, the Antidegradation Rule requires a specific amount of available capacity to be set aside to protect the overall health of the surface water ecosystem. All the surface waters in Ohio are assigned to a water quality category that prescribes a minimum percentage of available pollutant assimilative capacity needed to remain in that water quality category. Each percentage is known as "set-aside" to regulators and polluters. For example, imagine a company applies to discharge 100 gallons of a pollutant into the nearest surface water and the regulation for that surface water requires 25 percent set-aside. If the pollutant lowers assimilative capacity by one percent per gallon, then only 75 gallons of the pollutant is permitted by the agency for discharge. The amount of available pollutant assimilative capacity varies from water body to water body, and even among segments within the same water body. The ambient concentration of pollutants is dynamic, so pollutants are constantly being physically and chemically altered in a specific volume of surface water. This means each permit to discharge requires regulators to review the current available pollutant assimilative capacity.

A water quality criterion requiring available pollutant assimilative capacity to be set-aside could be considered additional protection. This raises the question: what are the economic benefits and costs associated with this additional protection? Applications to discharge usually come from industries increasing their production levels, growing communities needing to discharge more household waste, new businesses, and construction or development projects. Generally when there is a need to discharge more pollutants, there is the potential for economic growth in a community. Restricting economic growth invokes a cost in the lost opportunity for jobs and future tax revenue. Yet, there are also benefits from additional protection. Greater water quality could lead to an increase in ecosystem health, greater recreational values, lower drinking-water treatment costs, and increased property values.

VALUING WATER QUALITY

Contingent valuation is a frequently employed technique for valuing nonmarket benefits derived from environmental goods and services. The valuation estimates produced have been used in the legislative and judicial branches of our governmental bodies for decades, mainly to inform policymakers and assess compensation for natural resource damages. Contingent valuation is a survey-based technique which estimates the social benefits provided by a change in the level of environmental goods and services contingent on a market making them available for consumption.

Rivers can be considered public goods which provide environmental benefits that all consumers can consume jointly without any one consumer reducing the amount available for another to consume. Public goods are considered valuable to society, but are usually not included in a relevant observed market where their value can be expressed in monetary terms (McFadden and Leonard, 1993). Contingent valuation asks individuals to state their willingness to pay (WTP) for a specific change in the quantity of a public good contingent on the creation of a hypothetical market or other means of payment (Bishop et al., 1983). Because responses are contingent upon the hypothetical market described, this technique came to be called the contingent valuation method (Brookshire and Eubanks, 1978; Brookshire and Randall, 1978; Schulze and d'Arge, 1978).

Contingent valuation surveys should be composed of three parts: (1) a detailed description of the good being valued and the hypothetical market under which it is made available to the respondent; (2) questions that elicit a respondent's WTP for a specific change in the quantity of the good being valued; for example, "Would you be willing to pay \$___ to protect _____ amount of water quality?" and (3) questions about individual characteristics of the respondent. Previous studies identify a person's age, household income, and level of education as predictive of WTP, thus successful estimation with these variables could be partial evidence for reliability and validity of contingent valuation estimates (Mitchell and Carson, 1989).

A response to the WTP elicitation question infers what change in income, coupled with a change in the level of public good provided, leaves a respondent's utility level unchanged (Mitchell and Carson, 1989). Essentially, WTP represents the amount of income that a respondent would give up to make him or her indifferent between two scenarios: (1) their initial level of income and amount of public good, and (2) their income minus their WTP and the new amount of public good. Suppose $u(\mathbf{x}, q)$ is a person's utility function with a vector of private goods $\mathbf{x}$ available at the price vector $\mathbf{p}$, and a public good q available at price w. Prices, $\mathbf{p}$, are presumed to be determined in the market, but price w may not be determined by the market (Haab and McConnell, 2002). The utility function measures consumer preferences by ranking different bundles of x and q. We assume all individuals will maximize their consumption preferences subject to their budget constraints. We see this as:

$$\max_{x,q} u(\mathbf{x}, q) \tag{3.1}$$
$$\text{such that } \Sigma_i p_i x_i + wq \le y$$

where $y \equiv$ total household income. From this maximization problem we formulate the indirect utility function, $v(\mathbf{p}, q, y)$, as

$$v(\mathbf{p}, q, y) = \max_{x,q} \{u(\mathbf{x}, q) \mid \Sigma_i p_i x_i + wq \leq y\}$$

Looking at the indirect utility function of an individual, we can represent WTP as a specific amount of income spent to receive an increase in public good from q_0 to q_1.

$$v(\mathbf{p}, q_0, y) = v(\mathbf{p}, q_1, y - WTP) \qquad (3.2)$$

where an individual's utility changes from

$$u_0 \equiv v(\mathbf{p}, q_0, y)$$

to

$$u_1 \equiv v(\mathbf{p}, q_1, y) \geq u_0 \text{ as } q_0 \rightarrow q_1 \qquad (3.3)$$

with $v/\delta q > 0$ when $q_0 < q_1$.

The dual to utility maximization is expenditure minimization, where the expenditure function, $e(\mathbf{p}, q, u)$, is defined as

$$e(\mathbf{p}, q, u) = \min_{x,q} \{\mathbf{p}\mathbf{x} + wq \mid u_1(\mathbf{x}, q_1) \geq u_0(\mathbf{x}, q_0)\} \qquad (3.4)$$

WTP is considered the difference in expenditure functions, represented as

$$WTP \equiv e(\mathbf{p}, q_0, u_0) - e(\mathbf{p}, q_1, u_0) \qquad (3.5)$$

This represents the amount of income that a respondent would give up to make him or her indifferent between the original state, income level y and level of public good q_0, and the new state, income level $(y - WTP)$ and q_1 (Haab and McConnell, 2002). Essentially, WTP is the perceived value of the public good to the respondent. We are simply measuring "value" in dollar increments. So WTP equals value, and value equals benefits. Whenever WTP or benefits are mentioned, inherent value is inferred.

Once the mean WTP is estimated for a specific change in a public good, it is multiplied by the total number of people affected by this change to find the total benefits from the proposed change. To estimate net benefits, you subtract total costs from total benefits. With respect to efficiency, a positive net benefit economically justifies the proposed change in the level of the public good provided.

THE CONTINGENT VALUATION SURVEY

Assigning a value to setting aside available pollutant assimilative capacity would provide an estimate of the total social benefits from having this add-itional protection. These benefits should be incorporated into the benefit–cost analysis conducted by the regulator when evaluating permits to discharge pollutants that would lower the available capacity. The first step is to survey those who would benefit from setting aside available capacity. In November 2001, 3000 licensed automobile drivers in Ohio were randomly chosen to receive a contingent valuation survey.[2]

The survey began by stating the intention to ask questions related to pollution control in Ohio's surface waters and provided respondents with a definition of surface waters taken directly from the Antidegradation Rule (Ohio EPA, 2003). The first set of questions examined personal connections to surface water. Respondents were asked for the shortest distance from their home to surface water, how often they are around or in contact with surface water, and their connection to organizations that preserve or improve surface water. Variables such as distance, contact rates, and organizational ties are indicative of behavioral preferences that would normally be observed in an established market, thus providing one avenue for checking the validity of our nonmarket WTP estimates. Intuitively, if a respondent either lives close to surface water or is in regular contact with surface water, or both, they would be expected to be fairly knowledgeable about the water's quality and able to assign a value (WTP). Looking at Table 3.1, we see that respondents live close to surface water and are in regular contact with it. A higher proportion of respondents allocating time to organizations that protect or increase the quality of surface water would increase our mean WTP estimates. The time invested to water organizations might

Table 3.1   Personal ties to surface water

Variable	Mean
Distance	1.5 miles
Contact rate	67 times per year
Connection to surface water organization(s)*	23%

Note: * Percentage of respondents who stated that they were an employee, volunteer, or sent monetary contributions to organizations that preserve or improve surface waters.

Table 3.2   Water quality perceptions

Variable	Proportion
Average percentage of very clean water	18%
Average percentage of somewhat clean water	32%
Average percentage of somewhat dirty water	31%
Average percentage of very dirty water	19%
Proportion who stated "species diversity" as the best measure of water quality	48%
Proportion who stated nonpoint sources as the largest source of water pollution in Ohio	27%

relay stronger preferences for additional set-aside. Of the entire sample, 23 percent stated they worked, volunteered, or sent contributions to surface water organizations, with only 8 percent actually investing their own time.

The second section of the survey retrieves perceptions about the quality of surface waters. Respondents were asked to group all of Ohio's surface waters into various degrees of cleanliness, pick the best measurement of water quality, and define the largest source of water pollution in Ohio. Looking at Table 3.2, we see that respondents perceive an average level of cleanliness, almost half agree with what the Ohio Environmental Protection Agency (EPA) uses as their best measurement of water quality, and 27 percent acknowledge nonpoint sources as the major contributor of pollutants into Ohio's surface waters. These three questions measure how informed our respondents are about water pollution and the accompanying regulation. While it is difficult to quantify "somewhat clean", the Ohio EPA's 305(b) reports show surface waters being dirtier than an average level of cleanliness. Also, the diversity of species within surface water is the first test used by the Ohio EPA to find the overall quality of that particular water body. While discharge is important, the nonpoint source runoff from farms in Ohio contribute around 90 percent of the pollution found in surface waters. From these simplistic metrics, we get the impression that our respondents on average are not very knowledgeable about Ohio's current level of water pollution and its regulation.

The attitudes of respondents toward big business and environmentalism were also explored to check for possible protest bias or green bias. A high proportion of negativity toward big businesses could engender a protest against paying for additional water quality protection. Respondents may feel the polluter should pay for this added protection and understate their true WTP. Conversely, environmentalists may overstate their true WTP to make an "environmental statement". Mitchell and Carson (1989) and

Table 3.3   *General attitudes*

General attitudes toward business and the environment	
Proportion of respondents who believes businesses should be allowed to lower APAC	24%
Relative importance of improving or preserving the natural environment (scale: 1 = extremely important to 5 = not at all important)	1.8

Diamond and Hausman (1993) argue that contingent valuation respondents usually consider their WTP as a contribution to "general" environmental causes. In our case, there is the possibility of both a protest bias and a green bias. Table 3.3 shows that over 75 percent of the respondents are against businesses lowering available pollutant assimilative capacity. Plus, the average level of environmentalism is 1.8 on a scale of one to five, where the preservation or improvement of the natural environment being extremely important was coded as one and not at all important as five. How these biases influence our mean WTP estimates is uncertain. They may cancel each other out, but only a follow-up survey could determine the amount of bias.

Because we are valuing a state regulation, it is important to determine if our respondents are representative of Ohio's voting population. We compare results from the 2000 Census in Ohio (US Census Bureau, 2000) to the demographics from our survey, see Table 3.4. The contingent valuation survey respondents are older, with slightly higher incomes, and more years of education. There is an equivalent ratio of males to females, similar household sizes, number of urban versus rural households, and employment level characteristics. Overall, we have a reasonably representative sample.

In 1993, a blue-ribbon panel of experts organized by the National Oceanic and Atmospheric Administration (NOAA) defined methodological guidelines for a contingent valuation survey (NOAA, 1993). Following these guidelines we created a dichotomous choice referendum scenario where respondents voted on whether or not they would pay a proposed dollar amount to set aside 25, 50, 75, or 100 percent of available pollutant assimilative capacity. First, respondents were told two facts: (1) communities and businesses use surface waters as one way to dispose of pollutants, and (2) all surface waters have an EPA-defined water quality criterion, known as a minimum safety level, and that in some cases the quality of the water is above this level.

Each survey described one of four possible changes in the percent of set-aside to be enforced by the state. For a conceptual grasp of the change being

Table 3.4 Demographic comparison

Variable	2000 Census	CV survey respondents
Population (18 years or older)	8 464 801 people	548 people**
Average household income*	$51 996	$54 600
Average retirement income*	$14 132	$24 034
Employment 16 years or older in labor force		
Employed:	95%	87%
Unemployed:	5%	13%
Retired:	34%	41%
Gender		
Male:	49%	53%
Female:	51%	47%
Average age	36 years	59 years
Average household size	2.49 people	2.33 people
Geographic location of household		
Urban:	81%***	77%****
Rural:	19%***	23%****
Educational attainment (for people 25 years or older)		
8th grade or less	4%	1%
Some high school	12%	6%
High school diploma	39%	30%
Some college/associates degree	25%	35%
Bachelor's degree	14%	16%
Graduate or professional degree	7%	13%
High school graduate or higher	84%	94%
Bachelor's degree or higher	21%	29%

Notes:
*   Translated to 2001 US dollars with the consumer price index.
**   With 548 cases out of 560 responses, 1 respondent was 17 years old and
       11 respondents did not give their age.
***   Percentage of population living in a metropolitan area in July of 1999.
****   Based on respondent's zip code lying within a GIS population density polygon greater
       than 5000 people.

posed, the following example for 75 percent set-aside was provided, "if a river's safe level allows 100 gallons of a pollutant, this policy would only allow 25 gallons of it to be released into the water." Respondents were then asked if they understood the proposed change, and were told that if a majority voted for the change all Ohio taxpayers would make a one-time tax-deductible payment on next year's state income tax return to pay for the monitoring and enforcement costs. The survey declared that this would be the only payment required, that the money would be managed by a special fund which could only pay for the monitoring and enforcement costs and that without the proposed change, surface water would still be safe enough for humans and wildlife. After establishing these conditions, respondents were asked: "If an election was being held today and the one-time tax-deductible payment was $__, would you vote for protecting __% of the water quality above all safe levels?"[3]

The wording of our WTP elicitation question removes the complexities of pollutant types and presents a familiar scenario to the respondent. Simply, would you pay this price for this quantity of a specific good? Unfortunately, the question offers little information about what a person would actually pay. All we know is if they answered yes, their true WTP is greater than or equal to the proposed cost. If they answered no, their true WTP is less than the proposed cost.

Each survey differed in two ways: the proposed set-aside, and how much it would cost. The surveys were mailed out with a normal distribution of bid amounts having a mean of $50. Previous evidence of Ohio angler and boater WTP for water pollution control supports using this range of dollar amounts (Irvin, 2001). The response rate was 20 percent, which is lower than what should be expected with a mail survey. We were able to use 548 observations in our model, see Table 3.5.

ESTIMATING WILLINGNESS TO PAY

In 1976, Bruce Turnbull published a paper discussing the nonparametric estimation of a distribution function with incomplete data (Turnbull, 1976). Seven years later, Stephen Cosslett expanded Turnbull's work toward a consistent estimator that does not require assuming any functional form for the distribution of WTP, also known as the Turnbull distribution-free estimator (Cosslett, 1983). Boman et al. (1999) derive a lower-bound expected value function of WTP for the Turnbull estimator. We use this lower-bound Turnbull estimator because it offers the least restrictive approach to estimating WTP without the need to assume any arbitrary distribution of WTP (Haab and McConnell, 2002). Also, Vaughan et al. (2000) compared 12 methods of estimating WTP for a river improvement project in Brazil and discovered the Turnbull model as the most reasonable choice for a conservative lower-bound estimate. When evaluating changes in a regulatory policy as we are here, one should aim for conservative estimates. Haab and McConnell (2002) describe the Turnbull model as:

$$E(WTP) = \Sigma_i \, b_i (Z_{i+1} - Z_i) \ \forall \ i \epsilon [0, k] \qquad (3.6)$$

Table 3.5 *Survey distribution*

| Proposed dollar amount | Policy change proposed (minimum % of set-aside in all surface waters)) | | | | | | | |
| | 25% | | 50% | | 75% | | 100% | |
	Mailed	Responses	Mailed	Responses	Mailed	Responses	Mailed	Responses
$5	32	5	32	6	32	6	32	10
$10	37	6	37	6	37	6	37	4
$20	52	13	52	12	52	12	52	10
$30	77	17	77	18	77	12	77	14
$40	113	18	113	17	113	24	113	28
$50	128	25	128	23	128	17	128	30
$60	113	19	113	22	113	19	113	23
$70	77	18	77	15	77	6	77	14
$80	52	13	52	6	52	11	52	4
$90	37	12	37	4	37	5	37	6
$100	32	4	32	6	32	8	32	6
Total	750	150	750	135	750	126	750	149

where $Z_i = N_i / R_i$, $Z_0 = 0$, and $Z_{k+1} = 1$.
Let

$E(WTP)$ = expected lower-bound willingness to pay;
b_i = proposed dollar amount;
$\bar{Z}_i$ = monotonically increasing proportion of observed no responses to b_i;
k = number of proposed dollar amounts;
N_i = number of no responses; and
R_i = number of responses.

A monotonically increasing $\bar{Z}_i$ enforces our assumption that the proportion of no responses should continuously increase as b_i increases. Where there is not a monotonic increase, the proportions of no responses are pooled together. The model assumes that the proportion of respondents whose WTP falls between two proposed dollar amounts have a WTP equal to the lower of the two dollar amounts (Haab and McConnell, 2002). The model also assumes WTP is always greater than or equal to $0. Multiplying each proposed dollar amount by the probability of WTP being between that amount and the next highest amount results in a conservative lower-bound estimate for all distributions of WTP from zero to positive infinity (Haab and McConnell, 2002). The variance of $E(WTP)$ is shown by Haab and McConnell (2002) to be:

$$\mathrm{Var}(E(WTP)) = \Sigma_i (\bar{Z}_i (1 - \bar{Z}_i)/R_i)(b_i - b_{i-1})^2 \ \forall i \in [1, k] \tag{3.7}$$

Each of the proposed percentage changes in set-aside (25 percent, 50 percent, 75 percent, and 100 percent) were evaluated separately by the Turnbull model to find their lower-bound expected WTP. We assume people pay $0 for 0 percent set-aside, which results in five WTP estimates for different levels of the public good we are valuing. We found an expected WTP of $41.55 for setting aside a minimum of 25 percent available pollutant assimilative capacity in all of Ohio's surface water, $38.08 for 50 percent, $45.04 for 75 percent, and $43.38 for 100 percent. To illustrate the Turnbull model, the calculations for 25 percent are shown in Table 3.6.

SOME LIMITATIONS OF CONTINGENT VALUATION

A contingent valuation survey is hypothetical. We do not ask respondents to hand over the money they said they were willing to pay. As a result, some respondents may have stated a WTP different than what they would actually pay. There is also evidence of respondents tending to agree regardless of their

Table 3.6 *Expected lower-bound willingness to pay for a minimum of 25 percent set-aside in all surface waters*

b_i	R_i	N_i	Z_i^*	Z_i	$(Z_{i+1} - Z_i)$	$b_i(Z_{i+1} - Z_i)$	$(Z_i(1 - Z_i)/R_i)$ $\times (b_i - b_{i-1})^2$
$5	5	1	0.20	0.091	0.091	0.00	0.413
$10	6	0	0.00	Pooled	Pooled	Pooled	Pooled
$20	13	5	0.385	0.385	0.294	1.47	1.821
$30	17	9	0.529	0.392	0.007	0.14	1.402
$40	18	7	0.389	Pooled	Pooled	Pooled	Pooled
$50	25	10	0.400	Pooled	Pooled	Pooled	Pooled
$60	19	7	0.368	Pooled	Pooled	Pooled	Pooled
$70	18	5	0.278	Pooled	Pooled	Pooled	Pooled
$80	13	11	0.846	0.690	0.298	8.94	1.646
$90	12	8	0.667	Pooled	Pooled	Pooled	Pooled
$100	4	1	0.250	Pooled	Pooled	Pooled	Pooled
$100+	–	–	1.000	1.000	0.310	31.00	–

Notes:
$E(WTP) = \$41.55$.
$\mathrm{Var}(E(WTP)) = \$5.28$.
* Z_i = proportion of observed no responses to b_i without imposing a monotonic increase.

true preferences, known as "yea saying" (Blamey et al., 1999). To address the hypothetical bias in contingent valuation, List and Gallet (2001) compiled 29 experimental studies that compare what respondents state they are WTP to what they actually pay. Of these 29, there were 18 examples that ask a dichotomous choice WTP question like the one in our survey. They show the difference between stated and actual WTP in the form of a calibration factor, which equals the proportion of stated WTP to actual WTP. From these 18 examples, they found stated WTP being, on average, 2.27 times greater than what people were actually willing to pay. Assuming our results are hypothetically biased in a similar way, we divide our stated WTP estimates by 2.27 to estimate what our respondents would actually pay, see Table 3.7.

Actual WTP estimates were then used as the response variable in a bivariate second-order polynomial regression model to interpolate WTP estimates between our point estimates for 25, 50, 75, and 100 percent set-aside. The resulting WTP function is expressed as

$$E(WTP) = 0.6138q - 0.0044q^2 \ \forall \ q \in [0, 100] \qquad (3.8)$$

where $E(WTP)$ = expected lower-bound willingness to pay, and q = the percent of available pollutant assimilative capacity set-aside.

Table 3.7   Calibration for possible hypothetical bias

Minimum set-aside	Stated WTP	Calibrated actual payment
0%	$0.00	$0.00
25%	$41.55	$18.30
50%	$38.08	$16.78
75%	$45.04	$19.84
100%	$43.38	$19.11

Usually, contingent valuation surveys employ different econometric methods to estimate WTP. Vaughan et al. (2000) show how the same data can yield vast differences in WTP depending on the estimation method. Out of 12 different methods, Vaughan et al. (2000) estimated a maximum WTP of $140 per household and a minimum of $2.34 per household. Clearly, discrepancies of such magnitude require scrutiny when performing a benefit–cost analysis involving contingent valuation surveys.

In addition, Brown et al. (1996) demonstrate that estimates from dichotomous choice WTP questions are 2.45 times greater than "open-ended" questions for stated WTP, and 1.56 times greater for actual payments. This implies our estimates of actual payments could still be overstated even with the Turnbull model. Thus, we control for dichotomous choice and WTP characteristics when obtaining a calibration factor from the List and Gallet (2001) paper. The 18 experiments included valuing both public and private goods, in-person, mail, and telephone surveys, and comparing two estimates from the same person versus two estimates from different people. This may also introduce some measurement error to our calibration efforts.

Even if all we are assuming is correct and our WTP estimates are conservative, there will still be some level of asymmetric information favoring the polluter. When a polluter applies for a permit to discharge they must list the costs of alternative disposal methods. But it is almost impossible for the Ohio EPA to check the validity of these cost estimates with current resources. The difficulty of estimating benefits from setting aside available capacity is further compounded when moving from the valuation to the benefit–cost analysis stage because of a polluter's ability and incentive to overestimate the costs of alternative disposal scenarios.

SUMMARY AND CONCLUSIONS

The Antidegradation Rule outlines the minimum percent of available pollutant assimilative capacity required to be set aside based on the ambient

Table 3.8   Set-aside levels for Ohio EPA water quality categories as outlined in the Antidegradation Rule

Ohio EPA surface water quality categories	Minimum percent of set-aside required
Outstanding national resource waters	100%
State resource waters	70%
Superior high quality waters	35%
General high quality waters	0%
Limited quality waters	0%

quality of the receiving surface water (that is, background load), see Table 3.8 (Ohio EPA, 2003). We see that some surface waters already have a large percent of their capacity protected under the rule. Using a contingent valuation survey, we have shown Ohioans value this protection for all surface waters. In other words, our estimations for WTP apply not just to the surface waters with protection, but to all surface water in Ohio. The current regulation does not assign the additional protection in some surface waters. Thus, the Ohio EPA may not be providing the Pareto optimal allocation of a public good.

If we examine the relationship between levels of the public good provided and mean WTP in our regression model, we find requiring 20 percent set-aside across all surface waters equates to a mean WTP of $10.52 per person. This translates into $89 million in total social benefits, simply by aggregating across the residents of Ohio who were 18 years or older in 2001. Adult Ohioans are placing a mean value, based on their individual preferences, of $10.52 to protect 20 percent of available pollutant assimilative capacity in all of the state's surface waters.

If a 20 percent minimum does not occur, there would be a social opportunity cost of $89 million to the state. The opportunity for social benefits is possible but becomes an opportunity cost when a zero percent regulation is chosen instead of a 20 percent regulation. The same interpretation holds for intermediate changes. If the Ohio EPA started with a minimum of 20 percent and then decided to increase it to 40 percent, we would see total social benefits around $59 million, when moving from 20 percent to 40 percent. Again, there would be a social opportunity cost of $59 million if a 20 percent policy were maintained. What we find is Ohioans willing to pay more for a zero to 20 percent change than a 20 to 40 percent change, or diminishing returns from the additional protection of assimilative capacity.

An important point to remember is that these estimates are for changes in a statewide policy. It would be erroneous to apply these WTP estimates to specific cases of discharge. The reason is scale. Imagine that a company applies to increase their discharge of a particular pollutant that would lower available assimilative capacity by 10 percent within a 5-mile stretch along a specific river. Our respondents stated what they would pay for protection above all safe levels (that is, all Ohio's surface waters), not a 5-mile stretch of one river.

If you wanted to find the social benefits from discharges along a specific river, then you would survey the people affected by the discharge from that river. Also, these total benefits are estimated in 2001 dollars. Respondents were instructed to assume their payment was a one-time contribution. There is already an implicit discount rate for these total benefit estimates. They are total payments with an infinite time horizon, assuming the monitoring and enforcement costs will always be required.

A final finding is that as the requirement approaches 70 percent set-aside, the slope of the total WTP curve approaches zero and total benefits start to decrease as the amount of set-aside continues to increase. Ohioans are still receiving benefits but at a diminishing rate. This could be due to the realization that applying highly restrictive levels (70 percent to 100 percent) across all surface waters is not feasible. Realistically, there must be some pollutant discharge. Our communities could not exist at current living standards without creating some waste. The EPA requiring a minimum of 20 percent set-aside is more amenable than trying to set aside 70 percent. To immediately enforce highly restrictive regulations, like 70 percent, is irrational.

The use of contingent valuation is still evolving with more empirical applications developing at a rapid pace. Here we have provided estimates of the social benefits for different levels of additional protection for water quality in Ohio surface waters. The goal is for regulators to use these estimates when searching for the socially optimal level of pollution. Despite its limitations, when valuing changes in a broad regulation governing water quality across a spectrum of natural resources like surface water, the technique of choice is contingent valuation.

NOTES

1. Surface waters are defined as streams, rivers, creeks, ditches, lakes, reservoirs, ponds, marshes, wetlands, or other waterways.
2. A copy of the survey is available via the corresponding author. As an incentive to respond, we offered entry into a DVD-player raffle (the raffle had no statistical influence on the results).

3. Safe levels were defined in each survey as the minimum available pollutant assimilative capacity.

REFERENCES

Bishop, R., T. Heberlein, and M. Kealy (1983), "Contingent valuation of environmental assets: comparisons with a simulated market," *Natural Resources Journal*, **23**, 619–33.

Blamey, R., J. Bennett, and M. Morrison (1999), "Yea-saying in contingent valuation surveys," *Land Economics*, **75** (3), 126–41.

Boman, M., G. Bostedt, and B. Kristrom (1999), "Obtaining welfare bounds in discrete-response valuation studies: a non-parametric approach," *Land Economics*, **75** (2), 284–94.

Brookshire, D. and L. Eubanks (1978), "Contingent valuation and revealing actual demand for public environmental commodities," manuscript, University of Wyoming.

Brookshire, D. and A. Randall (1978), "Public policy alternatives, public goods, and contingent valuation mechanisms," paper presented at the Western Economic Association Meeting, Honolulu, Hawaii, March.

Brown, T., P. Champ, R. Bishop, and D. McCollum (1996), "Which response format reveals the truth about donations to a public good?" *Land Economics*, **72** (2), 152–66.

Cosslett, S. (1983), "Distribution-free maximum likelihood estimator of the binary choice model," *Econometrica*, **51** (3), 765–82.

Diamond, P. and J. Hausman (1993), "On contingent valuation measurement of nonuse values," in J. Hausman (ed.), *Contingent Valuation: A Critical Assessment*, Amsterdam: North-Holland.

Haab, T. and K. McConnell (2002), *The Econometrics of Non-market Valuation*, New Horizons in Environmental Economics Series, Aldershot, UK and Brookfield, US: Edward Elgar.

Irvin, S. (2001), "Estimating economic benefits to society from river and stream protection," MS thesis, The Ohio State University, Columbus, Ohio.

List, J. and C. Gallet (2001), "What experimental protocol influence disparities between actual and hypothetical stated values?" *Environmental and Resource Economics*, **20**, 241–54.

McFadden, D. and G. Leonard (1993), "Issues in the contingent valuation of environmental goods: methodologies for data collection and analysis," in J. Hausman (ed.), *Contingent Valuation: A Critical Assessment*, Amsterdam: North-Holland.

Mitchell, R. and R. Carson (1989), *Using Surveys to Value Public Goods: The Contingent Valuation Method*, Washington, DC: Resources for the Future.

National Oceanic and Atmospheric Administration (NOAA) (1993), "National resource damage assessments under the Oil Pollution Act of 1990," *Federal Register*, **58** (10), 4601–14.

Ohio Environmental Protection Agency (EPA) (2003), "A guide to Ohio's Antidegradation Rule," Division of Surface Water, Columbus, Ohio.

Schulze, W. and R. d'Arge (1978), "On the valuation of recreational damages," paper presented to the Association of Environmental and Resource Economists, New York, March.

Turnbull, B. (1976), "The empirical distribution function with arbitrarily grouped, censored and truncated data," *Journal of the Royal Statistical Society B*, **38** (3), 290–95.

US Census Bureau (2000), "U.S. Census 2000: Ohio," Washington, DC.

Vaughan, W., C. Russell, D. Rodriguez, and A. Darling (2000), "Cost–benefit analysis based on referendum CV: dealing with uncertainty," *Journal of Water Resources Planning and Management*, **126** (6), 351–7.

4. The economics of high-head dam removal in an ecological context: a case study of the Ballville Dam, Fremont, Ohio

Sarah A. Kruse, Timothy C. Granata, and Ulrike Zika

INTRODUCTION

Over the past two centuries the installation of dams, built mainly for economic reasons such as power generation, water supply, irrigation, or flood control, has transformed America's rivers. There are now over 76 000 registered dams (2 meters or higher) and an estimated 2 million dams of smaller size, and in many cases dams have led to environmental changes in both the river and surrounding habitat. More attention has been given recently to the effects of dams on the environment due to changing social values, safety issues related with aging structures, and an increase in scientific information on the long-term effects of dams (Heinz Center, 2002).

When assessing the discounted future flow of economic values for a dam, the typical life expectancy of the structure is normally considered to be 50 years. On the formal list of dams maintained by the United States Army Corps of Engineers (USACE), more than 30 percent are already over 50 years old, and by the year 2020 over 80 percent (60,000 dams) will have exceeded their typical life expectancy. In many cases, the structural integrity of the dam has been compromised or is obsolete, and the dam is also no longer being used. Of the dams officially accounted for in the United States, more than half will be up for license renewal in the next decade (Liggett, 2002), and for many, structural obsolescence will require that a decision be made to either remove or restore the dam.

When proposing a change such as dam removal, it is important to assess both the costs and benefits associated with such an action; however, one problem with such an analysis is that it may fail to accurately account for nonmarket values associated with the change. A change is said to have nonmarket value when society receives benefits, or incurs losses, from the change, but there is no observable market where that value can be expressed. Omission or undervaluation of such values may lead to an underestimation of the true social benefits of the proposed change. In the case of dam removal there is a wide array of complex issues that must be examined in order to make a comprehensive decision: ecology of the watershed, local riparian species, public recreation, economics of the local communities, and property rights.

The case study for this research project is the Ballville Dam in Northwestern Ohio. We perform a cost–benefit analysis to compare projected costs of dam removal with the estimated benefits of environmental improvements as suggested by the results of a contingent valuation survey. This study not only uses willingness to pay (WTP) estimates from a contingent valuation survey to estimate the benefits of dam removal, but also integrates research conducted by an ecologic engineer and aquatic ecologist in an effort to decrease the uncertainty often associated with certain aspects of a cost–benefit analysis.

ANALYTICAL OVERVIEW

Cost–benefit analysis (CBA) is a method frequently used by decision-makers to choose between policy alternatives, and in its most general sense is defined as a technique to determine economic feasibility by quantifying both the costs and benefits of a proposed project or policy. This broad definition has resulted in the application of CBA in a variety of fields, and in particular, environmental management. The protocol was first used by United States federal water agencies, including the US Army Corps of Engineers and quickly spread to other areas such as wildlife, recreation, health, and air quality. The protocols of cost–benefit analysis are long established, reasonably precise and, since the 1970s, have been required as part of environmental regulations by the United States government.

There are a variety of goods, sometimes referred to as nonmarket goods, for which obtaining dollar estimates can be extremely difficult (that is, estimating the value of an endangered species) or are not recognized as having value at the time the study is being conducted (Whitelaw and MacMullan, 2002). One of the first federal uses of CBA by the USACE was to assess the costs and benefits of dam construction. But it was only in the 1970s and 1980s, after the majority of United States dams had been built, that CBA began to focus on the importance of nonuse values. In an era where many dams are becoming structurally obsolete and/or are no longer economically viable, it is imperative that any assessment of the costs and benefits of dam maintenance or repair include nonmarket values.

Over the years a variety of techniques for valuing nonmarket goods have been developed, with the most commonly used methods being: the travel cost, hedonic pricing, and contingent valuation. The travel cost method is the oldest method and values nonmarket goods through the use of consumption behavior in related markets (Hanley and Spash, 1993). This method relies on the assumption of *weak complementarity*, which implies that when the cost of consuming the services of the environmental good is zero, then the marginal utility of the environmental good is also zero. Because of this assumption, the travel cost method can only measure use-values, and is used mainly to model and value outdoor recreation such as fishing, hunting, or boating.

Hedonic pricing establishes a statistical relationship between levels of an environmental good/change and a market, typically the housing or labor markets. The method relies on the assumption that the representative individual has a utility function that is *weakly separable*, and *weak complementarity* is also assumed. Weak separability implies that the marginal rate of substitution between two goods, *a* and *b*, in an individual's utility function, is independent of the quantities of all other goods. Because of these assumptions, hedonic pricing can also only measure use values. While both travel cost and hedonic pricing methods have the potential to work in certain dam removal scenarios, the particular application of this study involves a dam with few potentially affected properties and limited recreational activity. For this study, contingent valuation, explained in more detail later, has been chosen as the method that most accurately measures both the use and nonuse values of removing the Ballville Dam.

STUDY AREA

The focus of this study is the Ballville Dam, which spans the Sandusky River in Northwest Ohio, and was built in 1911 by the Ohio Power Company to be used as a source of hydroelectricity. In 1959, the dam was sold to the City of Fremont, Ohio and although it is no longer used for generating hydroelectric power, the reservoir behind the dam currently serves as a sole source water supply for the city. There is interest in removing the dam because of the potential to improve river quality and increase spawning habitat for walleye, as well as the fact that the dam structure is currently in need of repairs. The main issues under consideration are: (1) restoration of river quality, including improved water quality and increased availability of fish spawning habitat, (2) safety, and (3) water supply for the City of Fremont.

The Sandusky River is one of two major tributaries to the Western Basin of Lake Erie and is used by walleye for spawning. Walleye (*Sander vitreus*) were an important commercial fish species in the Great Lakes region (Leach and Nepszy, 1976). The Ballville Dam is the first major barrier in the Sandusky River for these anadromous fish and inhibits their access to spawning habitat upstream. There is only one suitable gravel bed of about $64\,000\,m^2$ below the dam, with potentially 10 times that area of habitat upstream.

The interdisciplinary nature of this study allowed for collaboration with an ecological engineer and an aquatic ecologist, whose research helped identify both the ideal spawning habitat for migrating walleye and the available habitat in the Sandusky River during different hydraulic conditions (see Box 4.1 and Box 4.2). This information, along with more specific research on larval migration, allowed the research team to identify with greater certainty the likely effects of dam removal on the walleye population. A mathematical, ecological model of early life-history stages of walleye was developed (Cheng et al., 2006) and coupled to a hydrodynamic model. Model simulations were run for two in-stream scenarios, with and without the Ballville Dam, to assess the potential benefit of dam removal. To validate the model, data were collected on egg deposition, hatching, and larval output in the Sandusky River (Zika, 2006). Simulation results showed that the current numbers of females spawning in the Sandusky River are insufficient to saturate the available spawning grounds below the dam with eggs. Therefore, no significant differences in egg deposition or larval production would occur in simulations without the Ballville Dam.

It should be noted that if dams are never removed, fish populations will never be able to use upstream habitat, which could provide more suitable grounds for spawning and the increased heterogeneity of the system might provide alternative spawning grounds during unfavorable conditions, such as floods or droughts, lacking downstream. In the case of a small population of spawners, it will take longer to reach a population level that saturates habitats both downstream and upstream of a dam. Only by removing the obstruction to spawning habitats (that is, the dams) can fish populations increase. Management of the river fishery and diligent monitoring in combination with river restoration could accelerate the recovery of the fish population in the Sandusky River.

The second issue is dam safety. The Ballville Dam is currently classified as a Class 1 (high hazard) dam, meaning that some loss of life is probable if the dam were to fail. Also, according to the Ohio Department of Natural Resources (ODNR) Dam Safety Office, the dam does not currently meet maintenance regulations under the Ohio Dam Safety Laws due to inadequate spillway capacity and the need for seawall stabilization. The cost of repairs is estimated to be around $700\,000$ (Brice, 2000).

BOX 4.1   INTEGRATING ECOLOGICAL ENGINEERING

Ecological engineering is a key component of dam removals and river restoration. Assessment of dam removal can be made using accurate hydraulic models to simulate river conditions and dam operation (Cheng and Granata, 2007). In the case of the Ballville Dam, a 1-D hydraulic river model was used to determine with and without dam water levels and velocities in numerous reaches of the river. Data were incorporated into habitat suitability indices to predict the effect of the restoration on fish habitat (Cheng et al., 2006). Results indicated that dam removal would benefit migration of adult fish by providing additional spawning habitat upstream of the dam. However, Zika (2006) found that while the Cheng model assumed a sufficient population of river spawners were present, consistent with best estimates by fisheries experts, the field data showed this number to be low, with the result that habitat was not limiting to spawners.

The hydraulic model can also be used in design for deconstruction of dams to investigate the propagation of the floodwave during the removal process. Granata (2006) has simulated controlled breaches of the Ballville Dam as a function of seasonal water levels in the Sandusky River. The model predicted the best time to remove the dam was during low river flows and low lake levels, usually in the summer. The best location to breach the dam was in the deepest sections (that is, thalweg) of the channel, which reduced the sediment scouring along the banks.

Finally, hydraulic models can give detailed two dimensional renditions of the river. Gillenwater et al. (2006) used a hydraulic model with a geographic information system (GIS) interface to predict habitat suitability downstream of the Ballville Dam. They found that even in high flows, refugia were found in most of the modeled reach.

Finally, the reservoir behind the dam is the sole source of municipal water for the City of Fremont. It has become a concern of the city that the reservoir is shrinking due to sediment build-up, and in its current condition it will not be able to meet the expected water demands of the city by 2030. According to Evans et al. (2002) from 1911 to 1993 the reservoir lost

BOX 4.2   INTEGRATING AQUATIC BIOLOGY

Dams block fish migration, inhibiting fish from using different habitats at different life history stages (Peter, 1998). This interruption of
river continuity can have drastic effects on migratory fish populations. The limitation of suitable spawning substrates can lead to
serious negative impacts on reproductive success. Dams have had
a major impact on the fish community of the Laurentian Great
Lakes. Since European settlement, nearly every river and stream
draining into the Great Lakes has been dammed (Jones et al.,
2003). The Sandusky River, a tributary to Lake Erie, provides one
of the major spawning areas for walleye. A portion of the walleye
population from the lake migrates into the Sandusky River to
reproduce (Regier et al., 1969). Walleye exhibit strong homing
behavior for their natal spawning grounds (Crowe, 1962; Jennings
et al., 1996). They are broadcast spawners but have a strong preference for gravel/cobble substrate (Eschmeyer, 1950). There are
currently four dams on the Sandusky River, the first and largest of
which is the Ballville Dam. Two kilometers downstream of the dam
is a gravel/cobble bed of approximately 64 000 m^2, representing
the only remaining suitable spawning habitat for walleye in the
Sandusky River. However, upstream of the dam about 10 times the
area could be available (Cheng, 2001). The loss of spawning
habitat has been implicated in the decline of the returning walleye
population in the river (Van Tea, 1999).

78 percent of its storage capacity due to sedimentation, and based on projected water needs for the city versus continued loss of storage capacity, the
study estimates inadequate water supply for the city within three to five
years.

COST–BENEFIT ANALYSIS

One of the difficulties in tailoring existing cost–benefit procedures to dam
removal is determining a point of reference; defined as the no-action alternative against which all beneficial and/or adverse affects are measured
(Heinz Center, 2002); however, in the case of dams, not taking action may
not be a viable alternative if the structural integrity of a dam is obsolete

and/or compromised. Therefore, the definition of a "no-action" alternative for dam removal must include whatever actions are necessary to comply with regulations and meet safety standards such as: repairs to the structure, spillway enhancements and/or dam maintenance. Were the dam to be removed, the elimination of these maintenance fees would fall on the benefit side of the analysis.

In the case of the Ballville Dam, the "no-action" alternative includes a number of repairs required to comply with Ohio Dam Safety regulations, the sum of which is in excess of $700 000. An assessment of the dam completed in spring 2004 by the ODNR Dam Safety Office showed that none of these repairs had been completed, and that the condition of the dam had worsened since the last assessment. This information suggests an even higher cost for the "no-action" alternative.

Another issue to consider is the valuation of both market and nonmarket goods that are economically relevant to the analysis. It is assumed that the goal of society is to maximize social welfare through maximizing the weighted sum of utilities across all individuals, and that utility is gained through consumption of both market and nonmarket goods. The environmental impacts of a project count as long as (1) they affect positively, or negatively, the utility of at least one individual, and/or (2) they change the level or quality of a commodity that has a positive value to society (Hanley and Spash, 1993).

For the purpose of this study, benefits will be defined as increases in the quantity or quality of a good that generate a positive utility, or a reduction in the price at which it is supplied. Similarly, a decrease in the quality or quantity of the good, or an increase in its price, will be defined as a cost. Goods such as dam services, or services provided to undertake the actual removal (for example, labor, machines), are all market goods, and market transactions provide the data necessary to calculate estimated costs. As discussed previously though, there exist a number of goods for which markets do not exist, nonmarket goods, such as recreational opportunities and environmental changes.

STRUCTURE OF A CBA

The first objective of a cost–benefit analysis is to define the project and identify the project impacts. The project should be defined in terms of the proposed change (that is, dam removal) and affected population (that is, Sandusky County residents). In the case of dam removal, defining the affected population may be more difficult than in other scenarios due to the number of nonmarket considerations.

In the case of the Ballville Dam, the size of the affected population was based on the ability of the researcher to access data, and the specific characteristics of the dam. The size and characteristics of the dam suggest that the impact of removal would be more local (as opposed to national), but potential linkage of increased spawning habit to Lake Erie walleye populations suggests a larger population might be affected if a direct link between the river and Lake Erie is confirmed. Using that information, two affected populations were chosen: *Sandusky County*, and a *30-mile radius* around the dam. For the purposes of the analysis, aggregation of costs and benefits were done for both populations.

The *Sandusky County* sample was chosen because it is believed that individuals in Sandusky County would be most familiar with the dam removal issue and most impacted by the potential changes. The *30-mile radius* sample was smaller than the one drawn for Sandusky County because of the belief that individuals living farther from the dam would be less familiar with the good being valued, and also less likely to be affected positively, or negatively, by the removal of the dam. Individuals less familiar and/or less knowledgeable about the dam may also have a more difficult time translating their preferences, if any, into dollar terms.

ESTIMATING THE COSTS OF DAM REMOVAL

Dam removal costs can be broken down into three major categories: dam deconstruction, lost services and external. Costs associated with dam deconstruction include those directly associated with removal of the physical structure such as: removal of the physical structure, sediment disposal and storage, and the disposal of waste material. At the time of this study, no dam the size of the Ballville Dam had been removed in the State of Ohio, though dams of similar size have been removed elsewhere in the United States. A study by Finkbeiner et al. (1999) estimates the cost of removing the dam to be $7–9 million dollars, not including dredging and disposal of reservoir sediments. Removal cost estimates updated into 2004 dollars put the cost of dam removal at just over $10.2 million.

The second category of costs includes lost dam services. In cases where the dam and/or dam reservoir are still being used in an economic capacity, such as power generation or as a water supply, this cost would be equal to the cost of providing an alternative source that generates at least the same level and quality of output.

In the case of the Ballville Dam, the reservoir behind the dam is the sole source of water for the City of Fremont, although it appears that in this scenario, this "loss" of water supply may not fall on the cost side of the analysis. The City of Fremont recently decided to go forward with the building of an up-ground water reservoir, and this decision appears to be independent of any decision to remove/restore the Ballville Dam. For this reason, the cost of the up-ground reservoir will not be considered a "cost" of dam removal.

The final category includes any external costs of removal, or in other words, the impacts dam removal has on the surrounding environment. The external costs of removal, while not necessarily the most costly category in dollar terms, are often the most difficult to estimate. As discussed previously, this category may include such effects as the temporary degradation of downstream habitat due to sediment flow and/or loss of aesthetics. Changes in the landscape caused by dam removal and the subsequent drawdown of the reservoir could have a negative effect on surrounding property values. According to the study by Finkbeiner et al. (1999) there are approximately 30 residences and two commercial establishments adjacent to the reservoir above the Ballville Dam. The largest projected impact on these residences would be the loss of a "lake type" atmosphere, but the study also suggests that impact may not be significant due to the limited use of the reservoir for recreational purposes.

Additional external costs that often involve a high degree of uncertainty include: (1) whether sediment behind the dam is contaminated, (2) how sediment moves after the dam has been breached, (3) whether the movement of the sediment has a positive or negative effect on downstream habitat, and (4) estimating the length of time required for sediment stabilization and regeneration of riparian vegetation. Both sediment contamination and movement are topics that could be very costly under a worst-case scenario, but in other scenarios may be trivial. Very few studies have attempted to address this uncertainty and improve cost estimates.

The interdisciplinary nature of this particular study has allowed for interaction with an ecological engineer, geologist and aquatic ecologist also doing research on the Ballville Dam. Working with these individuals provided valuable information not only on the sediment and contamination issues discussed above, but also on the likely impacts of dam removal on spawning habitats and aquatic species which will be discussed later (see Box 4.1 and Box 4.2).

It is known that contaminated sediments exist behind the Ballville Dam – there are DDT residues in the sediments from the 1940s and 1950s, and in 1988 there was an upstream toluene spill. Dr James Evans (personal communications, 2004) states, "The overall quality of the sediments is probably good enough to allow a release if the dam were removed." Unfortunately, the criteria used in determining if sediment is contaminated often vary by agency, and at this point it is unclear how the sediment behind the Ballville Dam would be classified. The cost estimate to sample and test for contaminated materials in the sediments may be as high as $200 000 if Ohio Environmental Protection Agency (OEPA) requirements are followed (Finkbeiner et al., 1999).

Based on the available information at the time of this study, a precautionary action would be to dispose of the dredged sediment in a landfill. A cost estimate for this scenario was done by Finkbeiner et al. (1999) and estimated at $5–8 million, with one-third to one-half of that cost being landfill disposal. If the material were disposed of in another fashion (for example, another fill site, left in place), then the cost should decrease significantly.

If the sediments are not considered hazardous, we suggest two options for the sediments in the reservoir, both of which involve sediment movement downstream. First, the dam could be notched and drawn-down slowly during the dry season. Grasses and trees would then be planted on the banks of the former reservoir to stabilize the sediment and for phytoremediation of metals. To smooth the transition in flow at the dam site, a series of steps could be used to reduce the river grade, and the energy grade, in the river to help maintain channel stability. Under this scenario, the only sediments moving downstream would be those in the deepest part of the river channel and they would cause only minimal disruption to downstream habitat.

The alternative is to not restore the channel and allow the sediments to freely travel downstream. The sediments will affect the downstream habitat and spawning grounds for an estimated one to two years before the entire load is washed downstream to Lake Erie. The disruption caused by this scenario, while greater than the previous, is not permanent and this alternative would be significantly less costly. With a restoration initiative and planting, it is estimated that the sediments would take less than two years to stabilize. In either case, the planting of vegetation on the riverbanks and a clear-cut river channel to transport sediments also would prevent the mudflats.

ESTIMATING THE BENEFITS OF DAM REMOVAL

The primary benefit of most dam removals is the restoration of environmental services. Dam removal allows the river or stream to flow freely again, and reconnects what were previously upstream and downstream sections. In economic terms, the values of restored environmental functions associated with dam removal fall into two categories: use values and nonuse values. Use values are defined as the economic measure of valuable environmental services that result from environmental functions (Heinz Center, 2002).

An example of a use value for removal of the Ballville Dam is the recovery and/or expansion of the fish-spawning habitat leading to an increase in the harvestable fish population. This increase in population could be converted into increased recreational opportunities to sport fishermen. Other use values may include increased canoeing and kayaking opportunities, or the creation of a riverfront revitalization project. Use values can be obtained through a variety of methods (discussed earlier) including travel cost, hedonic pricing and contingent valuation.

Individuals may also derive utility from dam removal even if they never visit the restored stream or river. Such values are not directly related to the economic functions of the dam or waterway, and are known as nonuse values. Often called intrinsic values, they are valued simply for their own existence (existence value), or the knowledge that the resource will be saved for future generations (bequest value) (Heinz Center, 2002).

Existence value is frequently mentioned with respect to endangered resources and species, or when the proposed action may cause impacts that are irreversible. Similarly, bequest value relates to the notion of preserving the good for use by future generations. The only way to obtain monetary values for intrinsic values is through the use of a stated preference method. For this reason, contingent valuation was chosen for this study.

One area of uncertainty often related to dam removal is the impact removal would have on in-stream species and their habitat. While it is known that the building of dams can have a negative impact on in-stream species, especially anadromous species, it is less clear the direction of impact dam removal would have. This is partially due to wide variability between dam removal scenarios and partially due to the limited amount of research done on the topic. In this situation, collaboration with an aquatic biologist helped decrease some of the uncertainty associated with this issue (see Box 4.2).

In the next section, Table 4.2 summarizes the economically relevant costs and benefits as they associate with those affected by the proposed removal of the Ballville Dam.

SOCIAL BENEFITS ESTIMATION RESULTS

When estimating the social benefits of nonmarket goods, economists use two valuation methods: revealed preferences, through which they observe behavior and infer values based on those observations; and stated preferences, where questions are posed to respondents and inferences are made based on those responses. The contingent valuation (CV) method is the most commonly used form of stated preferences.

Contingent valuation was first used by Davis in 1963, and by 1995 the methodology had been used in over 2000 studies (Carson et al., 1995). Contingent valuation provides a direct method through which the stated preferences of individuals can be calculated by asking a sample population their willingness to pay for an increase in a public good contingent on the creation of a market where all payments are hypothetical (Bishop et al., 1983; Freeman, 1993). Individual WTP estimates can then be aggregated to estimate the total economic value of the good to society.

For this study, a contingent valuation survey was mailed to two randomly selected samples and the survey results were used to estimate willingness to pay for removal of the Ballville Dam. The survey was composed of five subcategories: personal knowledge, self-reported behavior, opinion attitudes, willingness to pay, and demographics. There were two versions of the survey: one used an open-ended (OE) WTP question, and the other used a dichotomous choice (DC) question with a fixed bid value. A total of 974 surveys were mailed to a randomly selected population of Sandusky County residents and individuals that lived within 30 miles of the dam but not in Sandusky County.

The population over which the mean WTP values were aggregated is the total number of identifiable households for each sample. The US Census Bureau (2004) listed 23 717 households in Sandusky County. Estimating the total number of households within a 30-mile radius of the dam was slightly more difficult due to the partial inclusion of eight different counties in the sample. Based on best estimates, the number of households within a 30-mile radius is 309 529.

Table 4.1 lists the economic value estimates of dam removal to both Sandusky County residents and to *all* residents living within a 30-mile radius of the dam. Value estimates are also broken down by sample area.

An important step in the estimation of total social benefits is the calculation of a lower-bound estimate. Lower-bound estimates of total benefits were calculated using a Turnbull estimation, and are shown in Table 4.2.

Table 4.1   Mean WTP and estimates of total social benefits

	Observations	Mean WTP	Households	Estimated total value[a]
DC-Sandusky	134	$50.86	23 717	$1 206 246.62
DC-30 mile	175	$56.35	309 529	$17 442 522.65

Note: [a] These estimates do not include non-response to the WTP question and are based solely on surveys where the WTP question was answered.

Table 4.2   Turnbull mean WTP and lower-bound estimates of total social benefits

	Observations	Turnbull mean WTP	Households	Estimated total value[a]
DC-Sandusky	134	$36.38	23 717	$862 824.48
DC-30 mile	175	$38.95	309 529	$12 056 154.50

Note: [a] These estimates do not include non-response to the WTP question and are based solely on surveys where the WTP question was answered.

The study found no significant difference in WTP values between only Sandusky County residents and *all* residents; however, the aggregate benefits are significantly greater for the 30-mile radius due to the larger population of the region. The Turnbull low-bound estimate of social benefits for the 30-mile radius is over $12 million, a value that exceeds the estimated cost of removing the dam (excluding sediment dredging and disposal and the cost of building a supplemental water supply). On the other hand, the low-bound estimate of benefits to Sandusky County is approximately $860 000, which is less than the estimated cost of dam removal.

CONCLUSION

The removal of the Ballville Dam, and the subsequent restoration of the river corridor, is technically feasible, and the breaching of the dam could be done so as not to endanger the public. The hazard of releasing large volumes of sediment downstream could be reduced by breaching in the thalweg to de-water the reservoir, then stabilizing the banks with vegetation to prevent future erosion and avoid unsightly mudflats. The ecological benefits of the removal must be coupled to management of the river fishery to achieve success, otherwise it could take years for the fishery to recover.

In the case of the Ballville Dam, it appears that a population much larger than the City of Fremont or even Sandusky County would benefit from its removal, but the question remains, who would actually pay the removal costs? The City of Fremont owns the dam, and most likely would be responsible for most, if not all, of the removal cost, though recent informal discussions with the ODNR suggest they may help seek funds for the full cost.

This study has demonstrated that the net benefits of dam removal to a 30-mile radius, which includes Sandusky County are $13–17 million using conservative estimates, but the estimates for Sandusky County alone are a much lower $0.8–1.2 million. These distributional considerations are important not only for this particular scenario, but should be a factor in any decision-making process involving dam removal.

As of 2006, when this book was written, the removal of the Ballville Dam was finally being given consideration by the City of Fremont as a viable alternative to maintaining the status quo. We would like to think that the interdisciplinary research presented in this book has influenced that response, and hope it motivates other projects.

REFERENCES

Bishop, R.C., T.A. Heberlein, and M.J. Kealy (1983), "Contingent valuation of environmental assets: comparisons with a simulated market," *Natural Resources Journal*, **23**, 619–33.

Brice, M. (2000), "City officials say safe, adequate water supply key in final decision," *Fremont News-Messenger*, January 12, A1.

Carson, R.T., J. Wright, N. Carson, A. Alberini, and N. Flores (1995), *A Bibliography of Contingent Valuation Papers and Studies*, La Jolla, CA: NRDA.

Cheng, F. (2001), "Modeling effects of dam removal on migratory walleye life stages in a coastal watershed," master's thesis, The Ohio State University, Columbus, Ohio.

Cheng, F. and T.C. Granata (2007), "Sediment transport and channel adjustments associated with dam removal: field observations," *Water Resources Research*, **43**, W03444, doi: 10.1029/2005WR004271.

Cheng, F., U. Zika, K. Banachowski, D. Gillenwater, and T.C. Granata (2006), "Modelling the effects of dam removal on migratory walleye (*Sander vitreus*) early life-history stages," *River Research and Applications*, **22** (8), 837–51.

Davis, R.K. (1963), "Recreation planning as an economic problem," *Natural Resources Journal*, **3** (2), 239–49.

Eschmeyer, P. (1950), *The life history of the walleye (Stizostedion vitreum) (Mitchill) in Michigan*. Michigan Department of Conservation, Institute of Fisheries Research Bulletin no. 3.

Evans, J.E., N.S. Levine, S.J. Roberts, J.F. Gottgens, and D.M. Newman (2002), "Assessment using GIS and sediment routing of the proposed removal of Ballville Dam, Sandusky River, Ohio," *Journal of the American Water Resources Association*, **38**, 1549–63.

Finkbeiner, Pettis, and Strout (1999), *Raw Water Supply Study*, prepared for the City of Fremont, Ohio.

Freeman, A. Myrick, III (1993), *The Measurement of Environmental and Resource Values*, Washington, DC: Resources for the future.

Gillenwater, D.A., T.C. Granata, and U. Zika (2006), "GIS-based modeling of spawning habitat suitability for walleye (*Sander vitreus*) in the Sandusky River, Ohio, and implications for dam removal and river restoration," *Ecological Engineering*, **28** (3), 311–23.

Granata, T.C. (2006), "Modeling and measuring sediment transport following dam removal," proceedings of the ASCE Water Resources Conference, August 2005. Williamsburg, VA.

Hanley, N., and C.L. Spash (1993), *Cost–Benefit Analysis and the Environment*, Aldershot, UK and Brookfield, US: Edward Elgar.

Heinz Center (2002), *Dam Removal: Science and Decision-making*, Washington, DC: H. John Heinz Center for Science, Economics, and the Environment.

Jennings, M., J. Claussen, and P. David (1996), "Evidence for heritable preferences for spawning habitat between two walleye populations," *Transactions of the American Fisheries Society*, **125**, 978–82.

Jones, M., J. Netto, J. Stockwell, and J. Mion (2003), "Does the value of newly accessible spawning habitat for walleye (*Stizostedion vitreum*) depend on its location relative to nursery habitats?" *Canadian Journal of Fisheries and Aquatic Sciences*, **60**, 1527–38.

Leach, J. and S. Nepszy (1976), "The fish communities of Lake Erie," *Journal of the Fisheries research Board of Canada*, **33**, 622–38.

Liggett, J.A. (2002), "What is hydraulic engineering?" *Journal of American Society Civil Engineers*, **128**, 1–10.

Peter, A. (1998), "Interruption of the river continuum by barriers and the consequences for migratory fish," in M. Jungwirth, S. Schmutz, and S. Weiss (eds), *Fish Migration and Fish Bypass*, Oxford: Fishing News Books.

Regier, H., V. Applegate, and R. Ryder (1969), *The Ecology and Management of the Walleye in Western Lake Erie*, Great Lakes Fishery Commission, Technical Report # 15.

Tea, V. (1999), "Sandusky River walleyes. What does the future hold?" *Wild Ohio Magazine*.

US Census Bureau (2000), State and County QuickFacts found on quickfacts. census.gov/.

Whitelaw, E. and E. MacMullan (2002), "A framework for estimating the costs and benefits of dam removal," *BioScience*, **52**, 724–30.

Zika, U. (2006), personal communication.

5. The economics of low-head dam removal: a case study on the Salmon River in Fort Covington, New York

David Warren and Fred J. Hitzhusen

INTRODUCTION

Dams have been a common site on American waterways for hundreds of years, providing electricity, water supplies, and recreational opportunities for millions of citizens. In the 30 years since the "golden age of dam building" came to an end (Doyle et al., 2003b), however, a new trend involves the removal of dams for various socioeconomic and ecological reasons.

Of great concern to many proponents of dam removal is the safety hazard that aging structures pose to the general public. The life expectancy of a dam is generally about 50 years (FEMA, 1999; Heinz Center, 2002), but 25 percent of all dams in the US are already over 50 years old with estimates of 80 percent being past their life expectancy by the year 2020 (Heinz Center, 2002; NRC, 1992). Furthermore, many small dams were constructed over a century ago and are no longer fulfilling their intended uses while raising public safety concerns due to structural deterioration (Johnson and Graber, 2002). This is an obvious concern for states and local governments which must decide whether to repair dams, remove them, or do nothing and hope nobody gets hurt or incurs downstream flood damage.

Environmental benefits are also important factors driving the dam removal boom as advocates increasingly point to removal as a means of river restoration (Doyle et al., 2003a; Hart et al., 2002). In Lowry (2003), dozens of dam removal case studies involving goals of river restoration are discussed, including projects on the Neuse, Kennebec, Mississippi, Elwha, Osage, Missouri, and Snake Rivers. American Rivers (2000) touted the success of the removal of the Edwards Dam in improving the quality of the Kennebec River and also estimated that over 100 river restoration projects involving dam removal were proposed in the year 2000. Worth mentioning is the connection between environmental benefits and the recreational benefits that anglers and boaters may enjoy from potential increases in fish species and unimpeded streams.

Though safety and environmental concerns are at the top of the list of reasons for removing dams, economic concerns are evident in most removals. Born et al. (1998) noted that repairing small dams can cost up to three times more than removal. The economic benefits of improving anadromous fish runs by removing dams on the Snake River have appeared in removal debates in Idaho (Kareiva et al., 2000) while Loomis (1996) estimated a national willingness to pay (WTP) of between $3 billion and $6 billion to remove two large dams on the Elwha River in Washington to restore a famous anadromous fishery. A dissertation by Kruse (2004) employed contingent valuation using mail surveys and focus groups to estimate bid curves and WTP for the removal of a high-head dam on the Sandusky River in northern Ohio. Abdul-Mohsen (2005) estimated WTP and scope, scale, and context effects for river restoration projects that involve toxics and low-head dam removal on the Mahoning River in northeast Ohio.

Currently, there are 76 500 dams in the National Inventory of Dams, a database maintained by the US Army Corps of Engineers that lists high-head structures, the majority of which have a height of 4 to 16 meters (Poff and Hart, 2002). This quantity pales in comparison to the estimated number of small, low-head dams (2 meters or less), ranging from 2 million (Graf, 1993) to 2.5 million (Johnston, 1992).

STUDY AREA

The Town of Fort Covington, a small, rural community of about 1500 people near the Canadian border in upstate New York, began investigating the removal of such a dam from the Salmon River (see Figures 5.1 and 5.2). The low-head structure, surveyed at 5 feet high and 100 feet wide, was built over 100 years ago and was last repaired in the early 1900s when it was used to power lighting in the town. Today, the dam produces no electricity and has deteriorated (the west side of the dam is breached) to a point where residents feel it presents a potential safety hazard to the public, especially to children who are known to congregate on the crumbling western platform.

Aside from safety concerns, which the town would have to address with repairs and maintenance, the community was also interested in the potential for increases in the populations of certain fish species that dam removal could generate. Fisheries scientist John Farrell[1] collected data over a two year period above and below the dam in the Salmon River and estimated that walleye populations would be likely to increase after removal. Farrell also believed that removal of the dam, which would open up an additional

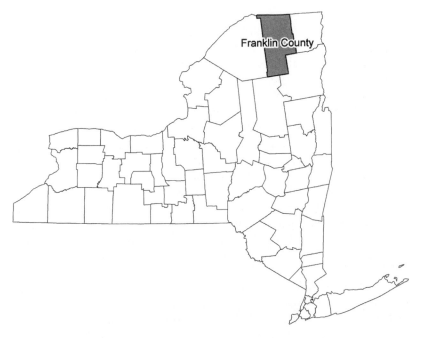

Figure 5.1   Map of New York State, with Franklin County outlined

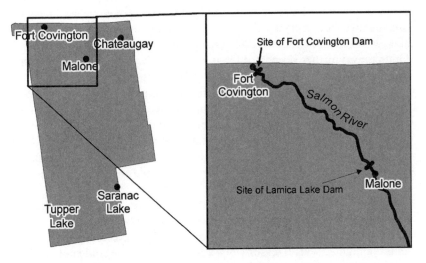

*Figure 5.2   Franklin County, New York, with Salmon River corridor
magnification*

15 miles of river habitat, would enhance the possibility for stocking the Salmon River with lake sturgeon, Atlantic salmon, and muskie. Other potential benefits included increasing the population of the threatened Eastern sand darter and reducing seasonal flooding that occurs upstream of the dam.

In 2002, an investigation into the possible removal of the dam became part of a broad dam removal study funded by the Great Lakes Protection Fund (GLPF, 2002). Support from the GLPF enabled an interdisciplinary team of researchers to examine the ecological, engineering, and economic feasibility of dam removal. The purpose of the research performed on the Fort Covington site was to investigate the support people had in the area for dam removal, including willingness to pay. Two biologists at the State University of New York College of Environmental Science and Forestry (SUNY-ESF) conducted biological research that was used by a state river organization, New York Rivers United (NYRU), to inform the community about issues related to the possible removal of the Fort Covington dam. The data from the biologists was also used in developing the contingent valuation survey.

The situation in Fort Covington was ideal for constructing empirical models of the economic benefits of low-head dam removal because most of the key variables suggested by the dam removal literature were present. In Lowry's analysis of 76 dam removal projects (2003), he found level of hazard, use of the dam, cost of maintenance, and desired ecological changes to be crucial determinants of dam removal. The Heinz Center (2002) included Lowry's (2003) variables and added the potential for increased "unregulated flow recreation" as another key driver in dam removal decisions. Johnson and Graber's (2002) documentation of the various benefits of dam removal further supported the use of the above variables in constructing empirical models of the economics of dam removal.

To value the removal of the Fort Covington dam, the contingent valuation method (CVM) was used for three main reasons. First, the area has a relatively small residential population and houses are sold infrequently throughout the county, especially within the Salmon River corridor. This ruled out the use of hedonic pricing due to limited housing price data. Second, the study was intended to estimate the value people place on a change in the river as a result of dam removal. This further rules out hedonics because two estimations would have been required (one before the project and one after the project) which would be costly and time-consuming (and impractical, given the aforementioned lack of housing price data). Third, discussions with residents highlighted several reasons for wanting removal that could not be investigated using methods that only elicit use-values. Among these were safety, flood prevention, and a desire to return the river to a more natural state. Using CVM allowed for the estimation of these potential benefits.

ANALYTICAL OVERVIEW

In order to estimate the economic benefits of the removal of the Fort Covington dam, CVM was implemented using surveys designed to elicit the WTP for dam removal. The survey was designed to allow for the estimation of WTP, and to evaluate the correlation between certain variables and WTP by estimating bid curves. An aggregate WTP was estimated for the town as well as for the entire county. These values, which represent the economic benefits of dam removal, were then compared to the economic costs of the removal in the cost–benefit analysis. The ultimate goal of the analysis was not only to inform decision-making for Fort Covington, but also to serve as a prototype decision-making tool for other potential low-head dam removals.

The primary hypotheses tested in the study were that economic benefits exceeded economic costs of dam removal and that variables such as income, education, environmentalism, and recreational behavior are significant predictors of WTP. Testing these hypotheses was done by applying CVM in the cost–benefit analysis.

Robert K. Davis's 1963 work on the economics of recreation planning was the first time CVM was used in practice (Hanley and Spash, 1993). However, the concept of CVM was first proposed in 1947, when Ciriacy-Wantrup brought up the idea of asking people what they would be willing to pay for improvements in public goods, such as decreased sedimentation in streams (Portney, 1994; Vaughn, 1997). Today's use of contingent valuation also owes much to John Krutilla (1967), who first discussed the presence of existence values in a paper that Portney (1994) said is "arguably the most influential paper ever written in [natural resource and environmental economics]." Researchers, especially those in the United States, increased their focus on CVM throughout the 1970s and 1980s with countless theoretical and empirical studies (Hanley and Spash, 1993). Following Ronald Reagan's 1981 Executive Order 12291, which required cost–benefit analyses on all government projects, the practice of CVM was promoted by federal agencies (US Water Resources Council, 1983), was used for the valuation of damages (US Department of the Interior, 1986), and has been upheld in federal courts (*State of Ohio* versus *US Department of the Interior*, 1989). Today, thousands of CVM studies can be found in the literature and efforts are being made by Environment Canada and US Environmental Protection Agency (EPA) to catalog such studies in the Environmental Valuation Reference Inventory (EVRI, 2004).

The predominant reason CVM was used in this study is that it allowed for an all-encompassing valuation of use values and those nonuse values that Krutilla (1967) introduced almost 40 years ago. While the different value categories are rather self-explanatory, a quick definition of each is in order. Use value refers to the value people derive out of some good or service by directly using it. For instance, an angler who uses the Salmon River to fish derives use value from the river. Nonuse value refers to value people have for something even though they do not directly use it. One category of nonuse value is existence value, or the value that people assign to the mere knowledge that some good or service exists. Another is bequest value, which refers to the value placed on the ability to pass the good or service down to future generations. A third major type of nonuse value is option value, meaning the value one places on the ability to use the good or service at some later point in time. All of these nonuse values were apparent during conversations with residents of Franklin County, leading to the logical selection of CVM for valuing the removal of the Fort Covington dam. Furthermore, previous CVM studies suggested large existence and bequest values for increasing salmon populations (Olsen et al., 1991), for the preservation of free-flowing rivers (Sanders et al., 1990), and for removal of dams (Loomis, 1996).

DEVELOPING THE CONTINGENT VALUATION (CV) SURVEY

Throughout the study, care was taken to adhere to the guidelines developed by the 1993 "blue ribbon" panel on contingent valuation (Arrow et al., 1993). Several drafts of the survey were created and revised, culminating in a "pre-test" of the survey on a diverse group of respondents. The results of the pre-test were used to ferret out confusing questions or terminology and to develop appropriate bid amounts for the payment question.

The hypothetical nature of CV surveys requires that information presented in the survey be understandable and realistic so that respondents can provide informed bids even if they have very little experience with the good in question (Mitchell and Carson, 1989). To accomplish this goal, the dam removal questionnaire included a page of information that informed respondents about the current state and use of the dam, reasons for the proposed removal, and the potential positive and negative consequences of removal. Following this information was a question matrix for the respondent to voice his or her opinions on the information provided. This was included to force the respondents to think carefully about the information presented to them.

Payment questions in CV surveys can take many forms, from those that allow open-ended bids to those that confine a respondent to answering yes or no to a specific payment. The latter form was chosen for this study in order to prevent strategic bidding by individuals who support dam removal. For example, in an open-ended or payment card (multiple choice of bids) format, those who value the good in question may be inclined to overestimate or underestimate their true WTP in hopes of producing an upward or downward bias on the results of the study. By using the dichotomous-choice format, the respondent can only answer yes or no to a specific dollar amount; those who would otherwise overestimate their true WTP will simply answer yes. In other words, the referendum format used in a dichotomous choice question is believed to be incentive compatible. This form of payment question was endorsed by the NOAA panel (Arrow et al., 1993) as a means of minimizing strategic bias and because the format, which resembles a referendum, is something people are familiar and comfortable with. Moreover, Mitchell and Carson (1989) assert that mail surveys are more susceptible to strategic bias given the greater amount of time that respondents have to think about the CV exercise.

The type of payment vehicle also demands careful selection in order to provide respondents a realistic scenario for bid elicitation. A voluntary contribution was not used because of the inherent potential for free-riding; those who are in favor of the project but feel others will contribute may decide to bid no because someone else will pay for it. The use of the word "tax" in the payment vehicle was avoided to make the vehicle less controversial (Hanley and Spash, 1993). The eventual payment vehicle chosen was "a one-time payment that would be used only to pay for the dam removal project" (Warren, 2004). This payment mechanism was placed in the context of a county-wide referendum, where the project would only happen if over 50 percent of the people voted for the project. Care was taken in the development of the survey to make the dam removal project a Franklin County issue, not just a Fort Covington one. Thus, the use of a county-wide referendum is realistic and plausible for the respondents (Hanley and Spash, 1993; Mitchell and Carson, 1989).

THE SAMPLE POPULATION

The population to be studied was first narrowed down to people within Franklin County, New York. This was decided because both the headwaters of the Salmon River and the Fort Covington dam are located within the county (see Figure 5.2). While the river flows north into the St Lawrence River in Quebec, Canada, Canadians were excluded from the sampling frame for two reasons. First, the predominance of French-speaking residents and a different postal system would have placed a large burden on the survey design and administration costs, especially given the relatively small budget for this research. Second, a drive through the Salmon River corridor in Quebec and examination of maps revealed few residential properties in the area, leading to an assumption that any WTP for a dam removal on the Salmon River would be by nonresidents and fairly small.

With the sampling frame selected to only include Franklin County residents, it was further decided to over-sample residents of Fort Covington. This is because Fort Covington residents would be most familiar with and impacted by the potential dam removal project, since the dam is located in the center of the town and many residents live close to the Salmon River. Moreover, only about 1500 of the approximately 50 000 Franklin County residents live in Fort Covington. With simple random sampling (SRS), only 3 percent of the sample would include residents of Fort Covington. As a comparison between the WTP of Fort Covington residents (near dam) and non-Fort Covington residents (not near dam) was desired, the decision was made to select a sample of 50 percent Fort Covington residents and 50 percent non-Fort Covington residents.

The survey administration process was done according to Dillman's (2000) "tailored design method," and employed two waves of mailings, each with concise cover letters detailing the rationale for the study. After the final surveys were returned, the sample populations for the town and the county were compared to the Census numbers for both municipalities (see Table 5.1). The Fort Covington sample was quite representative of the overall population, with the only major difference being the percent of respondents who were male. The Franklin County sample differed significantly from the total population, with the numbers suggesting that respondents were higher up on the socioeconomic ladder than the average resident.

By estimating the mean values for various social and environmental attitudes, a better understanding of the variation among respondents can be achieved. Tables 5.2 and 5.3 illustrate the responses to the first page of the survey (questions 1–8), which included questions regarding the respondents' awareness of the dam, knowledge about dam removal, and attitudes about social and environmental issues that are related to the potential dam removal project in Fort Covington. Means and confidence intervals are shown for both the Fort Covington and non-Fort Covington samples.

Evident in Table 5.2 are the differences in responses between the two sample groups. Fort Covington respondents demonstrate a greater familiarity with dam removal projects for environmental and safety reasons and are far more likely to know about the proposed dam removal project. This can probably be explained by the fact that Fort Covington residents are nearest to the dam and have had a greater chance of hearing about dam removal. Proximity also explains the differences between the two samples regarding boating and fishing frequency.

Table 5.1 Comparison between 2000 US Census data and the subsamples, with standard errors and 95 percent confidence intervals (CI) for the sample estimates

	Fort Covington (US Census)	Fort Covington (Survey)	Non-Fort Covington (US Census)	Non-Fort Covington (Survey)
People per household (mean)	2.65	2.625	2.46	2.75
Standard error		.1413104		.1512931
95% CI		[2.345, 2.905]		[2.45, 3.05]
Household income (mean)	$39 722	$41 087	$39 164	$49 245
Standard error		$2962		$4271
95% CI		[$35 282, $46 892]		[$40 874, $57 617]
Percentage Bachelor's degree	12.8%	17.4%	13.0%	27.6%
Standard error		3.65056		5.91997
95% CI		[10.20, 24.67]		[15.73, 39.44]
Percentage of whites	91.4%	94.5%	84.0%	100%
Standard error		2.1946		0
95% CI		[90.15, 98.85]		[100, 100]
Age of adults, 18 or over (mean)	48.01	54.578	45.01	52.45
Standard error		1.48634		1.872715
95% CI		[51.79, 57.37]		[48.70, 56.20]
Percentage male	47.6%	70.5%	54.9%	69.0%
Standard error		4.32704		.0612775
95% CI		[61.96, 79.11]		[56.69, 81.24]

From Table 5.3, several things are clear. First, both samples highly rated environmental protection and the protection of endangered species (ranked number 1 and 2 for both samples). Second, the greatest difference in ratings between the two samples is observed in the question regarding the level of concern over flooding problems in the county. Ratings from Fort Covington respondents produced a number 4 ranking for this variable versus a number 6 ranking for respondents outside of Fort Covington. Third, the greatest variations in responses are found in the flooding question and the "natural

Table 5.2   *Percentage and mean results with confidence intervals for*
               key survey questions for the Fort Covington and non-Fort
               Covington samples

	Fort Covington			Non-Fort Covington		
	Estimate	95% CI	n	Estimate	95% CI	n
Knew dam existed	98.21%	[.9572, 1.000]	112	62.07%	[.4920, .7494]	58
Heard of removals for environmental reasons	83.04%	[.7598, .9010]	112	62.07%	[.4920, .7494]	58
Heard of removals for safety reasons	73.21%	[.6489, .8154]	112	55.17%	[.4198, .6836]	58
Knew of proposed Fort Covington dam removal	82.88%	[.7577, .9000]	111	32.76%	[.2031, .4521]	58
Ever boated within sight of dam	58.93%	[.4968, .6818]	112	8.62%	[.0118, .1606]	58
Ever fished within sight of dam	62.50%	[.5339, .7161]	112	15.52%	[.0591, .2512]	58
Ever seen dam up close	83.93%	[.7702, .9084]	112	18.97%	[.0857, .2936]	58
Distance to dam in minutes	4.30	[3.594, 5.005]	112	39.16	[30.93, 47.38]	58
Distance to Salmon River in minutes	3.68	[3.018, 4.351]	112	30.36	[21.16, 39.57]	58

flow" question. This suggests that concern about flooding problems and
concern about making rivers flow more naturally may be significant variables that affect WTP for dam removal.

ESTIMATION OF WILLINGNESS TO PAY

While the percentage of those voting yes to the payment question is important for the econometric analysis of willingness to pay, it is also interesting
to observe how the dam removal "referendum" turned out. In Table 5.4, it

Table 5.3 *Mean ratings, standard errors, and the rankings of the mean ratings and standard errors for key survey questions*

	Fort Covington				Non-Fort Covington			
	Mean	Rank	Std error	Rank	Mean	Rank	Std error	Rank
How important do you consider environmental protection in general?	4.171	1	0.07876	6	4.259	1	0.10307	6
How important do you consider the protection of endangered species?	4.054	2	0.08398	4	4.172	2	0.11038	5
How concerned are you about safety issues on rivers in Franklin County?	3.884	3	0.08195	5	3.724	3	0.12731	3
How concerned are you about the cost of repairing and maintaining river structures (such as dams) in Franklin County?	3.661	5	0.08466	3	3.544	4	0.12281	4
How concerned are you about flooding problems along rivers in Franklin County?	3.866	4	0.09102	2	3.431	6	0.13271	2
How concerned are you about making rivers flow more naturally?	3.481	6	0.09621	1	3.456	5	0.13726	1

Table 5.4   *Number and percentage of people voting yes to payment, no to payment, or yes to dam removal but no to payment*

	Fort Covington	Percentage	Non-Fort Covington	Percentage
Voted yes to payment question	50	44.64	34	58.62
Voted no to payment question	62	55.36	24	41.38
Want dam removed but voted no for some reason	21	18.75	11	18.97

is evident that a minority of Fort Covington respondents voted yes to the payment question whereas a majority of non-Fort Covington respondents voted yes. In both samples, almost 19 percent of respondents voted against the payment but said they did indeed want the dam removed. By adding these individuals to the percent of those who voted yes to the payment question, it becomes clear that the great majority of respondents supported the dam removal project regardless of their willingness or ability to pay for it. In fact, about 63 percent of the Fort Covington sample and 78 percent of non-Fort Covington respondents wanted the dam removed.

Open-ended follow-up questions placed after the payment question were used to gauge respondents' voting rationale. Overwhelmingly, four specific reasons were cited by the respondents in their reasons for voting yes on the payment question: improving safety, reducing flooding, improving fishing/fish populations, and returning the river to a more natural state. This is extremely interesting because safety and flooding issues were barely mentioned in the information provided in the survey. Only six out of 49 lines of text (about 12 percent) were dedicated to these two concerns in the information section of the survey, with the majority of the remaining lines dedicated to environmental issues. Though both samples have a significant desire to return the river to a more natural state, the non-Fort Covington respondents cited it most as the reason for voting yes to the payment question; Fort Covington respondents ranked this category fourth. One surprise is the difference between the two samples regarding the elimination of costs associated with repair and maintenance of the dam. Only 2 percent of the Fort Covington sample cited this as a reason for voting yes versus over 17 percent of the non-Fort Covington respondents. Perhaps this is because those living outside of Fort Covington feel a sense of unfairness in that they would have to pay for repairs while a very small part of the county's population would reap most of the benefits.

The follow-up question regarding the reasons for voting no to the payment question was used to gain an understanding of which zero bids may actually be protest bids. Examples of protest bids include zero bids (or votes of no) that are made because the respondent believes somebody else should pay. In such a case, the respondent may actually derive positive economic value from the good but refuse to pay because of ethical or other considerations. Not all respondents who answer no to the payment question are considered protestors. Generally, bids of zero are treated as true zeros if the reason for the bid has something to do with the respondent's budget constraint. People who simply cannot afford the payment or someone who is already spending money on similar programs are considered to be giving true zero bids.

Respondents who voted no were allowed to choose any of five categories on the survey qualifying their response and were also given room to write an open-ended response to either expound on their choice(s) or offer a reason not provided in the choices. Most people selected an option and wrote a comment or two explaining their reasoning. Almost 50 percent of Fort Covington respondents who answered no to the payment question did so because they did not want the dam to be removed; however, a significant number of these respondents also noted that they felt somebody else should pay for the project. Comments written on the optional comment sheets that were provided with the survey confuse matters further, as many who said they did not want the dam removed spent a lot of time complaining that the people of Franklin County should not have to pay for the project. In short, it is difficult to tell if people who said they did not want the dam to be removed did so honestly or as some sort of strategy to avoid having to pay for the project.

For this study, all respondents who voted no for the dam removal project were left in the econometric analysis. This was done because written answers to the follow-up questions and comment sheets used by Fort Covington respondents provided evidence that there may actually be a significant number of people with negative WTP in the sample. If this is true, removing such individuals would bias the mean WTP upward, contrary to the goal of most WTP studies.

The mean WTP for the town of Fort Covington was estimated at $29.52 while the mean WTP for the rest of Franklin County was $70.80 (Table 5.5). Aggregating these values over their appropriate populations produced total social benefits of $18 331.92 for Fort Covington and $1 225 548.00 for non-Fort Covington residents. By adding these values, the total social benefits for the entire county amounted to $1 243 879.92. The lower-bound estimates of mean WTP using the Turnbull distribution-free estimator (Haab and McConnell, 2002) were $18.70 for Fort Covington respondents and $41.08 for non-Fort Covington respondents, providing a lower-bound estimate of total social benefits for Franklin County of

Table 5.5   Mean WTP estimates and total social benefits and costs

	Fort Covington households	Non-Fort Covington households
Mean WTP	$29.52	$70.80
Turnbull estimate of WTP	$18.70	$41.08
Households	621	17310
Lower bound estimate of total PV social benefits	$11 615.77	$711 012.90
Lower bound estimate of total PV social benefits for Franklin County	$722 628.67	
PV cost estimate for dam removal project	$167 876.45	

$722 628.67. Compared to the $167 876.45 in estimated removal costs (Kwasnowski, 2004), even the lower-bound estimate produces a benefit–cost ratio for the county greater than 4:1.

The finding in this study that the mean WTP was higher for people who lived farther away from the dam is consistent with the high-head dam removal study by Loomis (1996). In that study, it was found that residents of the state of Washington were willing to pay more for removal of the Glen Canyon dam ($73) than residents of the county in which the dam was located ($59). In that case, all residents could benefit from the restoration of salmon in the Elwha River, but residents closer to the dam would also be losing fishing and boating venues. While the Fort Covington dam is a low-head structure, the situation is somewhat similar. In Franklin County, all residents would stand to benefit from improved conditions for fish species, but the removal would take away a popular fishing location for residents living close to the dam.

The difference in WTP also highlights a crucial point of concern with respect to the benefits and economic feasibility of low-head dam removal in Franklin County. Given the estimated total cost for the dam removal project, it is obvious that the total social benefits to the county outweigh the costs. But social benefits to the town of Fort Covington amount to less than $20 000, far less than the cost of the project. The problem then becomes one of who should pay for the project. Fortunately for Fort Covington, a grant will by paying for most, if not all, of the dam removal. Without the grant, however, it is difficult to imagine the town itself paying for removal. Even though it has been demonstrated in this study that total social benefits to the county could be close to $1 million, the benefit–cost ratio for the town would be less than 1:8. This problem cannot be overstated and should be taken into consideration by any group of people contemplating dam removal, especially in small municipalities like Fort Covington.

The data collected in this study provide no way of testing exactly why Fort Covington residents had a lower WTP than non-Fort Covington residents, but it can be hypothesized that a significant number of Fort Covington residents actually had a negative WTP for dam removal. Many open-ended responses to the survey included phrases such as "I like hearing the water fall over the dam" or "the dam is my favorite fishing location." Whether from the aesthetics or the convenient fishing location it provided, many residents derived utility from the dam. Those who did not live in close proximity to the dam were less likely to get any utility from it. Indeed, most non-Fort Covington respondents said they had never seen the dam and some did not know it existed. For these respondents, the only decision to be made was whether or not they wanted to pay the specified bid value for the potential benefits of dam removal. For the Fort Covington respondents, they had to decide whether or not they wanted to pay for the dam removal and, if so, whether or not the benefits they would derive out of the removal would exceed the benefits they may already derive from the dam in its current state.

This has important implications for dam removals throughout the country. First, if benefits are not equal, who should pay for the dam removal? In this case, grant money will likely pay for the removal of the Fort Covington dam, which should prevent controversy over the town paying for a project that mainly benefits outsiders. Even so, it is possible (from the anecdotal evidence collected in the surveys) that some Fort Covington residents will be worse off after the dam is removed. Thus, it behooves proponents of dam removal projects in other areas to address distributional issues.

Implications are also evident from the significant variables affecting WTP for the two samples. The variable representing the importance a respondent places on the protection of endangered species was highly significant in both models. This suggests that people may be WTP more to remove a dam if the removal would benefit an endangered species. In the Fort Covington case, it was stated that dam removal would be beneficial to a threatened species, the Eastern Sand Darter.

The "price" of the dam removal (the bid value in the payment question) for each respondent was also highly significant and negatively correlated with WTP. While this is consistent with economic theory and not at all unexpected, it does show that proponents of dam removal projects can expect more support from people if the per capita cost of the project is low. Many respondents who were not willing to pay for the project noted that they did not object to the project but that the supporters should apply for grants to cover the cost.

While household income was a significant variable in the non-Fort Covington model, it was insignificant in predicting the WTP of Fort Covington residents. As non-Fort Covington household incomes increased, they were more likely to vote yes to the payment question. In Fort Covington, income simply did not matter.

The WTP was also positively correlated with the following variables: Fort Covington respondents' knowledge about dam removal projects to improve safety conditions, membership in environmental organizations, and by level of concern regarding flooding issues along the Salmon River (all three were significant). The second correlation was expected, but the first and the third are rather interesting. The fact that the probability of a yes response increased if the respondent knew about safety-oriented dam removals suggests that people who are informed about such projects are more likely to vote for them. This sounds like common sense, but it should be instructive to proponents, especially if they are proposing the removal of dams that pose safety problems. The positive correlation of flooding awareness with WTP suggests that people who are concerned about flooding believe that dam removal can help alleviate the problem.

One of the most interesting findings in this study was the insignificance of all variables relating to fishing and boating on the Salmon River. This is especially perplexing given that the majority of the information about the dam removal project in the survey was about the potential fishing and boating benefits. The insignificance of variables representing the ways people use the river and the significance of variables representing concern for endangered species suggest that the majority of the value assigned to the removal of the Fort Covington dam is actually nonuse or passive-use value.

CONCLUSION

The CVM study showed that removal of the Fort Covington dam would indeed produce benefits far exceeding costs – even the conservative, lower-bound estimate of WTP resulted in benefits four times greater than the costs. Interestingly, survey responses and higher WTP outside of Fort Covington suggest nonuse values may be driving the low-head dam removal trend. At least, that is the case in this study despite significant evidence that pointed towards increased fishing and recreational opportunities post-removal.

While the benefit–cost ratio exceeded one, significant spatial differences emerged. Like previous studies showed, removal of the Fort Covington dam stands to produce greater benefits outside of the most affected area. This reality demands attention, especially in rural areas like Franklin County, New York, as disparities in benefits can lead to controversies over who should pay. More extreme cases of disparity may exist in other parts of the country. For instance, there may be low-head dams that provide so much utility to residents in close proximity to them that total WTP could be negative. If WTP farther away is high enough to push the total benefit–cost ratio over one, even greater controversy may arise regarding not just who should pay, but whether or not the dam should be removed at all.

In the end, benefit disparities are not enough to refute the fact that low-head dam removal, at least in the case of Fort Covington, is economically prudent. Indeed, existing low-head structures are holding back more than just water.

NOTE

1. John M. Farrell, PhD, is director of the Thousand Islands Biological Station, Department of Environmental and Forest Biology, State University of New York, College of Environmental Science and Forestry.

REFERENCES

Abdul-Mohsen, A. (2005), "Economic efficiency and income distribution evaluation of toxics and dam removal using contingent valuation," dissertation, The Ohio State University.

American Rivers (2000), "Kennebec recovery well underway a year after removing Edwards Dam," *American Rivers*, **28**, 2–6.

Arrow, K., R. Solow, P. Portney, E. Leamer, R. Radner, and H. Schuman (1993), "Report of the NOAA Panel on Contingent Valuation," *Federal Register*, **58** (10), 4602–4614.

Born, S.M., K.D. Genskow, T.L. Filbert, N. Hernandez-Mora, M. Keefer, and K. White (1998), "Socioeconomic and institutional dimensions of dam removals: the Wisconsin experience," *Environmental Management*, **22**, 359–70.

Dillman, D.A. (2000), *Mail and Internet Surveys: The Tailored Design Method*, 2nd edn, New York: John Wiley & Sons.

Doyle, M.W., J.M. Harbor, and E.H. Stanley (2003a), "Toward policies and decision-making for dam removal," *Environmental Management*, **31** (4), 453–65.

Doyle, M.W., E.H. Stanley, J.M. Harbor, and G.S. Grant (2003b), "Dam removal in the United States: emerging needs for science and policy," *EOS, Transactions, American Geophysical Union*, **84** (4), 29–36.

Environmental Valuation Reference Inventory (EVRI) (2004), accessible online at http://www.evri.ca.

Federal Emergency Management Agency (FEMA) (1999), *Availability of Dam Insurance: A Report to Congress*, Washington, DC: National Dam Safety Program, FEMA Mitigation Directorate.

Graf, W.L. (1993), "Landscapes, commodities, and ecosystems: the relationship between policy and science for American rivers," in Water Science and Technology Board, National Research Council, *Sustaining Our Water Resources*, Washington, DC: National Academy Press, pp. 11–42.

Great Lakes Protection Fund (GLPF) (2002), *Coupling Ecological, Economic, and Engineering Studies to Formulate Guidelines for Dam Removal and River Restoration in Great Lakes Watersheds*, T.C. Granata, F. Hitzhusen and U. Zika, GLPF Proposal 671.

Haab, T.C. and K.E. McConnell (2002), *Valuing Environmental and Natural Resources*, Cheltenham, UK and Northampton, MA, USA: Edward Elgar.

Hanley, N. and C.L. Spash (1993), *Cost–Benefit Analysis and the Environment*, Aldershot, UK and Brookfield, US: Edward Elgar.

Hart, D.D., T.E. Johnson, K.L. Bushaw-Newton, R.J. Horwitz, A.T. Bednarek, D.F. Charles, D.A. Kreeger, and D.J. Velinsky (2002), "Dam removal: challenges and opportunities for ecological research and river restoration," *BioScience*, **52** (8), 669–81.

Heinz Center (2002), "Dam removal: science and decision making," The H. John Heinz III Center for Science, Economics, and the Environment.

Johnson, S.E. and B.E. Graber (2002), "Enlisting the social sciences in decisions about dam removal," *BioScience*, **52** (8), 731–8.

Johnston, L.R. (1992), *A Status Report on the Nation's Floodplain Management Activity: An Interim Report*, Washington, DC: Federal Interagency Floodplain Management Task Force, contract no. TV-72105A.

Kareiva, P., M. Marvier, and M. McClure (2000), "Recovery and management options for spring/summer Chinook salmon in the Columbia River Basin," *Science*, **290**, 977–9.

Kruse, S. (2004), "Creating an interdisciplinary framework for economic valuation: a CVM application to dam removal," dissertation, The Ohio State University.

Krutilla, J. (1967), "Conservation reconsidered," *American Economic Review*, **56**, 777–86.

Kwasnowski, D. (2004), personal communication.

Loomis, J.B. (1996), "Measuring the economic benefits of removing dams and restoring the Elwha River: results of a contingent valuation survey," *Water Resources Research*, **32** (2), 441–7.

Lowry, W.R. (2003), *Dam Politics: Restoring America's Rivers*, Washington, DC: Georgetown University Press.

Mitchell, R.C. and R.T. Carson (1989), *Using Surveys to Value Public Goods: The Contingent Valuation Method*, Washington, DC: Resources for the Future.

National Research Council (NRC) (1992), *Restoration of Aquatic Ecosystems: Science, Technology, and Public Policy*, Washington, DC: National Academy Press.

Olsen, D., J. Richards, and R.D. Scott (1991), "Existence and sport values for doubling the size of the Columbia River basin salmon and steelhead runs," *Rivers*, **2** (1), 44–56.

Poff, L.N. and D.D. Hart (2002), "How dams vary and why it matters for the emerging science of dam removal," *BioScience*, **52** (8), 659–68.

Portney, P.R. (1994), "The contingent valuation debate: why economists should care," *Journal of Economic Perspectives*, **8** (4), 3–17.

Sanders, L., R. Walsh, and J. Loomis (1990), "Toward empirical estimation of the total value of protecting rivers," *Water Resources Research*, **26** (7), 1345–58.

State of Ohio versus *US Department of the Interior* (1989), US District Court of Appeals (for the District of Columbia), number 86-1575, July 14.

US Census (2000), *United States Census 2000*, The United States Census Bureau, accessible online at www.census.gov/main/www/cen2000.html.

US Department of the Interior (1986), "Natural resource damage assessments, final rule," *Federal Register*, **51** (148), 27 614–27 753.

US Water Resources Council (1983), *Economic and Environmental Principles for Water and Related Land Resources Implementation Studies*, Washington, DC: US Government Printing Office.

Vaughn, G.F. (1997), "Siegfried von Ciriacy-Wantrup and his safe minimum standard of conservation," *Choices*, **12** (4), 30–33.

Warren, D. (2004), "An estimation of the economic benefits of low-head dam removal," MS thesis, AED Economics Department, The Ohio State University, Columbus, Ohio.

6. Economic analysis of infrastructure and water quality improvements in the Muskingum River Corridor

Fred J. Hitzhusen, Radha Ayalasomayajula, and Sarah Lowder

INTRODUCTION

The Muskingum River, which flows 75 miles through four counties in an economically depressed region of southeastern Ohio in The Great Lakes region of the US provides an example of the roles a river can play in regional development. Although the Muskingum tributary is small relative to the Mississippi Basin of which it is a part, it illustrates many important issues of public policy. Throughout the length of the river are 10 sets of locks and dams that were constructed between 1837 and 1841 to facilitate transport of products by barge (see Figure 6.1). The original features of the locks have been maintained throughout the century, making them an interesting attraction for boaters and anglers as well as for tourists, even though little cargo moves through them now.

The Muskingum River has the designation of an American Heritage River which implies keen interest in improvements in the river to develop the potential of the river as an economic resource. In the first stage, this study developed methodologies to estimate the current or without improvements annual recreation and tourism expenditures related to the river, and to estimate the impact of property, community and environmental attributes on values of residential properties along the river. In the second stage, the study determined the costs and benefits of residential property value impacts in addition to proposed river corridor improvements including: (a) improving water quality in the river, (b) developing a bike trail/greenway along the river, (c) repair of locks and dams on the river, and (d) zoning and subdivision restrictions in Muskingum, Morgan and Washington counties.

The methods applied for estimating costs in this study are market-based opportunity cost concepts. Benefits are more difficult to observe in market

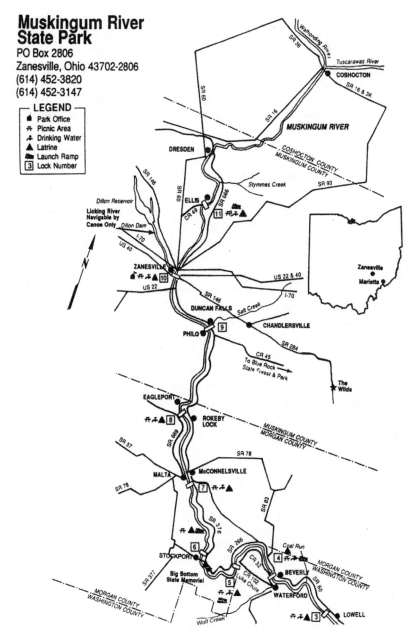

Source: Ohio Department of Natural Resources – Division of Parks and Recreation.

Figure 6.1   Muskingum River State Park

transactions for each of the corridor improvements, so the authors used hedonic pricing and contingent valuation survey methods, benefit transfer from previous related studies and benefit capture. In all cases conservative assumptions are made in order to provide lower-bound estimates of net benefits and to avoid overstating the economic merits of the selected corridor improvements. In order to easily compare benefits and costs that are occurring over time, both the benefits and costs are expressed in 1999 dollar values at a 10 percent discount rate.

RECREATION AND TOURISM USE DATA

The majority of the recreation and tourism use data was obtained from records maintained by Blue Rock State Park in Muskingum County. These data represent the annual use for the locks and dams located on the river. Because of significant asymmetry in the data between years, an average of the values was taken from 1995–97. Lock users were categorized into six categories: lock boaters, other boaters, fishermen, picnickers, visitors, and programs. The number of lock boaters is defined as the total number of people in the boats that go through the locks; other boaters are those who launch from boat ramps in the pools and do not use the locks. The fishermen are those people who fish in the river but do not use the locks; these users may be fishing either from boats or along the river banks. Picnickers are those who are at the site primarily to picnic and therefore are counted separately from those who are only touring the lock. Programs are considered to be any sort of explanation provided by the technician regarding the function or history of the locks; this value is not reflected in the visitor count.

It was possible to get a spatial perspective on lock boaters from the 1995–97 time period by address of origin. The results reveal that 775 boats used the locks during this time period. Of this total, 26 boats (3.3 percent) were from 10 states outside Ohio (West Virginia, Pennsylvania, Illinois, Missouri, Tennessee, Indiana, Alabama, Michigan, Missouri, and Virginia) and of the remaining 745 boats from Ohio, 404 or 52 percent were from 15 cities in Ohio. Zanesville ranked first, followed by Columbus, Marietta, Lowell and McConnelsville in origin and number of boats using the locks.

The data are collected daily by the technicians at each lock and are fairly reliable. The boaters are physically counted as they go through the locks, although the numbers for the remainder of the activities are estimated by the technicians. The chief problem with these data is that the users are counted only as far as the lock master can see in either direction from the lock; therefore, some use in the pools is omitted. As a result, the estimated economic value of the corridor may be undervalued, and further data collection would be beneficial in providing a more accurate estimate.

In addition to the lock use data, annual visitation and revenues were obtained from several of the river-related businesses in the corridor. These businesses include sternwheelers in Marietta and Zanesville and the Ohio River and Campus Martius museums. Also, the annual revenues of two marinas can be approximated from information provided by the owners regarding fees and the number of club members. These annual revenues are comparable and additive to the values obtained from the benefit transfer applied to the lock use data.

Benefit transfer is becoming an increasingly widely used method of valuing nonmarket resources for policy decisions. This process involves the transfer of data from existing studies (study site) to a new study which differs from the previous work (policy site). Several problems are inherent in the transfer process, for example, the commodity valued at the study site must be identical to the commodity to which the results are being transferred. Also, the site and population characteristics of the area being used as the study site must be identical to those of the new study. Despite these complications, however, benefit transfer has many advantages. Collection of primary data is time consuming and expensive, and many studies are constrained by budget and time requirements (Boyle and Bergstrom, 1992). Benefit transfer, if used carefully, allows additional studies to be conducted at a lower cost and over a shorter period of time. The results presented later in this chapter are the product of a simple benefit transfer which was performed in order to obtain an initial, lower-bound estimate of the economic benefits that are provided by recreation and tourism in the Muskingum River corridor.

METHODS FOR COSTS AND BENEFITS OF IMPROVEMENTS

A well-developed method called *hedonic pricing* was chosen to measure the effect of corridor improvements such as zoning and septic systems on residential property values. Hedonic pricing is a method of statistically determining the amount paid for housing and community attributes as well as for environmental goods. A basic concept of the hedonic model is that the value of an asset, in this case a home, is a function of a set of characteristics; this function is known as the hedonic price function. This can be expressed as: $P=f(S,C,Q)$, where P is the price or value of the house, S is a vector of housing characteristics, C is a vector of community characteristics and Q a vector of environmental characteristics. Hedonic pricing involves decomposing property prices into their relevant components (as expressed above) to reveal the amount by which consumers value the environmental amenities and disamenities being studied. Using the hedonic function, we can estimate the change in the asset value, in this case property value, as a result of a change in any characteristic, while holding all other characteristics constant. This change is measured by the coefficient by which that characteristic is multiplied.

Zoning regulations are included in the hedonic equation developed by Ayalasomayajula (2000) to represent one community characteristic. Jud concluded in his study on the effects of zoning on residential values in North Carolina, "purchasers of residential housing seek a uniformity in neighborhood land use . . . and are willing to pay a premium for it" (1980, p. 150). An important purpose of zoning is to protect the neighborhood residents from externalities (such as decreased property value) arising from undesirable uses of land in the same area. Zoning increases the value of land in the neighborhood by preventing these uses. The purpose of zoning in any city or township is to promote the health, safety, and welfare of the citizens of that region. It is considered to be an important factor in the allocation of property rights to the residents of the region. Further, zoning contributes to the tax base of the region and it is generally the case (for example, Hite, 1995) that property bidders include the higher tax rate when bidding for a property with such attributes.

Another set of community characteristics is represented by the cost and quality of the school system; "high school graduation rate" was included as a proxy output. Expenditure per pupil was not included as an input variable, because the school districts in the corridor were of vastly different sizes. Distance to the three urban centers (Marietta, McConnelsville and Zanesville) is intended to provide a measure of relative locational advantage. A dummy variable specifying whether a property has direct river access or not, is intended to measure an environmental amenity, but lack of data made it difficult to include water quality in our model. Earlier work by Epp and Al-Ani (1979) found that river water quality has a positive impact on nearby nonfarm residential property values.

A *contingent valuation* survey of the general adult population of Ohio (a random sample of licensed drivers) was designed based on the standard reference: *Using Surveys to Value Public Goods: The Contingent Valuation Method* by Carson and Mitchell (1989). See Appendix 6A.1 for examples of the payment card format used to determine willingness to pay for a bike path extension and improved treatment of household waste. In order to identify the characteristics of people who are willing to pay for the locks and dams, bike trail, and/or septic program, we utilized bid functions. A bid function explains willingness to pay (WTP) as a function of various demographic and other characteristics of the respondent. Community leaders and policy-makers could use this information to identify what constituency they should be targeting in legislative, referendum, or fund raising efforts. By contacting or soliciting only those people who are likely to vote favorably or contribute, transaction costs could be reduced and the probability of success increased.

The benefit transfer values used for this study were derived from a 1992 meta-analysis published by Walsh et al. (1992). The authors reviewed 120 outdoor recreation studies from sites in the US between 1968 and 1988. They estimated benefits resulting from various recreational activities including camping, fishing, boating, hunting, picnicking, swimming, and sightseeing. In their article, Walsh et al. gave the activities and their median values per recreator day in 1987 dollars. The values from Walsh et al.'s study were appreciated to 1999 dollars using a consumer price index (CPI).

For this study we deflated the day use values to reflect the median household income for the three-county area, which is lower than that of American households which are more relevant to the Walsh study. Because the proportion of motorized to nonmotorized boating on the river was unknown, the average of the two values was used to calculate the benefits. On average, lock visitors probably do not spend more than an hour at a site and it is unknown whether or not they stop at more than one lock, or other river businesses. Furthermore, the magnitude of the average annual visitation to locks was suspiciously large. Therefore, a very conservative assumption was made and the value of visitation supplied by the Walsh study was divided by eight for use in this study. This resulted in a value of $3.11.

In environmental economics *benefit capture* generally relates to attempts by environmental economists to estimate nonmarket or extra market values for various natural resource projects or policy initiatives. Pearce and Kerry (1990) have suggested that environmental economics is concerned with not just the measurement or estimation but also the capture and internalization of benefits and costs from environmental service and residual flows. Considerable research activity over the past 20 years or more has been concerned with nonmarket valuation techniques for measuring (for example, Bishop et al., 1983) and transferring the economic benefits including nonuse values of various environmental goods and services (for example, Boyle and Bergstrom, 1992; French and Hitzhusen, 2001; Walsh et al., 1992). Less attention has been given to how some of these benefits could be captured and by whom in a real world policy context. This chapter explores two approaches (first-stage hedonic price model linked to tax revenue functions and Contingent Valuation Model [CVM] bid functions) for answering these questions in the context of a benefit–cost analysis of several proposed upgrades to the Muskingum River corridor in southeastern Ohio (Hitzhusen et al., 2000).

RESULTS OF ANALYSIS

Recreation/Tourism Annual Benefits

The conservative estimate of recreation and tourism annual values (1995–97) in the Muskingum River corridor is $7.3 million. If one adds the annual rental equivalent value of residential properties of $13.5 million the corridor total is $20.8 million annually for recreation, tourism and residential rent equivalents. The recreation and tourism values are lower bound estimates and the rental equivalent values are upper bound estimates, at least for residential property. However, commercial and industrial property in the corridor is not included, so both estimates and thus the totals are probably conservative.

Several models of statistical inference including fisherman use, Washington, Morgan and Muskingum property values and Morgan County property values were estimated to determine what factors influence corridor value. The statistical results identified key statistically significant explanatory variables and their relationship to fisherman use and residential property values. For example, fisherman use is influenced by presence of a dock, accessibility of the lock and dam from highway 60 or 669, availability of fuel and presence of a restaurant nearby. Variations in residential property value are explained by several characteristics of the property itself, plus existence of zoning or subdivision controls, availability of septic and gas hook-up and proximity to the river. These statistical results provide a starting point for determining the economic payoff that might be expected from various improvement proposed for the corridor.

Infrastructure Results

Earlier US Army Corps of Engineers analysis (1991) projected large increases in Muskingum River corridor recreation; and maintained that these values justified large future investments in lock and dam improvements. Analysis by Hitzhusen et al. (2000) shows that recreational use values *do not* offset the costs of lock and dam repair/upgrades. This is demonstrated with evidence that repairs and upgrades made in recent years have not resulted in any measurable increases in recreation use. Decreases in lock use have in fact been the norm. This evidence was combined with benefit transfer techniques and day use values for various types of recreation (for example, boating, fishing, picnicking and visiting) common in the Muskingum Corridor.

Since use values are inadequate, nonuse (existence, historic preservation) values were explored by implementing a contingent valuation survey of willingness to pay for lock and dam repair by a sample of the adult residents of Ohio. These results suggest benefits large enough to exceed the discounted present value costs of repairing, maintaining and operating the locks and dams; the benefit cost ratio is 1.51 and the net present value \$5 876 000 (see Table 6.2).

The proposed extension of the Zane's Landing bike trail was evaluated with a similar approach. Construction cost estimates were available for the proposed trail and it was possible to get information on annual operating and maintenance costs from other trails in Ohio. The benefits were estimated by aggregating the results from the aforementioned contingent valuation survey and the forecasted trail use. Once again the findings are supportive; the benefit cost ratio is 6.49 and the net present value (NPV) \$11 261 000.

Zoning and Septic-System Results

The costs of zoning and improved household septic systems were determined from interviewing those involved in the provision of each. The analysis of the benefits was more complex. Both zoning and household septic systems are expected to impact residential property values, so a hedonic pricing method was chosen to estimate this effect. Hedonic pricing statistically decomposes the housing/property values into house, community, and environmental attributes and estimates the relative values of each of these attributes. In the case of household septic systems it was presumed appropriate to assess benefits accruing to other stream users besides river corridor residents. Thus, the contingent valuation survey was utilized to approximate these values and the results were combined with the hedonic estimates.

The hedonic price function for the model developed for the Muskingum River Corridor is expressed as: $Value = \beta_1 + \beta_2 \text{ zoning} + \beta_3 \text{ electricity} + \beta_4 \text{ water} + \beta_5 \text{ sewer} + \beta_6 \text{ gas} + \beta_7 \text{ septic} + \beta_8 \text{ basement} + \beta_9 \text{ nacre} + \beta_{10} \text{ lnggla} + \beta_{11} \text{ room} + \beta_{12} \text{ bathroom} + \beta_{13} \text{ heat} + \beta_{14} \text{ ac} + \beta_{15} \text{ riverdist} + \beta_{16} \text{ garage} + \beta_{17} \text{ age}$.

The transformed model was estimated using the assessed values as the dependent variable. The results are presented in Table 6.1. All the coefficients except electricity, sewer, basement, and air-conditioning were significant at .05 level of significance. All the coefficients had expected signs

Table 6.1   Parameter estimates

Variable name	Estimated coefficient	Standard error	T-ratio
Zoning	0.33354	0.083	3.997
Electricity	0.07421	0.291	0.254
Water	−0.22670	0.168	−1.348
Sewer	0.07545	0.079	0.946
Gas	0.24464	0.087	2.810
Septic	0.11912	0.105	1.132
Basement	0.02589	0.104	0.248
Ln acre	0.16451	0.031	5.183
Ln GFLA	0.23710	0.112	2.114
Room	0.03778	0.019	1.914
Bathroom	0.13893	0.067	2.061
Heat	0.47661	0.104	4.558
AC	−0.02828	0.076	−0.368
Riverdist	0.21043	0.058	3.597
Garage	0.26720	0.085	3.132
Lnage	−0.23437	0.069	−3.393
CONSTANT	8.6876	0.848	10.240

except basement, which is negative but not significant. The reasoning is that presence of a basement may decrease the assessed value of the house since the basement may be subject to flooding in the river corridor.

Most of the estimated parameters are statistically significant. The coefficients larea and lgfl are the elasticities, interpreted as percentage change in the value of property due to a 1 percent change in land or parcel area and square foot of residence respectively. The elasticity of Y (dependent variable) with respect to X (independent variable) is

$$\eta = (dy/y)/(dx/x) = (X/Y)(dy/dx)$$

The other coefficients represent change in the price due to a unit change in the respective variables. As area of the property increases by one percent, the value of the property is expected to increase by 0.165 percent approximately. Similarly, as the area of the house (gfla) increases by one percent, value of the property will increase approximately by 0.27 percent. On the other hand, a one-year increase in the age of the property will result in an expected decrease in the value of the property by $230. The value of the property is expected to increase if an additional room were added to the house by $37 and by approximately $140 if an additional bathroom were added. Provision

Table 6.2 *Summary of aggregate benefit–cost results in 1999 dollars,*
i = 10 percent

	Present value of benefits	Present value of costs	Net present value (B−C)	Benefits/ costs (ratio)
Zoning	$774 000	$144 000	$630 000	5.39
Septic (cost-sharing)	$6 692 000	$4 641 000	$2 051 000	1.44
Bike trail	$13 311 000	$2 050 000	$11 261 000	6.49
Lock and dam	$17 511 000	$11 635 000	$5 876 000	1.51
Total	$38 290 000	$18 470 000	$19 816 000	2.07

of heating is expected to increase property value by $470 and a basement would decrease the value of the house by $25. Most importantly for this study, the value of the property is expected to increase by nearly $330 if the property is located in a zoned area, and by $210 if the property has direct access to the river.

From the hedonic model it was possible to determine the effect of the presence of zoning, central sewer system, individual household septic system and river proximity on residential property values in the corridor. The aggregate values are as follows: zoning $912 000; central sewer $678 000; household septic systems $1 470 000; and river proximity $637 000. The hedonic benefits for zoning when compared with costs show a benefit–cost ratio of 5.39 and NPV of $630 000. The combined hedonic and CVM results for household septic systems (with a local government 50 percent cost share of installation and full coverage of repair and cleaning) showed a benefit–cost ratio of 1.44 and NPV of $8 274 812. The results of a program of full governmental subsidization were a benefit–cost ratio of 1.39 and NPV of $2 051 000. Full subsidization is not economically viable; the benefit cost ratio is 0.72 and NPV is −$2 590 000.

At a 10 percent discount rate (a discount rate commonly used in this type of analysis) it is instructive to compare and aggregate the net present value and benefit–cost ratio results for the corridor improvements. Table 6.2 presents these results.

When using the benefit cost ratio efficiency criterion, the bike trail extension and zoning rank first and second respectively followed by lock and dam operation and repairs and upgraded household septic systems. With the net present value criterion, which is influenced by the scale or size of investments, the bike trail ranks first, followed by the locks and dams, the upgraded household septic systems and zoning respectively. In total, the four improvements have a net present value of $19.8 million and a B/C ratio of 2.07.

Benefit Capture Results

Regarding benefit capture, the hedonic based tax revenue functions showed increases in tax revenue from zoning accruing to the cities of Zanesville and Marietta (see Table 6.3) to be about two times larger than the increases from improved household rural septic systems in Muskingum and Washington counties. The hedonic-based tax revenue functions for school districts in Muskingum and Washington counties (see Table 6.4) showed sixfold differences between zoning and improved septic-system impacts. However, the annual revenue increases from zoning and household septic-system improvements are generally larger to the school districts than to the local governments.

Table 6.3   Estimated annual property tax revenue increases from corridor improvements

City	Tax millage ($)	Coefficient estimate	Number of houses in the area	Tax revenue increase ($)
Zoning				
Zanesville	44.22	269	485	5782.21
Marietta	43.18	269	464	5389.55
				$\Sigma = 11\,172$
Septic system				
Muskingum	44.22	67	1002	2975.38
Washington	43.18	67	726	2100.36
				$\Sigma = 5076$

Table 6.4   Estimated annual school district tax revenues generated by zoning and septic system

City	Tax millage ($)	Coefficient estimate	Number of houses in the area	Increase in tax revenue ($)
Zoning				
Muskingum	24.61	269	1487	9844.07
Washington	26.23	269	1190	8396.49
				$\Sigma = 11\,172$
Septic system				
Muskingum	24.61	67	1002	1652.60
Washington	26.23	67	726	1275.70
				$\Sigma = 2928$

The CVM instrument was not originally designed with bid function estimation in mind, and a limited number of observations were available, but these limitations can be resolved in future work. However, the aggregate evidence on WTP from the CVM survey resulted in benefit cost ratios of 1.4 to 6.5 for the four river corridor improvements (see Table 6.2). This, in turn prompted two river advocacy groups, Rivers Unlimited and Community 20/20, to work with US Senator DeWine in developing a $3.4 million appropriation request which was progressing through the political process until the 9/11 terrorist attack. Despite the bid function limitations, there are some general conclusions that can be drawn regarding what groups of people are more likely to have positive WTP for the three amenities.

The CVM bid function results show that previous boaters on the Muskingum River and museum visitors are likely to have higher WTP for the locks. These two groups can be easily solicited using address lists of museum visitors and lock users. Museum visitors are, however, less likely than non-museum visitors to have positive WTP for the bike trail or the septic program. This would suggest that the museum visitors should only be solicited for the locks and not for bike trail or the septic program. Users of bike trails that are adjacent to rivers other than the Muskingum are more likely to have positive WTP for both the bike trail and the septic program; this group of people could be targeted for both programs (see Hitzhusen et al., 2002 for more details).

CONCLUSIONS AND IMPLICATIONS

Any research endeavor has limitations and this study of the Muskingum River is no exception. In an ideal world, better water quality data and higher response rates on the CVM survey would have been preferred. More evidence on establishment and opportunity costs for zoning, and the economic value as well as any environmental consequences of using river water for American Electric Power's cooling needs in electric power generation would all improve the study results. More detailed estimation of economic internal rate of return and development of bid functions for the CVM survey results would improve the accuracy, generalization, and explanation of results.

These research results have some important policy implications in spite of the limitations highlighted and the need for further research. First, the methods and results demonstrate that it is possible to develop economic metrics for the costs and benefits of selected river corridor attributes. In addition, these results provide evidence for ranking corridor improvements based on the benefit–cost ratio and net present value of each attribute.

However, if magnitude or scale of the attribute improvements varies considerably, the ranking of attributes according to benefit–cost ratio and net present value may be different.

Benefit–cost ratios greater than one and positive net present values were evident at the 10 percent discount rate for all Muskingum River Corridor attributes and improvements except for fully subsidized household septic systems. So, in general, the economic rationale for river improvement and restoration is supported. As an investment strategy one might propose to proceed by implementing corridor improvements on the basis of their relative economic efficiency based on their benefit–cost ratios. Some caution must be exercised. One might expect improved septic systems, lock and dam restoration and the bike trail extension to result in increased economic well-being in the Muskingum River Corridor. However, limited opportunity may exist for additional municipal zoning and hence it is unlikely that additional benefits from zoning will occur in the future.

There are some benefit capture implications from the hedonic model – tax revenue and bid function results. The absolute numbers, for example annual property tax revenue increases from zoning in the small cities of $11 172 and from improved household septic systems in two rural counties of $5076 may not seem large, but at the margin these may not be trivial increases to small municipal and rural county governments. The annual increases in school district tax revenues in Muskingum and Washington counties from zoning and improved household septic systems totaled $21 169. Explanatory evidence from the CVM bid functions can be used to target fund-raising from individual citizen-consumers as indicated, but this evidence could also be strengthened and combined with the CVM aggregate WTP evidence to develop a political economy approach and generate majority support for legislative and referendum efforts. This would seem to be a promising area for future research to assist initiatives for restoration and/or protection of rivers and other natural resource systems.

One potential advantage of these economic methods and results is to reduce conflict and transaction costs in the policy process. For example, applying a common economic metric to river corridors and other natural systems may make it possible for state departments of natural resources and economic development to find more common ground in improving the well-being for state citizens. Business and environmental interest groups may also be able to build more consensus and lower decision-making (for example, litigation) costs. Economic analysis of a river corridor or basin as a hydrologic unit may also facilitate cooperation across political boundaries for more optimal public policy and management of this natural resource system. Further analysis of selected river systems in the Great Lakes US region is presented in other chapters in this book with the hope of developing templates useful for generalizing these results to other river systems in the US and elsewhere.

REFERENCES

Ayalasomayajula, R. (2000), "Economic valuation of river corridor attributes: a hedonic and NIE approach," unpublished master's thesis, The Ohio State University.

Bishop, R., T.A. Heberlein and M.J. Kealy (1983), "Contingent valuation of environmental assets: comparisons with a simulated market," *Natural Resources Journal*, **33**, 619–33.

Boyle, K.J. and J.C. Bergstrom (1992), "Benefit transfer studies: myths, pragmatism and idealism," *Water Resources Research*, **28**, 657–63.

Carson, R.T. and R.C. Mitchell (1989), *Using Surveys to Value Public Goods: The Contingent Valuation Method*, Washington, DC: Resources for the Future.

Epp, D.J. and K.S. Al-Ani (1979), "The effect of water quality on rural nonfarm residential property values," *American Journal of Agricultural Eonomics*, **61** (3), 529–34.

French, D. and F. Hitzhusen (2001), "Status of benefits transfer in the United States and Canada: a comment," *Canadian Journal of Agricultural Economics*, July, 259–66.

Hite, D. (1995), "Welfare measures for an environmental disamenity in the residential real estate market," unpublished PhD dissertation, The Ohio State University.

Hitzhusen, F.J., R. Ayalasomayajula and S. Lowder (2002), "Some conceptual clarification and empirical evidence on benefit capture: a river corridor case," AEDE Working Paper, The Ohio State University, September.

Hitzhusen, F.J., S. Lowder and R. Ayalasomayajula (2000), "Muskingum River economic valuation," AED Economics Department, The Ohio State University, Summer.

Jud, D.G. (1980), "Effects of zoning on single-family residential property values: Charlotte, North Carolina," *Land Economics*, **56** (2), 142–53.

Pearce, D.W. and T.R. Kerry (1990), *Economics of Natural Resources and the Environment*, Hemel Hempstead: Harvester Wheatsheaf.

United States Army Corps of Engineers (1991), "Muskingum River lock and dam study: reconnaissance report," Huntington District, Huntington, WV., December.

Walsh, R.G., D.M. Johnson and J.R. McKean (1992), "Benefit transfer of outdoor recreation demand studies, 1968–88," *Water Resources Research*, **28**, 707–13.

APPENDIX 6A.1:   CVM SURVEY

There is currently a short bike path (2.7 miles long) located in northern Zanesville. An extension of this path has been proposed that will run north to Dresden. Imagine you are approached by someone who asks you to donate towards the extension of the Zanesville trail. How much would you pay (as a one-time donation) towards funding the extension of the Zanesville bike trail along the Muskingum River?

$0.00	❐
$10.00	❐
$25.00	❐
$50.00	❐
$75.00	❐
$100.00	❐

more than $100.00 (please specify amount) _____.

The effectiveness and existence of household waste treatment systems varies across households in the Muskingum River. That is, some households have septic systems that are in good working order, others have septic systems that are not functioning well and still others do not have septic systems and are not connected to a sewage treatment plant. Because household waste is emptied directly into the river after it has or has not been treated, it is regarded as a threat to the water quality of the Muskingum River.

Imagine you were asked to contribute towards an effort to improve the treatment of household waste produced by homes that are located on the banks of the Muskingum River. This effort would involve installation of treatment plants in areas where doing so is economically feasible (due to large enough household density). In areas where individual septic systems are necessary, the local health departments would service (replace baffles, repair motors, etc.) and pump out every household's septic system at no cost to the owner. How much would you pay (as a one-time donation) to help install, upgrade, and maintain household septic and sewage treatment along the Muskingum River?

$0.00	❐
$10.00	❐
$25.00	❐
$50.00	❐
$75.00	❐
$100.00	❐

more than $100.00 (please specify amount) _____.

7. Economic analysis of water quality and recreational benefits of the Hocking River Valley

Allan Sommer and Brent Sohngen

INTRODUCTION

Outdoor recreation is a highly valued resource to a large number of consumers in the US. Bergstrom and Cordell (1991) suggest that outdoor recreation in the United States is worth $172 billion per year (1997 US dollars). Water-based recreation in particular is an important activity, however, long-term degradation to water quality can reduce its social value. While many watershed groups and grass-roots organizations work locally to try to improve water quality conditions in rivers and streams, these groups unfortunately, do not have access to economic information that can help them make better decisions. Local groups increasingly are searching for information on the benefits of recreational and other uses of river water resources in their regions.

When information is not available, as is often the case in small, rural watersheds, groups can choose to go without data or they can work to develop estimates. To develop estimates relevant for their local region, economists suggest that groups have two choices. They can rely on benefit transfer (Smith et al., 2002; Walsh et al., 1992), a method that adopts results from studies in other regions, or they can collect and analyze data on their own. While benefit transfer holds promise as a low-cost method to provide data for local groups, this study presents an example where primary data were collected locally, and used to estimate benefits of water quality improvements. Data collection can be costly and time-consuming, but when local watershed groups work with researchers, meaningful results can be obtained without exceptionally large expenditures.

Having access to information on the benefits of environmental improvements can help local watershed groups in many ways. Today, more than ever, local groups are being asked to show the efficiency of expenditures with federal or state grants. Information on the dollar value of benefits provided can be a strong argument in favor of continued funding. Groups also often make difficult choices about which activities to undertake locally. Information on benefits can be used to help determine which activities are most important to tackle first. Such information may also help groups target expenditures within a watershed. Finally, many rural watersheds may in fact be overlooked by funders simply because the perceived benefits lie more heavily in populated areas.

To address these important benefit–cost questions, this chapter examines the benefits of improving water quality in a rural watershed of southeastern Ohio. This region is heavily influenced by acid mine drainage. Although over 4000 miles of streams in the Eastern United States (Kim et al., 1982) and 5000 to 10 000 stream miles in the West (USDA Forest Service, 1993) are affected by acid mine drainage, only a few studies investigate the recreational benefits of mitigating acid mine drainage (Farber and Griner, 2000; Hitzhusen et al., 1997; Huszar et al., 2001; Shaw, 1991; Shaw and Lambert, 2000). Unfortunately, cleaning up acid mine drainage has proven to be an expensive proposition, as it often involves expensive technological fixes like redirecting water around old mines, or installing limestone spillways to treat water as it leaves mines. Having estimates of the value of such improvements can help local groups secure funds for reclamation, and the values can help state and federal policy makers evaluate different options.

We build upon recent advances in survey techniques and valuation methods that link revealed and stated preference to show how individuals value specific improvements in water quality in this region (that is, Adamowicz et al., 1994; 1997; Earnhart, 2001; Huang et al., 1997; Kling, 1997; Whitehead et al., 2000). Questionnaires were administered to anglers and boaters in a seven county area surrounding the Hocking River Valley (HRV) in southeastern Ohio. The results show that recreational water users in this region of Ohio would value water quality improvements and change their trip-taking behavior if water quality were improved. Anglers are more sensitive than boaters to the changes and they consequently obtain most of the increase in value when water quality changes. The results also suggest that alternative sites outside the Hocking River Valley behave as complements in demand, suggesting that if water quality improvements in the Hocking River Valley increase trips, those outside the region will not necessarily decline.

DATA

The study area for this analysis is the Hocking River Valley (HRV) located in southeastern Ohio (Figure 7.1). The HRV contains six sub-watersheds

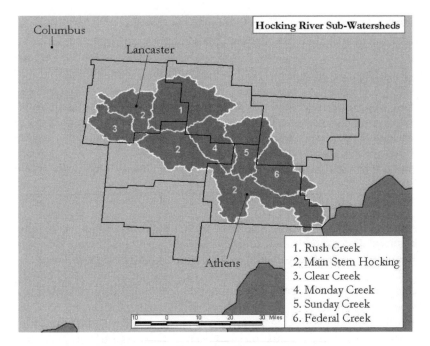

Figure 7.1   Hocking River Valley and surrounding counties

separated by steep ravines and deep hollows. The streams in the watershed are typically narrow and shallow with gravel bottoms. Although the HRV differs from the western part of Ohio, there are many similar sites nearby. The impacts of coal mining activity, from the 1800s to the present, heavily influence water quality in this region. With little to no regulation on the historic mining operations or the clean-up of the abandoned mining sites, the HRV is plagued with numerous mines producing acid mine drainage (AMD).

The data for this analysis was collected with a mail questionnaire to 1000 randomly selected individuals from databases of registered boaters and licensed fishers. Names and addresses for individuals with registered boats and fishing licenses were obtained from the Ohio Department of Natural Resources. Our sample was restricted to individuals from the seven counties in and around the HRV (Figure 7.1). Registered boaters were removed from the fisher database to ensure that multiple questionnaires were not mailed to the same individual. Because the total number of registrants in each county varies, the sample was stratified by county to ensure adequate responses from all counties within the HRV. To increase response rates, a follow-up questionnaire was sent two weeks after the initial mailing, and a reminder postcard was sent after four weeks. The overall response rate for

Table 7.1   Summary statistics for sample (n = 190)

	Average
Mapquest distance (miles)	13.36
Number of single day trips to HRV	2.86
Total recreational trips	20.7
Number of additional adults in party	2.18
Number of children in party	0.85
Hours spent per trip	6.99
Expenditures per trip ($)	$84
Household income	$52 529

the questionnaire was 23 percent, after accounting for questionnaires returned undeliverable. Due to the stratification, sample weights for observations are developed and used in the empirical analysis that follows.

Each questionnaire had user or activity specific questions (that is, boating and fishing), while general recreation, perception and demographic questions were identical for all questionnaires. The survey instrument collected information on trip-taking behavior within the six sub-watersheds and the respondent's primary recreation site. Given that boaters are likely to fish and anglers are likely to use boats, boaters were asked about their fishing behavior, and anglers were asked whether or not they used boats. The results revealed that 59 percent of the boaters reported that fishing is their primary activity while boating, and 50 percent of the anglers use boats when fishing. In general, respondents were found to take 2.9 single day trips to the HRV each year, and 20.7 single day recreational trips overall (Table 7.1). There are few other recreation surveys of anglers and boaters in this part of Ohio, so it is difficult to compare our survey results to other estimates. One statewide survey of registered boat owners was conducted in 1999. Individuals in these same counties in that survey indicated that they take 17 trips per year (Hushak, 1999). This difference makes sense since our survey results also indicate that those who only boat take fewer trips per year than anglers, and our survey has a large proportion of anglers. Average household income for the respondents in our survey is $52 529 and median income is $45 000, which is slightly higher than the US Census estimate of median household income for this region of $41 987 (US Census Bureau, 2000). This also makes sense because Hushak (1999) also finds that in Ohio, boaters tend to have higher income on average than the general population.

Table 7.2 presents water quality in the six sub-watersheds of the HRV and the number of trips to each watershed reported by the respondents. Water quality measures were obtained from the Ohio Environmental

Table 7.2   Water quality and average number of trips to sub-watersheds in the Hocking River Valley

	Baseline % streams meeting water quality standards	Additional trips		
		Baseline	Small change	Large change
Sunday Creek	4	0.3	0.3	0.5
Monday Creek	10	0.1	0.2	0.3
Main Stem Hocking	25	0.8	1.1	1.9
Rush Creek	25	0.8	0.5	0.9
Clear Creek	59	0.9	0.8	1.3
Federal Creek	84	0.1	0.2	0.4
Total trips in HRV	–	2.9	3.1	5.4
Total trips outside HRV	–	11.6	–	–

Protection Agency (EPA) (1998). Their measures take into account dissolved oxygen, pH, biological criteria, and other pollutant concentrations. Two of the sub-watersheds in the HRV have conditions with less than 10 percent of the streams in the sub-watershed meeting state standards, while 84 percent of streams in Federal Creek meet state standards. The primary cause of impairment in this region according to the Ohio EPA is acid mine drainage. Acid mine drainage results in low pH levels, precipitation of heavy metals and increased turbidity.

To assess how individuals may respond to hypothetical changes in water quality respondents were provided with information on baseline water quality conditions for each of the sub-watersheds. This information was provided in two places. A map was provided on the first page of the questionnaire showing each sub-watershed graphically, and the proportion of streams in that sub-watershed meeting water quality standards. A stated preference question providing baseline water quality measures and hypothetical improvements then asked individuals to state how many trips they would take to each sub-watershed. The stated preference question is shown in Appendix 7A.1. Table 7.2 presents baseline trips and the additional annual trips individuals stated they would take under improved water quality conditions.

One problem with the questionnaire employed for this research is that we did not control for the information treatment. That is, even though most respondents stated that water quality was important or very important to them, it is possible that they did not know the "objective" quality of water before we presented it to them in the questionnaire. Simply providing the objective measures of water quality to the respondents could influence their stated behaviors. Unfortunately, we are unable to test specifically whether the revelation of water quality information had a separate influence on the stated results from the two hypothetical treatments. It is unclear whether this omission should bias the results upwards or downwards, however, because individuals may have had better or worse opinions about water quality in the region.

Several potential changes in behavior are evident in the raw data. First, the results in Table 7.2 indicate that some respondents would change their site choices from the baseline scenario to the alternative scenarios. In the baseline, 70 percent of the trips taken are to the individual's primary recreational site, however, in the two scenarios, only about 39 percent of the additional trips are taken to this primary site. Second, under the small and large change scenarios, approximately 17 percent and 42 percent of respondents respectively, who currently take no trips into the HRV under baseline water quality conditions, indicate that they would begin taking trips there.

TRAVEL COST DEMAND ANALYSIS

To estimate the welfare effects associated with the hypothetical changes in water quality, a travel cost demand function is estimated using a Poisson random effects panel model. Count models such as this predict the number of trips as a function of price, income, and other variables. We begin by assuming that the trip decision follows a Poisson process, where the probability of observing a particular number of trips, t_i, is assumed to be drawn from a Poisson distribution with parameter λ_i. This probability is given as:

$$\text{Prob}(T=t_i)=(e^{\lambda i})(\lambda^{ti}_i)/(t_i!) \tag{7.1}$$

For the random effects model proposed for this analysis, we are interested in the number of trips for each of three scenarios – a baseline, and two changes in water quality, small and large. Thus, the probability of observing $t_{i,j}$ trips for person i in scenario j is given as:

$$\text{Prob}(T=t_{i,j})=(e^{\lambda ij})(\lambda^{tij}_{i,j})/(t_{i,j}!) \tag{7.2}$$

Following Greene (1997) the mean of the distribution is $\lambda_{i,j}$, which can be parameterized as:

$$Ln(\lambda_{i,j})=\text{B'}X_{i,j}+u_i \tag{7.3}$$

where *B* is a set of parameters, $X_{i,j}$ is a set of explanatory variables, and u_i is a random effect for each group. The random effect captures unobserved correlation in the responses for individuals across the different scenarios. For the empirical results, we assume that u_i is distributed normally.

For the analysis, we assume that trips include all single day trips taken within the HRV. Prices are the mechanical costs of accessing the sites (that is, the direct costs of driving an automobile), plus opportunity costs of time (*TC_C*). Hourly opportunity costs of time are estimated as 30 percent of the value of the individual's wages (Cesario, 1976), where hourly wages are total income divided by 2000 working hours per year. The equation used to calculate the travel costs is presented below:

$$TC\_C = Distance(0.35) + \{(Distance/40)(Income/2000)(.30)\} \quad (7.4)$$

Since most individuals primarily visited only one of the six potential sites in the HRV under both the baseline and the proposed improvements, we use the price for accessing this primary site in the analysis. For individuals who indicated that they took zero trips to the HRV under current conditions, or would take zero trips under the two improved scenarios, the price for traveling to the center of the Main Stem Hocking sub-watershed was used.

Travel costs to a nearby recreational site, Buckeye Lake, are also included (*TC_BUCK*) in the estimation. Buckeye Lake is located just outside the HRV, and many individuals stated in their response that they took trips to this site during the season. This site is a reservoir providing both boating and fishing opportunities. Since 77 percent of respondents indicated that their primary activity on trips to the HRV was fishing (whether they were drawn from the boater or fisher samples), for the empirical analysis we include a dummy variable for individuals who indicated that their primary activity was fishing (*FISH*). In addition to these variables, income is included in the model (*INCOME*). Fixed effects and interaction terms are included in the model to account for changes in the demand function across the three scenarios considered (baseline, and two hypothetical changes in water quality). A fixed effect for each panel is included, where *P2* is a fixed effect for the small water quality change and *P3* is a fixed effect for the large water quality change. Interaction between these fixed effects and other variables are noted as *P#VARNAME*.

Table 7.3 presents the results for the full panel Poisson model (panel 1) with interaction terms for income, travel cost, travel cost to the substitute site, and whether or not the primary activity on trips is fishing. A model that includes only fixed effects for the two stated preference scenarios (panel 2) is also presented in order to test the restrictions that set these interaction

Table 7.3   Regression results – Poisson model on baseline data alone and random effects panel model with all three panels

| | Panel 1 | | Panel 2 | |
	Coefficient	Standard error	Coefficient	Standard error
Constant	−0.119	0.194	0.331**	0.104
INCOME	0.006**	0.002	−0.019**	0.001
TC_C	−0.042**	0.002	−0.029**	0.001
TC_BUCK	−0.014**	0.002	0.012**	0.001
FISH	1.836**	0.145	0.941**	0.072
P2	−0.347	0.273	0.739**	0.033
P2INCOME	0.007**	0.002		
P2TC_C	0.007**	0.002		
P2TC_BUCK	0.003	0.002		
P2FISH	0.482*	0.229		
P3	0.212	0.233	1.065**	0.029
P3INCOME	0.009**	0.002		
P3TC_C	0.008**	0.002		
P3TC_BUCK	0.004*	0.002		
P3_FISH	0.088	0.164		
Observations	190		190	
Log likelihood	−1267.44		−1295.90	

Notes: ** significant at $p = 0.01$; * significant at $p = 0.05$.

terms to 0. A likelihood ratio test comparing the two panel models suggests that the additional parameters are appropriate, and therefore the discussion focuses on the panel 1 model.

The signs for the panel 1 model generally follow theoretical predictions. Income is positive indicating that increases in income increase recreational trips. The travel cost parameter is negative, as expected. Interestingly, the parameter for the substitute site is negative, indicating that the alternative site is a complement, that is, a reduction in the price of trips to the alternative site will also increase trips to the HRV. *FISHER* is positive and significant, suggesting that anglers take more trips to the HRV than those who only boat.

The parameters for *P2* and *P3* both are insignificant. Many of the terms interacted with the fixed effects for water quality changes, however, are significant, indicating that individual characteristics, such as income, prices or dominate activities (that is, fishing) influence the change in trips with improvements in water quality. Specifically, individuals with higher incomes tend to be more responsive to water quality changes. The interaction terms on travel costs (price) for both scenarios are positive; indicating that the demand curves become more inelastic when water quality improves. Own-price elasticity in the baseline case is -1.02, declining to -0.44 under the small change, and -0.32 under the large change in water quality. Individuals appear to become less sensitive to price changes as water quality increases. The interaction term on the travel cost to Buckeye Lake is not significant for the small change in water quality, and it is positive and significant for the large change. This suggests that as water quality changes become larger, the alternative site shifts towards becoming a substitute site rather than a complementary site.

To measure welfare effects of changes in water quality, we compare annual consumer surplus in the baseline to the annual consumer surplus for the two policy scenarios. Specifically, the change in consumer surplus is estimated as:

$$\text{Change in Welfare} = \int_{P^1}^{P^{1*}} D(p)dp - \int_{P^0}^{P^{0*}} D(p)dp \qquad (7.5)$$

where P^1 is the price of the marginal trip under the policy change, P^{1*} is the choke price for the demand function with the policy change, P^0 is the marginal trip price under the baseline, and P^{0*} is the choke price for the baseline demand function.[1] For the Poisson model estimated in this chapter, equation (7.5) is calculated as:

$$\text{Change in Welfare: } \frac{\exp(x^{1\prime}b)}{b_{tc}^1} - \frac{\exp(x^{0\prime}b)}{b_{tc}^0} \qquad (7.6)$$

Estimates of predicted trips and annual consumer surplus for anglers and boaters are calculated below by producing predictions for the entire sample and then averaging across the boaters or anglers separately.

For the baseline water quality, average annual consumer surplus for boaters and anglers is $24 per trip, individuals take 1.3 trips per year, and gain $30 in annual consumer surplus from trips to the HRV (Table 7.4). Given the dummy variable for individuals who claim fishing as their main activity, predicted trips and annual surplus is estimated for anglers and boaters separately. Anglers are predicted to take 1.6 trips per year in the baseline and to accrue $37 in annual consumer surplus, whereas individuals who only boat are predicted to take less than 0.1 trips per year and to accrue $2 per year in annual surplus.

Under the two scenarios with improvements in water quality, per trip consumer surplus is estimated to increase. Relative to the baseline, both the small and the large increase in water quality provide approximately $5 in

Table 7.4   *Trips, consumer surplus per trip, annual consumer surplus, and*
                change in consumer surplus for the baseline and two proposed
                changes in water quality

	Baseline	Small change	Large change
CS per trip ($$ per trip)	$23.55	$28.43	$28.68
Change in CS ($$ per trip)	–	$4.88	$5.13
Predicted trips (#) – All	1.28	2.44	3.27
Angler predicted trips	1.59	3.05	4.02
Boater predicted trips	0.07	0.1	0.2
Annual CS ($$ per year) – All	$30.14	$69.37	$93.78
Angler annual CS ($/yr)	$37.44	$86.71	$115.29
Boater annual CS ($/yr)	$1.65	$2.84	$5.74

additional per trip consumer surplus. This makes sense because the parameter on *P3TC_C* is slightly larger than *P2TC_C*. It is nevertheless somewhat surprising that the large change scenario results in only a small
improvement in consumer surplus. One explanation is that the large proposed change actually results in improved water quality in only four of the
six sub-watersheds relative to the small change scenario. Thus, the actual
gain in water quality going from the small to the large change scenario is
less than the change going from the baseline to the small change.

The number of predicted trips and consumer surplus per trip increase for
the two policy scenarios. For a small change in water quality, angler trips
increase by approximately 91 percent while they increase only 43 percent
for boaters. For the larger change in water quality, angler trips increase 152
percent while they increase 185 percent for boaters. Boaters appear to
require larger changes in overall water quality to change the total trips they
will take to a particular region. Because anglers take more trips, they also
gain the most from water quality improvements. Annual consumer surplus
for anglers rises from $37 per year to $87 and $115 per year respectively in
the small and large water quality change scenarios.

Using the results presented in Table 7.4 it is possible to estimate the potential aggregate benefits of water quality improvements for boaters and
anglers in the region. For this calculation, we use "Annual CS ($ per year) –
All" in Table 7.4, which represents an estimate of average consumer surplus
per year for an average individual from our sample (weighted by the
stratification procedure described above). These results can be applied to the
total population of anglers and boaters in the region, 83 385. Baseline
consumer surplus from recreational boating and angling trips to the HRV
is $2.5 million. For a small and large change, annual consumer surplus is

$5.8 and $7.8 million respectively, indicating that the annual welfare gain from an improvement in water quality could range from $3.3 to $5.3 million per year for the small and large changes in water quality respectively.

SUMMARY AND CONCLUSIONS

This study estimates the value of water quality improvements in a rural watershed of southeastern Ohio. The water in this region is heavily influenced by acid mine drainage, a problem facing many watersheds across the United States. Our methods combine revealed and stated preference techniques to estimate a panel data model that captures the welfare effects of changes across two scenarios of water quality improvements. The data are derived from a survey of 1000 boaters and anglers during 2001. A total of 193 responses were obtained, of which 190 were usable for the estimates presented in this paper. When bad addresses were removed from the total sample, the effective response rate was 23 percent. A comparison of the respondents in our survey with US Census data indicates that our respondents have slightly higher income than the population in the region in general.

Individuals were queried on current recreational trips to the HRV, and their stated trips under hypothetical improvements in water quality. Survey results reveal that anglers and boaters take 1.3 single day trips per year within the HRV under baseline water quality conditions. The stated preference questions in the questionnaire provided individuals with baseline water quality data, and queried respondents on trip-taking behavior under small and large improvements. Baseline water quality within the region ranged from watersheds where 4 percent of streams meet water quality standards to watersheds with 84 percent meeting water quality standards. Under the small change, this range shifts to 25–100 percent and for the large change, the range shifts to 50–100 percent. With the proposed water quality changes, average trips would increase 1.2 trips per year (or 91 percent) for a small change in water quality, and 2.0 trips per year (or 155 percent) for a large change. For the most part, these increased trips accrue to anglers, who consequently are estimated to gain the most from the water quality improvements.

The model results suggest that trips to the HRV are normal goods (that is, higher income increases trips), and the demand for these trips becomes more inelastic as water quality improves. The most common alternative site outside the HRV is found to be a complement with the HRV, rather than a substitute. Many travel cost models, particularly random utility models, treat alternative sites as substitutes so that improved environmental quality will have offsetting effects because individuals reduce trips elsewhere. Our results indicate that improvements in water quality within the HRV may have little effect on trips outside the HRV. We do find that as water quality improvements become larger, the strength of the parameter on the alternative site diminishes; however, it appears to take a relatively large change in water quality for the cross price parameter to change in a significant way for our sample.

Using the data on current visitation, and our estimate of the annual benefit of trips to the HRV ($30 per person per year in the baseline), consumer surplus for visitation to the HRV is approximately $2.5 million per year under current water quality conditions. Under the small and large hypothetical improvements the annual consumer surplus is predicted to increase by $40 and $64 respectively. When extrapolated to the full population, a small or large improvement in water quality could have a social benefit ranging from $3.3–$5.3 million per year.

One concern that could be raised is that with a small sample of only 1000 anglers and boaters, and a relatively small number of usable responses (190), the results may be inaccurate. Our results on per trip values, however, fit within the ranges of values suggested in Bergstrom and Cordell (1991) and Walsh et al. (1992). Further, we were able to address questions the local group specifically had (for example, what would be the value of meeting EPA water quality objectives?). For watershed groups in rural areas, results from sampling efforts like this could provide useful information to assist with local efforts to improve water quality. Surprisingly, when combining local resources with research resources, it was possible to conduct this particular survey for relatively low cost. The total direct survey cost of this study was approximately $3000. Obviously, additional resources would need to be applied for developing the questionnaire, testing it, and analyzing the data.

NOTE

1. Choke price is defined as the price at which the demand function crosses the price axis, that is, the price when the quantity of trips demanded becomes 0.

REFERENCES

Adamowicz, W., J. Louviere, and M. Williams (1994), "Combining revealed and stated preference methods for valuing environmental amenities," *Journal of Environmental Economics and Management*, **26**, 271–92.
Adamowicz, W., J. Swait, P. Boxall, J. Louviere, and M. Williams (1997), "Perceptions versus objective measures of environmental quality in combined revealed and

stated preference models of environmental valuation," *Journal of Environmental Economics and Management*, **32**, 65–84.

Bergstrom, J.C. and H.K. Cordell (1991), "An analysis of the demand for and value of outdoor recreation in the United States," *Journal of Leisure Research*, **23** (1), 67–86.

Cesario, F.J. (1976), "Value of time in recreation benefit studies," *Land Economics*, **52** (1), 32–41.

Earnhart, D. (2001), "Combining revealed and stated preference methods to value environmental amenities at residential locations," *Land Economics*, **77** (1), 12–29.

Farber, S. and B. Griner (2000), "Valuing watershed quality improvements using conjoint analysis," *Ecological Economics*, **34**, 63–76.

Greene, W. (1997), *Econometric Analysis*, 3rd edn, Upper Saddle, NJ: Prentice-Hall.

Hitzhusen, F.J., L. Friedman, K. Silva, and D. Hite (1997), *Hedonic Price and Travel Cost Estimation of Stripmining Impacts on Lake-Based Property and Recreation Values*, ESO 2376, Department of Agricultural, Environmental, and Development Economics, The Ohio State University.

Huang, Ju-Chin, T. Haab, and J. Whitehead (1997), "Willingness to pay for quality improvements: should revealed and stated preference data be combined?" *Journal of Environmental Economics and Management*, **34**, 240–55.

Hushak, L.J. (1999), *Recreational Boating in Ohio: An Economic Impact Study*, The Ohio Sea Grant College Program, OHSU-TB-040, November.

Huszar, E.J., N. Netusil, and D. Shaw (2001), "Contingent valuation of some externalities from mine dewatering," *Journal of Water Resources Planning and Management*, **127** (6), 369–77.

Kim, A.G., B. Heisey, R. Kleinmann, and M. Duel (1982), *Acid Mine Drainage: Control and Abatement Research*, US DOI, Bureau of Mines IC 8905, p. 22.

Kling, C. (1997), The gains from combining travel cost and contingent valuation data to value nonmarket goods, *Land Economics*, **73** (3), 428–39.

Ohio Environmental Protection Agency (1998), *1998 Addendum: Stream Segment Summaries (95–96)*, Division of Surface Water Monitoring and Assesment Section.

Shaw, D. (1991), "Methods of assessing the sensitivity of fishing demand to acid precipitation," *Environments*, **21** (1), 45–53.

Shaw, D. and J. Lambert (2000), "Agricultural and recreational impacts from surface flow changes due to gold mining operations," *Journal of Agricultural and Resource Economics*, **25** (2), 533–46.

Smith, V.K., G. Van Houtven, and S.K. Pattanayak (2002), "Benefit transfer via preference calibration: 'prudential algebra' for policy," *Land Economics*, **78** (1), 132–52.

US Census Bureau (2000), *United States Census 2000*, United States Department of Commerce, Census Bureau, http://www.census.gov/main/www/cen2000.html.

USDA Forest Service (1993), *Acid Mine Drainage From Mines on the National Forests, A Management Challenge*, Program Aid 1505, p. 12.

Walsh, R.G., D.M. Johnson, J.R. McKean (1992), "Benefit transfer of outdoor recreation demand studies, 1968–1988," *Water Resources Research*, **28** (3), 707–13.

Whitehead, J., T. Haab, and J. Huang (2000), "Measuring recreation benefits of quality improvements with revealed and stated behavior data," *Resource and Energy Economics*, **22**, 339–54.

APPENDIX 7A.1:   WORDING OF STATED PREFERENCE QUESTION

Given the hypothetical small and large improvements in water quality proposed below, how many *additional* boating trips would you take *during a calendar year* to each watershed in the **Hocking River Valley**? The map on page one and the table below show current water quality conditions in the watersheds. *Mark 0 if you would take NO additional trips.*

Water Quality Rankings

Excellent = **75%** or more of all waters meet natural conditions
Good = **50–74%** of all waters meet natural conditions
Fair = **25–49%** of all waters meet natural conditions
Poor = **0–24%** of all waters meet natural conditions

	Current Conditions	**Small Water Quality Improvement**		**Large Water Quality Improvement**	
		Becomes	Additional Trips	Becomes	Additional Trips
Sunday Creek	**Poor**	Fair:		Good:	
Monday Creek	**Poor**	Fair:		Good:	
Main Stem Hocking	**Fair**	Good:		Excellent:	
Rush Creek	**Fair**	Good:		Excellent:	
Clear Creek	**Good**	Excellent:		Excellent:	
Federal Creek	**Excellent**	Excellent:		Excellent:	

8. Effects of pesticide use and farming practices on water treatment costs in Maumee River basin communities

D. Lynn Forster and Chris Murray

INTRODUCTION

Nonpoint source (NPS) water pollution has been a concern for several decades. Farming practices and pesticide use are sources of NPS surface water pollution in farming communities. Farm management practices, including tillage and pesticide application methods, can influence the local water quality by affecting the amount of NPS particulates and chemicals that enter nearby water (Fawcett et al., 1994; Forster et al., 2000a; 2000b; Gaynor et al., 1995; Kenimer et al., 1997; Myers et al., 2000). Besides other social and ecological impacts that these NPS pollutants might have, studies suggest that water quality can influence the cost of treating water for consumption (Dearmont et al., 1998; Forster et al., 1987; Holmes, 1988). It follows that if the suggested cause and effect relationships exist, farm management practices and land use should affect downstream water quality and community drinking water treatment costs. The objective of this study is to examine relationships between (a) land use and farm management practices and (b) downstream water quality and community water treatment costs by investigating evidence from 11 communities in the Maumee River basin.

Earlier studies have investigated water quality and drinking water treatment costs. Forster et al. (1987) investigates water treatment costs using volume treated, turbidity, soil erosion rates, and storage capacity as the explanatory variables in a Cobb-Douglas cost function. Holmes (1988) uses sediment loads by region along with streamflow and storage capacity to estimate a water quality function. Using the water quality function and cost estimates for several standard water treatments, Holmes estimates the additional treatment costs from sediment loads at a regional level. Dearmont et al. (1998) examine the relationship between treatment costs and the turbidity and chemical content of the source water for treatment plants in Texas. Their cost function includes volume, a turbidity measure, rainfall, and a dummy variable for treatment plants whose source water had high levels of chemical contaminants. This chapter goes beyond the earlier studies by including both tillage practices and pesticide application rates in the model. By doing a more comprehensive approach such as this, we can make a more direct connection between farm management practices and water treatment costs within a watershed. These results may be useful when discussing the spillover effects of different farming practices.

STUDY AREA AND SAMPLE

The Maumee River basin is located in northwestern Ohio and contains a large amount of agricultural land use; 88 percent of the 4.2 million acre basin is used for this purpose. Furthermore, the Maumee River basin is located within the Lake Erie–Lake Saint Clair drainage basin that has some of the highest use of agricultural chemicals. The United States Geological Survey (USGS) estimates that herbicide concentrations in the Lake Erie–Lake Saint Clair basin are in the top 25 percent in the nation. They also note that many communities use surface water for drinking water and are required to treat the water for herbicide removal (Myers et al., 2000). In 1999 Bowling Green, Ohio, joined Iberville Parish Waterworks of Iberville Parish, Louisiana in a civil action suit against Novartis Crop Protection, Inc., the maker of Atrazine, to try and recover the cost of treating contaminated water for consumption (Forrest, 1999). Data collected for this study indicate that the surface water treatment plants (Figure 8.1) in the basin exceeded Environmental Protection Agency (EPA) maximum contaminant levels an average of 19 times a year or 1.5 times per plant for Atrazine, a widely used herbicide. These characteristics of the Maumee River basin make it an ideal location for a study of farm management practices and drinking water treatment costs (Table 8.1).

MODEL FORMULATION

As in Forster et al. (1987), Holmes (1988), and Dearmont et al. (1998), we focus on the variable costs of treating water. It is assumed that the fixed costs will not change significantly during the five-year period of this study, and in fact none of the plants in our study made any significant capital investments during the study period. Therefore, the focus of the model is

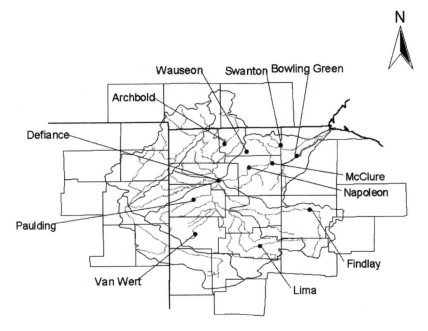

Figure 8.1   Location of water treatment plants in study area

the relationship between treatment variable costs and upstream land and chemical use.

Discussions with water treatment plant managers suggested that chemical costs are a large portion of variable costs. Chemicals such as alum, chlorine, activated carbon, and polymers are used to clarify and balance the pH of the water. It is during this stage of water treatment that most agricultural chemicals are removed from the water. Because of this, we assume that chemical treatment costs that will be affected by changes in the quality of influent water. On the other hand, nonchemical treatment costs (for example, labor and energy costs) are a function of the treatment technology and volume of water treated. As a result we developed two different variable cost relationships, one for average variable costs less chemical costs and one for average chemical costs.

Similar to the earlier studies, we assume turbidity is a good measure of water quality. However, we assume that turbidity of the water is a function of upstream farming practices and land use. Forster et al. (1987) used a soil erosion rate and the turbidity removed directly in their cost function. Holmes (1988) also used a sediment loading rate variable in his cost function. Dearmont et al. (1998) used the observed turbidity rate in their cost

Table 8.1 *Characteristics of treatment plants that participated in the study*

Drinking water treatment plant	No. of surface water intakes	Raw water storage (1000 gals)	Activated carbon used*	Population served	Largest treatment expense	Average annual million gallons treated	Average annual operating budget 1995–99 ($1000)**
Archbold	1	300 000	PAC	5 114	Softening	674	$1075.40
Bowling Green	1	170 000	NONE	40 000	Softening	1671	$896.58
Defiance	2	0	PAC	17 000		1523	$2865.00
Findlay	3	6 400 000	NONE	40 000	Softening	2599	$1580.19
Lima	3	3 141 000	PAC	74 000	Softening	5149	$1747.53
McClure	1	0	PAC	850	Softening	22	$148.00
Napoleon	1	0	PAC	10 500	Softening	497	$408.51
Paulding	1	500 000	PAC	3 318	Softening	158	$343.20
Swanton	1	110 000	PAC	4 000	Softening	190	$391.87
Van Wert	2	780 000	PAC	11 000	Clarification	642	$0.38
Wauseon	1	350 000	PAC	8 000	Power	365	$450.44
Average	1.5	1 068 272		19 435		1226	$900.64

Note: * PAC = powdered activated carbon; ** inflated to May, 2000 dollars using CPI.

118

function. We go beyond the earlier studies and develop a turbidity function that we estimate separately from the treatment cost function to capture the effects upstream practices have on water treatment costs.

For these reasons we decided to have three separate functions for the water treatment cost model to capture the complex relationships between upstream causes (land use and farming practices), and downstream consequences (turbidity and water treatment costs): a variable cost less chemical cost function, a chemical cost function, and a turbidity function. The following set of equations model these relationships:

$$AVC - ACC = f(V, A, S) \tag{8.1}$$

$$ACC = f(V, P, TR) \tag{8.2}$$

$$TR = f(TL, A, E, S) \tag{8.3}$$

where AVC is the average annual variable cost, ACC is the average annual chemical cost, V is the annual volume treated, A is the area of the watershed, S is raw water storage capacity, P is annual pesticide use, TR is turbidity, TL is a vector of land use (tilled farmland, non-tilled farmland, and so on), and E is a measure of annual erosion. We do not include precipitation as an independent variable because, after inspection of rainfall data, there was not enough variation in the annual averages among watersheds in this relatively small study area. Furthermore, studies suggest that significant rainfall events are the ones most likely to impact soil and pesticide runoff (Jaynes et al., 1999; Kenimer et al., 1997; Laroche and Gallichand, 1995). We felt annual average rainfall measures did not adequately capture these heavy rain events.

We expect the cost relationships expressed in equation (8.1) and equation (8.2) to be nonlinear, in part because of the economies of scale that are evident in the earlier studies of water treatment costs; as the volume treated increases, the average variable costs per unit decrease. We also anticipate a nonlinear relationship for equation (8.3). For example, as the storage capacity increases, we would expect the turbidity to decrease at a slower rate. Because of the nonlinear relationships, Cobb-Douglas type functions are used to estimate the relationships among the variables. Expanding equations (8.1) through (8.3) respectively to include specific variables and converting them to a log-linear form:

$$\log (avc - acc) = b_0 + b_1 \log (v) + b_2 \log (a) + b_3 \log (s) \tag{8.4}$$

$$\log (acc) = c_0 + c_1 \log (v) + c_2 \log (p) + c_3 \log (tr) \tag{8.5}$$

$$\log (tr) = d_0 + d_1 \log (cn\_low) + d_2 \log (cn\_high) + d_3 \log (u)$$
$$+ d_4 \log (nt) + d_5 \log (a) + d_6 \log (e) + d_7 \log (s) \qquad (8.6)$$

where avc is the average annual variable costs per million gallons in 2000 dollars, acc is the annual chemical costs per million gallons in 2000 dollars, v is the annual water volume treated in gallons, a is the area of the watershed in acres, s is the raw water storage capacity of the water treatment plant in gallons, p is the amount of pesticides applied annually per tilled acre, tr is the average water inflow turbidity rate in nephelometric turbidity units (NTUs), cn_low is the proportion of tilled farmland in the watershed in conventional tillage with 0 to 15 percent residue, cn_high is the proportion of tilled farmland in the watershed in conventional tillage with 15 to 30 percent residue, u is the proportion of total land in the watershed in nonagricultural use, nt is the proportion of farmland that is not cultivated or "non-tilled farmland" in the watershed, e is a weighted average of the 1992 soil erosion rate for corn and soybeans, and b, c, and d are the coefficients being estimated by their respective regressions.

We expect there to be a negative relationship between volume and the average cost variables in equations (8.4) and (8.5). As mentioned before, there is evidence of economies of scale and as the volume treated increases, costs per unit should decrease. The area of the watershed is included to act as a measure of water supply. The larger the watershed the more likely there is to be more water available for treatment. Storage capacity is expected to decrease average variable cost less chemical costs. Reservoirs may allow sediments in water to settle, and as a result, treatment costs may decrease.

Since chemicals are used in the treatment process to control for turbidity and pesticides, increases in these variables are anticipated to increase chemical costs. Forster et al. (1987) and Dearmont et al. (1998) provide evidence that water turbidity increases the cost of water treatment. The results from Dearmont et al. (1998) also suggest that the chemical content of the pretreated water, including pesticides, increase the cost of water treatment. We anticipate that the more pesticides that are applied in a watershed, the greater the amount of pesticides in the pretreated water. This would result in higher chemical costs to remove these contaminants.

The amount of pesticides applied is not the only variable that may impact the amount of pesticides in surface water. Tillage practices have also been shown to influence the amount of pesticides in surface water (Fawcett et al., 1994; Forster, 2000; Kenimer et al., 1997). There are two possible reasons for this. The first is that conservation tillage techniques tend to require the use of more pesticides for weed control and the second is reduced surface runoff would prevent some of the pesticides from reaching the surface water.

A more recent study done by Homes et al. (2001) that investigates herbicide loss and watershed characteristics found no relationships between tillage practices or watershed area and herbicide concentrations, suggesting that these variables may be insignificant. We anticipate that these effects, if any, are captured by the turbidity equation.

The relationship between turbidity and the independent variables in equation (8.6) is more difficult to predict. It is expected that conventional tillage would increase the turbidity, with the smaller the residue, the greater the turbidity. However, it may be the case that conventional tillage is employed in areas where erosion rates are lower. By including the erosion variable, we are hoping to capture this effect. Farmland that is not cultivated is expected to decrease turbidity since the soil is left undisturbed. Land that is in nonagricultural use is anticipated to have a positive effect on turbidity. Although much of this land is also undisturbed, it is more likely to contain paved areas such as parking lots and roads. These areas funnel water and their debris into storm overflows that are expected to increase turbidity by concentrating sediments and increasing water flow.

Area of the watershed is also expected to increase turbidity. A larger area causes more sediment to flow into the source water. Storage is anticipated to reduce turbidity. Reservoirs allow the sediments in pretreated water to settle to the bottom; however, since reservoirs also restrict the flow of water, the water they contain may be more conducive to algae growth, which would increase turbidity levels. We anticipate a positive coefficient estimate for erosion rates. As more soil enters the water source there is more likely to be a greater amount of suspended sediments that would increase turbidity.

DATA COLLECTION

We collected both primary and secondary data for this study. A mail survey was used to collect primary data from treatment plant managers including plant characteristics, turbidity, variable cost data, and a flow chart to diagram the plant's treatment process. Annual data were collected for the 1995 to 1999 period. The average annual total variable costs were just over $1 million per treatment plant, while annual average chemical costs are about one-tenth of these variable costs. Table 8.2 lists the total variable costs and chemical costs for each treatment plant, the costs per million gallons treated, and average turbidity. All the treatment plants use similar treatment technology, and all but one listed a chemical component of the treatment process as its greatest cost.

Table 8.2   *The total variable costs, chemical costs, chemical costs per million gallons, and average turbidity for each treatment plant*

Water treatment plant	Total variable costs ($1000)	Chemical costs	Chemical costs per million gallons treated	Average annual turbidity (NTUs)
Archbold	$1 075	$113 784	$166.48	9.37
Bowling Green	$897	$205 043	$127.50	78.19
Defiance	$2 865	$224 763	$147.08	97.67
Findlay	$1 580	$191 581	$73.38	6.04
Lima	$1 748	$354 854	$68.66	6.48
McClure	$148	$4 035	$181.97	51.72
Napoleon	$409	$74 285	$149.44	72.77
Paulding	$343	$36 204	$216.74	72.77
Swanton	$392	$25 993	$139.17	3.02
Van Wert	$0.38	$72 963	$113.76	8.86
Wauseon	$450	$43 751	$123.25	5.70
Average	$901	$122 478	$137.04	37.51

We collected secondary tillage and pesticide use data. Tillage data were collected from the Conservation Technology Information Center (CTIC) at Purdue University. The data consist of five categories: conventional tillage 0 to 15 percent coverage, conventional tillage 15 to 30 percent coverage, conservation ridge-till, conservation mulch-till, and conservation no-till. Data are in acres per tillage practice for each county and were for the period of 1995 to 1998. Data are not available for 1999 because CTIC changed their survey that year. After testing for time related trends in the 1995 to 1998 data, we chose to use the 1998 data for 1999.

Pesticide application data were collected from the US Department of Agriculture National Agricultural Statistics Service (USDA NASS) Agricultural Chemical Usage, Field Crop Summaries for 1995 to 1999. In order to estimate pesticide use in the watersheds, we collected data on the acres of each crop planted in the watersheds from the Ohio Agricultural Statistic Service county profiles. Using these data and the statewide application rates collected from USDA, we estimated pesticide application rates for each watershed in the study. Table 8.3 lists estimates of these variables for the treatment plant watersheds in the study.

We also collected precipitation and soil erosion data. Precipitation data were collected from the Midwestern Regional Climate Center for nine different weather stations in the basin. Finally, average annual soil erosion

*Table 8.3   Estimates of the pounds of pesticides applied per acre per year
and the acreage of tillage practices for the water treatment
plant's watershed*

Water treatment plant watershed	Average pounds of pesticides per acre per year	Conventional tillage		Conservation tillage		
		0 to 15% residual	15 to 30% residual	No-till	Ridge-till	Mulch-till
Archbold	1.43	29 792	16 481	57 357	629	23 272
Bowling Green	1.44	1 238 215	292 409	1 245 279	4 518	327 044
Defiance	1.61	58 121	14 737	70 635	5	7 918
Findlay	1.64	41 800	12 127	37 150	180	12 575
Lima	1.76	25 019	7 929	30 235	106	11 668
McClure	1.39	1 238 215	292 409	1 245 279	4 518	327 044
Napoleon	1.38	1 129 976	268 683	1 207 957	3 315	286 557
Paulding	1.18	57 763	10 363	52 375	0	13 257
Swanton	1.85	4 588	1 162	6 796	172	2 140
Van Wert	2.21	4 472	298	4 113	0	880
Wauseon	2.32	839	213	1 243	31	391
Average	1.66	348 073	83 346	359 856	1 225	92 068

data for each watershed were obtained from the 1992 National Resources
Inventory.

REGRESSION ANALYSIS AND RESULTS

We use ordinary least squares to solve equations (8.4), (8.5), and (8.6).
Although we can combine equations (8.5) and (8.6), we choose to solve the
equations separately so that we can estimate how changes in land use and
farming practices affect turbidity. To strengthen the statistical relationship
between equations (8.5) and (8.6), we use the predicted turbidity values
from (8.6) as the independent turbidity variable in equations (8.5). (We estimated equation (8.5) using the actual turbidity data and had similar
results.) The following results were obtained for equations (8.4) and (8.5)
respectively with *t*-values below each coefficient:

$$\log (avc-acc) = 16.68 - 0.41 \log (volume) - 0.089 \log (acres)$$
$$(13.77)^{**} \quad (-6.22)^{**} \qquad (-1.86)^{*}$$

$$- 0.024 \log (storage) \qquad (8.7)$$
$$(-1.80)^{*}$$

$$\log(acc) = 7.77 - 0.17 \log(volume) + 0.27 \log(pesticide\ use)$$
$$(11.82)^{**}\ (-5.88)^{**} \qquad\qquad (1.36)$$
$$+\ 0.30 \log(predicted\ turbidity) \qquad\qquad\qquad (8.8)$$
$$(3.53)^{**}$$

where ** indicates that the coefficient estimate is significant at the five percent level and * indicates significance at the 10 percent level. The adjusted R-squares are 0.679 and 0.595 respectively.

Since this study also investigates the relationship between land use practices and water treatment costs, it is worthwhile to consider the predicted turbidity equation. This allows us to see how turbidity is affected by various land uses in the watershed. The following results were obtained using ordinary least squares on the predicted turbidity equation:

$$\log(turbidity) = 3.10 + 1.34 \log(<15\%\ residual) + 0.10 \log(15\ to\ 30\%$$
$$(1.26)\quad (1.96)^{*} \qquad\qquad\qquad (1.30)$$
$$residual) + 2.01 \log(nonagr.\ use) + 0.07 \log(non\text{-}tilled$$
$$(2.75)^{**} \qquad\qquad (0.23)$$
$$farmland) - 1.91 \log(weighted\ average\ of\ soil\ loss)$$
$$(-1.70)^{*}$$
$$+\ 0.35 \log(area\ of\ watershed) - 0.04 \log(raw\ storage)$$
$$(3.16)^{**} \qquad\qquad\qquad (-2.29)^{**} \qquad (8.9)$$

The adjusted R-square for this regression is 0.808. Because log-linear equations are regressed, the coefficients represent elasticities for their respective independent variables.

The relationship between total variable costs less chemical costs and the volume treated, acreage of the watershed, and raw water storage capacity are estimated in equation (8.7). The estimated coefficients for volume and storage have the expected negative sign. As volume and storage capacity increase, economies of scale occur and the variable costs per million gallons decrease. More specifically, a 1 percent increase in volume treated causes a 0.41 percent decrease in variable costs other than chemical costs, holding all other variables constant. It is not surprising that volume treated has a greater impact on these variable costs than storage. Most of these costs are probably associated with maintenance and electricity costs that vary more with changes in volume than changes in storage capacity or watershed area.

Equation (8.8) estimates how chemical costs per million gallons at water treatment plants are influenced by the volume treated, the per tilled-acre amount of pesticides used in each watershed, and the predicted turbidity from the reduced form equation. All of the estimated coefficients have the expected sign. A 1 percent increase in the amount of pesticides used or a 1 percent increase in the turbidity of the water would cause a 0.27 percent increase or a 0.30 percent increase in chemical costs respectively. A 1 percent increase in the volume treated would cause a decrease of 0.17 percent in the chemical costs. Both the volume and predicted turbidity are significant at the 1 percent level indicating that the coefficient estimates are significantly different from zero. The pesticide coefficient is significant at the 20 percent level.

Equation (8.9) investigates the relationship between the inflow turbidity rate and various land uses, area of the watershed, erosion rate, and storage capacity. The conventional tillage coefficient estimates have the expected positive sign and magnitude. A 1 percent change in the amount of conventional tillage with 0 to 15 percent residue increases turbidity by 1.34 percent, but conventional tillage with 15 to 30 percent residue has an insignificant effect. These results suggest that conventional tillage may increase water turbidity, and the amount of crop residue and soil surface coverage can influence turbidity.

Regardless of the type of conventional tillage being used, the coefficient estimates in equation (8.9) suggest that the proportion of tilled farmland in the watershed has less of an impact than land in nonagricultural use. Land in uses other than agriculture has the expected positive sign on turbidity; a 1 percent increase in nonagricultural use causes an estimated 2.01 percent increase in the average turbidity. The increase is most likely caused by the channeling of urban waters and their particles to storm sewer overflows that are being released directly into streams. Other studies of land use and water quality find similar results (see for example Ferrier et al., 2001). We anticipated that non-tilled farmland would have a negative influence on turbidity since it is much less disturbed than tilled farmland. However, the small t-value indicates that the coefficient estimate is not significantly different from zero.

The coefficient estimate for the acreage of the watershed is as expected. The larger the watershed, the more likely there is to be additional turbidity. A 1 percent increase in the area of the watershed would cause an estimated 0.35 percent increase in the average turbidity. The coefficient estimate for erosion, however, suggests a 1 percent increase in the erosion rate could cause a decrease of 1.91 percent in the average turbidity. It is also significant at the 1 percent level. This result is most likely caused by soil particle size. Soil particles are likely to be larger on the more sloping, erosive areas. When these courser particles erode they have a greater tendency to settle rather than be suspended in the water. Similarly, flat, non-erosive areas contain more clay soils with finer particles. These particles are more likely to become suspended in water and cause greater turbidity. The coefficient for the erosion variable may be partially capturing differences in soils among the watersheds in the study.

The raw water storage capacity coefficient is significant at the 1 percent level and has the expected negative sign. A 1 percent increase in the storage capacity would cause an estimated 0.04 percent decrease in the turbidity of the water. The storage of the water prior to intake allows many of the suspended particles to settle resulting in clearer water.

DISCUSSION

Using the cost data collected and the coefficient estimates from equation (8.8), it is possible to estimate the monetary change a 1 percent reduction in the pounds of pesticides applied per tilled acre. A 1 percent reduction in the application rate would be approximately 44 676 pounds of pesticides, which would result in an average decrease of $0.37 in the chemical costs of treating a million gallons of water. These results suggest that a 10 percent decrease in the chemical application rate would decrease the annual chemical costs by $4530 at the average treatment plant. These results are substantially different than the $94.75 per million gallons reported by Dearmont et al. (1998). One reason for this large difference may be that Dearmont et al. used a dummy variable for treatment plants that had exceeded maximum contaminant levels, therefore only capturing the effect of large amounts of chemicals in the water. They also investigated the cost of removing contaminants from groundwater, which is more likely to have a greater impact on treatment costs. Surface water is more susceptible to spikes in the contamination level making it possible for surface water treatment plants to only have to treat for contaminants several times a year. This additional cost would be minimal when addressing annual costs. However, contaminated groundwater may need to be treated year round therefore significantly increasing the costs. Furthermore, a study done by Miltner et al. (1989) suggests that powdered activated carbon used to control for taste and odor adequately removed pesticides for surface water treatment plants.

Our turbidity elasticities are similar to those found in other studies that estimate the effects of water quality on the costs of treating drinking water. The 0.30 turbidity elasticity presented here is close to Forster et al.'s (1987) 0.119 percent and very similar to Dearmont et al.'s (1998) 0.27 percent. We estimate a $0.41 increase in chemical costs per million gallons treated with a one percent increase in turbidity. Using the average annual volume treated for the treatment plants in this study, our results suggest that a 10 percent decrease in turbidity would result in an annual savings of $5034 for the average treatment plant.

This study goes beyond estimating the change in chemical costs due to changes in turbidity and includes a turbidity function that captures the affects of upstream farming practices and land use on the cost of treating drinking water. The results of equation (8.9) allow us to estimate how changes in tillage practices and land use affect the chemical costs of treating drinking water. A 1 percent increase in conventional tillage would increase turbidity 1.34 percent, and a 10 percent increase in conventional tillage would increase chemical costs by $6750 annually at the average treatment plant. Surprisingly, non-agricultural use has the greatest impact on turbidity; a 1 percent increase in the acreage of non-farmland causes a 2.01 percent increase in turbidity and a $0.83 increase in the average chemical costs of treating a million gallons, and a 10 percent increase in nonagricultural use acreage would increase chemical costs by $10 120 annually at the average plant.

ACKNOWLEDGEMENTS

Rivers Unlimited and the Joyce Foundation provided funding for this project. The authors would like to thank Diane Hite and Hyojin Jeong for their valuable contributions.

REFERENCES

Dearmont, D., B.A. McCarl, and D.A. Tolman (1998), "Costs of water treatment due to diminished water quality: a case study in Texas," *Water Resources Research*, **34** (4), 849–53.

Fawcett, R.S., B.R. Christsensen, and D.P. Tierney (1994), "The impact of conservation tillage on pesticide runoff into surface water: a review and analysis," *Journal of Soil and Water Conservation*, **49** (2), 126–35.

Ferrier, R.C., A.C. Edwards, D. Hirst, I.G. Littlewood, C.D. Watts, and R. Morris (2001), "Water quality of Scottish rivers: spatial and temporal trends," *The Science of the Total Environment*, **265**, 327–42.

Forster, D.L., C.P. Bardos, and D.D. Southgate (1987), "Soil erosion and water treatment costs," *Journal of Soil and Water Conservation*, **42** (5), 349–52.

Forster, D.L., R.P. Richards, D.B. Baker, and E.N. Blue (2000a), EPIC modeling of the effects of farming practice changes on water quality in two Lake Erie watersheds, *Journal of Soil and Water Conservation*, **54** (1), 85–90.

Forster, D.L., E.C. Smith, and D. Hite (2000b), "A bioeconomic model of farm management practices and environmental effluents in the western Lake Erie Basin," *Journal of Soil and Water Conservation*, **55** (2), 177–82.

Forrest, J. (1999), *Protect Our Dinking Water and Prepare Farmers for the Future*, Cleveland, OH: Ohio Citizen Action.

Gaynor, J.D., D.C. MacTavish, and W.I. Findlay (1995), "Atrazine and metolachlor loss in surface and subsurface runoff from three tillage treatments in corn," *Journal of Environmental Quality*, **24**, 246–56.

Holmes, T.P. (1988), "The offsite impact of soil erosion on the water treatment industry," *Land Economics*, **64** (4), 357–65.

Homes, M.J., J.R. Frankenberger, and B.A. Engel (2001), "Susceptibility of Indiana watersheds to herbicide contamination," *Journal of the American Water Resources Association*, **37** (4), 987–1000.

Jaynes, D.B., J.L. Hatfield, and D.W. Meek (1999), "Water quality in Walnut Creek watershed: herbicides and nitrate in surface waters," *Journal of Environmental Quality*, **28**, 45–59.

Kenimer, A.L., J.K. Mitchell, A.S. Felsot, and M.C. Hirschi (1997), "Pesticide formulation and application technique effects on surface pesticide losses," *Transactions of the ASAE*, **40** (6), 1617–22.

Laroche, A.-M. and J. Gallichand (1995), "Analysis of pesticide residues in surface and groundwater of a small watershed," *Transactions of the ASAE*, **38** (6), 1731–6.

Miltner, R., D. Baker, and T. Speth (1989), *Treatment of Seasonal Pesticides in Surface Waters*, American Waterworks Association, September, 43–52.

Myers, D.N., M.A. Thomas, J.W. Frey, S.J. Rheaume, and D.T. Button (2000), *Water Quality in the Lake Erie–Lake Saint Claire Drainages: Michigan, Ohio, Indiana, New York and Pennsylvania, 1996–1998*, USGS Circular 1203.

9. Economic efficiency and distribution evaluation of dredging of toxic sediments and selected dam removal in the Mahoning River

Ashraf Abdul-Mohsen and Fred J. Hitzhusen

INTRODUCTION

Contingent valuation (CV) has been used extensively to value nonmarketed environmental resources and public policies. Despite its sound theoretical background as a direct measure of welfare change and its ability to measure nonuse (existence) values, the validity of CV hypothetical estimates of value is still being debated. Of equal importance is the issue of equity or income distribution impacts of environmental change and how to incorporate equity into public policy analysis without sacrificing economic efficiency. This chapter examines the theoretical validity of dichotomous choice CV as well as the distributional effects of river contamination and clean-up including stated preference evaluation of environmental improvements. The study case is restoring the Lower Mahoning River in northeast Ohio through dredging of toxics and/or selected dam removal.

The Mahoning River drains 1133 square miles in northeastern Ohio and northwestern Pennsylvania. Over the years, sediments in the river have become contaminated with a variety of chemicals. Contaminated sediments in the river are primarily from waste disposal of the steel and related industries, which were operating along the riverbanks, as well as waste disposal from adjacent communities into the river. Although pollutants' concentrations in the water are now lower than before 1970 (USACE, 1999), some hazardous chemicals such as polynuclear aromatic hydrocarbons (PAHs) and heavy metals are still absorbed in the bottom sediments and prevent recovery of the ecosystem (Testa, 1997). As a result, the Ohio Department of Health (ODH) has issued an advisory against swimming and wading in the stretch of the Mahoning River from the Northwest Bridge Road in Warren, Ohio, extending downstream to the Pennsylvania border (ODH, 2001). The advisory affects both Mahoning and Trumbull counties. The ODH recommended also that consumption of fish caught in the advisory area is strongly prohibited, especially fish such as carp and catfish, which usually feed in the bottom sediments.

Currently, The US Army Corps of Engineers (USACE) is considering several options to restore ecological conditions in the Mahoning River to pre-industrialization conditions. The USACE has estimated the cost of three remedial alternatives (projects) for Mahoning River sediments. These costs (presented in 1999 dollars) ranged from $66.5 million for the minimum cost alternative (hydraulic dredging of sediments with no dam removal) to $101.3 million for the maximum cost alternative (complete dredging – hydraulic and mechanical – of the river sediments, excavation of contaminated bank materials, and the removal of all nine dams in the study area). The third alternative (intermediate cost) costs $91.5 million and entails both hydraulic and mechanical dredging of sediments, excavation of bank materials, and selective removal of five dams.

The policy objective of this research is to estimate both the economic benefits and distribution impacts of the removal and disposal of contaminated sediments from the lowest 30 miles of the river in the State of Ohio. Benefits will be estimated utilizing contingent valuation models for two alternatives: with and without removal of the low-head dams. This is expected to restore the aquatic ecosystem within the study area to the biotic integrity in a model reach on the Mahoning River just upstream of the study area, and help eliminate the ODH human health advisories. The upper portions of the river, upstream of Warren, are cleaner and known as monitoring sites. This is because Ohio Environmental Protection Agency (EPA) officials monitor water quality in these sites and their water quality levels meet EPA standards. These monitoring sites host many recreational activities such as fishing and boating and hence could be used as a benchmark for targeted water quality in the impacted area.

METHODOLOGY

Contingent valuation, a stated preference method, is defined by Randall (1987, p. 260) as follows: "contingent valuation methods (CVM) attempt to determine the amount of compensation paid (WTP) or received (WTA), that will restore the initial utility level of an individual who experiences an increment or decrement in the level of Q [some nonmarketed good]." Data required for a contingent valuation study may be collected through surveys or economic experiments. In any case, a properly designed CV instrument must accomplish the following tasks:

1. Establish the baseline conditions or the status quo (Q) regarding the availability of the environmental resource and distribution of property rights over that resource.
2. Describe the change in Q that would result from the proposed change in policy.
3. Establish a contingent market, in which participants may, hypothetically, obtain the change in Q by paying a specified amount of money through a specified payment vehicle that is both relevant and familiar to respondents (for example, increases in taxes, good prices, and utility fees).
4. Elicit participants maximum willingness to pay (WTP) for the proposed change in Q either directly through open-ended, bidding, or payment card vehicles or indirectly through referenda.

The hypothetical nature of contingent valuation might affect the accuracy of stated WTP if individuals treat the whole experiment as hypothetical or inconsequential. This, in turn, can lead individuals to give meaningless responses that do not represent their true valuation of the public good in question. Another problem with CV is strategic behavior where individual respondents try to influence the outcome of the policy through their actions. Carson and Mitchell (1989) argue that the possibility of respondents giving meaningless (hypothetical) values is a much more serious problem than the possibility of them giving untruthful (strategic) values because of the effect of the former on the validity of WTP as a measure of value. They concluded that unfamiliarity with the public good in question or with how it will be provided and paid for characterizes most of the difficulties posed by the hypothetical nature of CV.

The validity of stated willingness to pay as a measure of value has been examined extensively in the literature (for example, Hoehn and Randall, 1989; Kahneman and Knetsch, 1992b; Mitchell and Carson, 1989; Smith, 1992). The validity of a measure, as defined by Mitchell and Carson (1989, p. 190), is "the degree to which it measures the theoretical construct under investigation." Three types of validity are distinguished in contingent valuation method (CVM) studies – content validity, criterion validity, and theoretical (construct) validity. Content validity is concerned with how a CVM questionnaire presents the market structure and defines the amenity in a way that accords with well-defined preferences. Content validity is typically assessed through subjective examination of the instrument typically for wording and question ordering. Criterion validity is concerned with whether the measure of interest could be related to other measures considered to be criteria for the construct in question. A criterion is a measure of value, which is closer to the construct than the measure being validated.

Theoretical validity is concerned with the degree to which the outcomes of a CVM study – for example, the sign and magnitude of the estimated coefficients in the bid functions and the relative magnitude of willingness to pay under different split-sample conditions – are consistent with expectations of economic theory.

One way to examine the theoretical validity of a CVM study is to compare WTP estimates of different scenarios for which theory suggests statistically different or similar values. For example, economic theory would predict that the greater the amount of the public good being offered, the more an individual would be willing to pay for that amount. This has been known in the literature as scope or scale effect or part-whole effect (Whitehead et al., 1998). Theory would also suggest that the value of an environmental good is independent of the serial position of the good in a sequence of other environmental goods (sequence or order effects) and independent of the context in which the good is presented or what is known as context effects (Carson et al., 2001). The last two effects (order and context effects) constitute what has been known in the literature as the embedding effect: the value of a particular good depends upon whether it is valued alone or as part of a more inclusive agenda or package (Loomis et al., 1993). Split sampling is usually used to test for the presence of these effects and hence for the validity of contingent valuation.

Specifying and estimating a parametric model for dichotomous choice contingent valuation responses serves two objectives: first, to calculate willingness to pay for the prescribed amenity, and second, to study the effects of respondents' characteristics (demographic or behavioral) on WTP. The basic model for analyzing dichotomous CV responses is the random utility model first developed by McFadden (1974). The following presentation of the model follows that of Haab and McConnell (2002).

Suppose that an individual j is confronted with a choice between a program to provide an environmental amenity, for example restoring a contaminated river to improve recreation experience and other services provided by the river, and the status quo which is doing nothing about contamination in that river. The indirect utility function for respondent j is

$$u_{ij} = u_i(y_j, X_j, \varepsilon_{ij}) \tag{9.1}$$

where $i = 1$ if the proposed program is implemented (the alternative state), and $i = 0$ for the current state; y_j is household j's discretionary income; X_j is a vector of household-specific and choice-specific characteristics; and ε_{ij} is a random preference component that is known to the respondent but not observable by the researcher.

Respondent j would be willing to pay a specified sum (t_j) for the proposed program if his utility with program net of the payment (t_j) exceeds his utility without the program; that is, if

$$\Pr(yes_j) = \Pr(u_1(y_j - t_j, X_j, \varepsilon_{1j}) > u_0(y_j, X_j, \varepsilon_{0j})) \tag{9.2}$$

Another, and more direct, way to model dichotomous CV responses is to specify a model for the random willingness to pay function. The question imposed by the dichotomous valuation scenario then is whether WTP for respondent j exceeds the offered price t_j; that is, the respondent answers yes to the CV valuation question if his true WTP for the proposed scenario exceeds t_j:

$$WTP(Z_j, \eta_j) > t_j \tag{9.3}$$

where Z_j is a vector of respondent's characteristics, which may include household income, and η_j is a stochastic error term that is distributed with mean zero and constant variance σ^2. This function could be estimated by specifying a functional form for WTP and a distribution for the stochastic error term. Let us assume that WTP is exponential, the functional form chosen in the current CV study:

$$WTP_j = e^{\Theta Z_j + \eta_j} \tag{9.4}$$

Where Θ is a vector of coefficients to be estimated that corresponds to the vector of covariates Z. The probability of a yes response by individual j to the offered price t_j is:

$$\Pr(yes_j) = \Pr(WTP_j > t_j)$$
$$= \Pr(e^{\Theta Z_j + \eta_j} > t_j) \tag{9.5}$$
$$= \Pr(\eta_j > \ln(t_j) - \Theta Z_j)$$

Normalizing the above inequality function by the unknown standard error σ, the probability of yes can be written as follows:

$$\Pr(yes_j) = \Pr\left(\frac{\eta_j}{\sigma} > \frac{1}{\sigma}\ln(t_j) - \frac{\Theta}{\sigma}Z_j\right)$$
$$= \Pr(\theta_j > \alpha \ln(t_j) - \beta Z_j) \tag{9.6}$$

where $\theta_j = \eta_j/\sigma$ $\alpha = 1/\sigma$, and $\beta = \Theta/\sigma$. Assuming that η_j is distributed normally then θ_j is distributed as standard normal with mean zero and unit variance and the resulting model is estimated using a probit model. Likewise, if we assume that the error term is distributed logistically, the resulting model is estimable using a logit model. Assuming a normal distribution for the error term, the last inequality can be rewritten as a standard normal *cdf* function as follows:

$$\Pr(yes_j) = 1 - \Pr(\theta_j < \alpha \ln(t_j) - \beta Z_j)$$

$$= 1 - \Phi_\theta(\alpha \ln(t_j) - \beta Z_j) \tag{9.7}$$

Where Φ_θ is the cumulative distribution function for the normalized error term θ. Consequently, the probability that respondent j answers no to the offered price is:

$$\Pr(no_j) = \Phi_\theta(\alpha \ln(t_j) - \beta Z_j) \tag{9.8}$$

Suppose that the sample size is N and let $I_j = 1$ if respondent j answers yes, parameters α and β are estimated by maximizing the likelihood function:

$$L(\alpha,\beta|Z,t) = \prod_{j=1}^{N} [1 - \Phi_\theta(\alpha \ln(t_j) - \beta Z_j)]^{I_j} [\Phi_\theta(\alpha \ln(t_j) - \beta Z_j)]^{1-I_j} \tag{9.9}$$

This model can be estimated using any of the available econometric software programs such as Limdep and SAS. The estimated coefficients are then used to calculate WTP for the mean or median individual in the survey.

In order to examine theoretical validity in the current CV study, two projects for restoring the Mahoning River were considered: dredging only and dredging plus dam removal. The reason to include dam removal is that toxics removal might restore aquatic resources in the river but for a short period of time. Eventually, sediments will rebuild behind dams and cause ecological problems in the future. Although these sediments will not be as toxic as the current deposits, dam removal per se has some advantages like improving the flow of water along the river, which leads to improvements in fish habitat and better navigation for some types of boating. It is clear now that there are two different goods for respondents to value and indirectly decide if dam removal should be considered in addition to dredging. Each good produces multiple benefits. For dredging only, these benefits include a healthier ecosystem, recreational activities (fishing, boating, hiking, and so on), lifting the human health advisory, and economic return to businesses and residents of the river valley. For dredging plus dam removal, the benefits include all of the above for a longer period of time in addition to enhancing fish habitat and allowing more navigation along the river.

To test for scope, sequence, and context effects, four scenarios were sent out randomly to four groups of respondents. The first scenario asks a respondent to value dredging only. The second scenario asks another respondent to value dredging plus dam removal. The third asks a third respondent to value dredging only and dredging plus dam removal with the dredging only option offered first. The fourth scenario asks a respondent to value dredging plus dam removal first, and then asks him to value dredging only. The purpose of using the last two scenarios is to test for sequence effects; the maintained hypothesis is that an environmental good is less valued by a respondent, the later it is offered to him or her in a sequence of goods (Carson et al., 2001). Comparing the first and second scenarios allows testing for scope effects since one good (dredging only) is nested within the other good (dredging + dam removal). The testable hypothesis here is that respondents are insensitive to the scope (quantity) of the good being valued. Carson and Mitchell (1995) developed a "component sensitivity test", which rejected the hypothesis that respondents are insensitive to scope effects. This means that respondents in their study were able to perceive different levels of provision of the environmental good and took this difference into account when asked to state a value for that good.

Finally, comparing scenarios one and three, and two and four respectively allow testing for context effects. This test looks at how CV responses are affected by the context in which the valuation question is asked. The question here is: does WTP for a particular public good depend upon whether it is being valued on its own or within an agenda? Hoehn and Randall (1989) have argued that conventional benefit–cost methods in which public goods are valued independently will overstate the measure of benefits for each good. According to this argument, scenarios one and two are expected to overstate the values of (dredging only) and (dredging plus dam removal) proposals respectively compared to scenarios three and four. We test for this proposition by comparing scenarios one and two (in which dredging and dredging plus dam removal are valued independently) with scenarios three and four (in which each proposal is evaluated first in a sequence containing both proposals), respectively.

SAMPLING AND DATA COLLECTION

Choice of the population to survey is a very important factor in CV experiments since the estimated value of mean/median WTP and aggregate WTP are both dependent on the choice of survey population and the size of the population. In general, people who benefit or will benefit from the project in the future should be included, regardless of the type of benefits enjoyed (use or nonuse values). In the Mahoning River case, direct use benefits are classified by Schroeder (1998) into recreational (for example, canoeing, bird watching, hiking, and so on), ecological functional (for example, flood mitigation, pollution abatement, and biodiversity), social (for example, aesthetic and psychological benefits), in addition to economic development and lifting the ODH public health advisory. These benefits will be enjoyed by most if not all the residents of the Mahoning Valley from the city of Warren to the Ohio/Pennsylvania state line, and may also be realized by some residents in the unimpacted area upstream. Besides, residents of the Mahoning Valley in Pennsylvania could benefit indirectly (indirect use value) from the restoration efforts in Ohio since the actions taken in Ohio are expected to increase potential benefits of the subsequent actions in Pennsylvania, as shown before. Originally, Lawrence County in Pennsylvania was included in the survey but was excluded later from the sample used in model estimation because responses from this county were too few to estimate WTP in Pennsylvania.

Nonuse values, such as knowing that the Mahoning River is restored or continues to be restored for future generations, are likely to be enjoyed by all the residents of the valley along the river. The geographic zone for nonuse values might be extended to a wider area like the state of Ohio and some parts of Pennsylvania. However, we chose to limit the sample population to residents of the river valley in Ohio in order to obtain conservative and more defensible estimates of willingness to pay.

A mail survey was used to collect primary data from a randomly selected sample of respondents in northeastern Ohio. Data collected included preference and behavioral characteristics with respect to environmental issues, demographic characteristics, past and current use of the Mahoning River and substitute sites and WTP answers (for referendum as well as open-ended questions). The payment vehicle was a one-time contribution that the respondent would be asked to pay through a multi-county trust fund that could only be used for river restoration purposes. The actual response rate was 19 percent. In addition to the survey, secondary census data on demographics (such as income, race, gender, level of education, and unemployment rate) for the selected counties were used to compare between respondents and census statistics for representativeness of responses and for the environmental justice analysis.

To test for scope and other effects four scenarios of the CV survey were sent out to households in seven counties within the Mahoning River Watershed (MRW). Scenario 1 contained a contingent market for the dredging only (D) program. Scenario 2 contained a contingent market for the dredging and dam removal program (D-DR) program. In scenario 2, we specified that partial dam removal would be undertaken in addition to dredging and then explained the benefits of dredging (as in scenario 1) and the additional benefits of dam removal. Scenario 3 contained a contingent market for an agenda in which (D) is valued first then (D-DR) is valued second. Scenario 4 contained a contingent market for an agenda in which (D-DR) is offered first then (D) is offered second. Scenarios 3 and 4 are identical in every way except for the order of the WTP questions.

REGRESSION ANALYSIS AND RESULTS

We first test for scope effects using scenarios 1 and 2 in which each good is valued independently. The parametric model used to estimate willingness to pay from the dichotomous contingent valuation responses is the random willingness to pay *probit* model, in which the probability of a "yes" response is a function of some explanatory variables including socioeconomic and behavioral characteristics. Only significant covariates are reported in the regression tables below. A respondent answers yes to the dichotomous choice valuation question if his WTP exceeds the offered bid amount (t_j):

$$\Pr(yes_j) = \Pr(WTP(y_j, X_j, \varepsilon_j) > t_j) \qquad (9.10)$$

Where X is the vector of independent variables, y_j is income of household j, and ε is a normally distributed random error term with mean zero and constant variance σ_2. Estimating a parametric model for dichotomous choice contingent valuation questions involves two linked stages. In the first stage, a preference function or willingness function is estimated and then estimated parameters are used to calculate willingness to pay in the second stage.

We test for sensitivity to scope using a dummy variable for the more inclusive good (D-DR) in the probit equation while holding constant other potentially influential variables. Our regression model assumes an exponential WTP function, which bounds WTP from below to be non-negative and does not bound it from above. The functional form is:

$$WTP_j = e^{\beta X_j + \varepsilon_j} \qquad (9.11)$$

where β is the vector of parameters that corresponds to the vector of covariates X. Mean and median WTP from the probit model are calculated using the following equations:

$$E_\varepsilon(WTP/X_j, \beta) = e^{\beta X_j + 0.5\sigma^2} \qquad (9.12)$$

$$MD_\varepsilon(WTP/X_j, \beta) = e^{\beta X_j}$$

Table 9.1   Scope results

Variable	Coefficient	*t*-value
Constant	−.96	−.94
Protect	.55***	3.93
Lakes	.03**	2.07
Income/1000	.01***	3.63
D-DR	−.2	−.75
Log (bid)	−.47**	−2.36
ΔWTP	$10.74	
Log likelihood function	−91.82***	

Notes:
Sample size = 167, σ^2 = 1.03.
*   Significant at the .10 level.
**   Significant at the .05 level.
*** Significant at the .01 level.

Since expected WTP for the exponential model is increasing in σ^2, the difference between mean and median WTP will be bigger for higher values of σ^2 (Haab and McConnell, 2002). For the current data, $\sigma^2 = 1.03$ so the difference between the mean and the median is relatively large (of a degree of magnitude). As such, the more conservative estimate of WTP (the median) is used in the analysis.

Table 9.1 shows results of the probit regression on data from Versions 1 and 2 only. The coefficient on the (D-DR) dummy variable is insignificant at the .10 level, meaning that respondents are not willing to pay more for the dredging with dam removal project relative to the dredging only project. The importance of protecting the environment and income coefficients are significantly different from zero at the .01 level while the lakes and bid price coefficients are significant at the .05 level. All coefficients except for the D-DR coefficient have the expected signs. That is, WTP is increasing with increasing household median income, whether the respondents sees that protecting the environment is an important national goal, and whether the respondent recreates on lakes in the Mahoning River Valley. As expected, WTP is decreasing in the logarithm of the bid price. With regard to scope effects, WTP is decreasing with greater scope of the good but the relationship is insignificant as indicated by the insignificant coefficient on the dummy variable for D-DR at the .10 level. Moreover, the difference in WTP between the two scopes of the good is $10.74 – median WTP is $93.23 for D and $82.49 for D-DR) – and is insignificantly different from zero at the .10 level based on comparison of the 90 percent confidence intervals for the two goods – confidence intervals are [$51–$162] for

Table 9.2   Scope results based on past use of the river

Variable	User		Nonuser	
	Coefficient	*t*-value	Coefficient	*t*-value
Constant	3.96	1.62	−2.64**	−2.18
Protect	1.33**	2.48	0.49***	3.09
Lakes	0.06*	1.84	0.03	1.14
Income/1000	0.02	1.63	0.01***	2.98
D-DR	1.91***	2.62	−0.91***	−2.72
Log (bid)	−2.44***	−3.22	−0.01	−0.05
N	44		123	
Log likelihood	−15.7***		−65.6***	

Notes:
*   Significant at the .10 level.
**   Significant at the .05 level.
***   Significant at the .01 level.

the dredging only policy and [$28–$126] for the dredging plus dam removal policy.

In order to study the effect of past use of the Mahoning River on sensitivity to scope in the current CV survey, the pooled sample from scenarios 1 and 2 was classified according to responses to the question about recreation on the Mahoning River in the past year into two separate subsamples, past users and nonusers. Then, a scope test was conducted on each sub-sample. Table 9.2 shows the estimated probit equations for both users and nonusers. Comparing the two regressions, users of the Mahoning River also visit other lakes and reservoirs in the area more than nonusers and this has a positive effect on WTP for river restoration.

Household income has positive and more significant effect on WTP for nonusers than for users of the Mahoning, indicating that income is a more restrictive factor for WTP of nonusers. For past users of the Mahoning, the scope coefficient (D-DR) is positive and significant at the 1 percent level indicating that users of the river were sensitive to the scope of the restoration program and willing to pay more for the benefits of dredging with dam removal ($213) than for the benefits of dredging only ($97). On the other hand, nonusers of the river were insensitive to scope of the good and their responses do not conform to expectations of economic theory, the coefficient on scope (D-DR) is negative and significant at the .01 level.

In the current study, we explicitly test for context and sequence effects using the Mahoning River survey data. First, we test for context effects by comparing Versions 1 and 2, in which D and D-DR are each valued alone,

Table 9.3   Context effects

Variable	Coefficient	t-value	Coefficient	t-value
	D		D-DR	
Constant	2.402***	2.61	1.696	1.41
Parks	0.077***	2.53	0.093**	2.70
Own boat	0.102	0.41	0.655***	2.12
Age	−0.015***	−2.39	−0.005	−0.74
Scenario 3	−0.013	−0.07		
Scenario 4			0.380	1.67*
Log (bid)	−0.387**	−2.23	−0.441**	−2.05
Log likelihood	−121.82		−88.22	
Sample size	190		152	

Notes:
*   Significant at the .10 level.
**   Significant at the .05 level.
*** Significant at the .01 level.

to Versions 3 and 4, in which D and D-DR are valued first in an agenda, respectively. Next, we test for sequencing by comparing scenarios 3 and 4, in which both goods are valued within an agenda but in a different sequence.

Table 9.3 shows a multivariate analysis of the context effect, in which a dummy variable for the multiple-program scenario is included as a covariate. In the second column, the coefficient on the "scenario 3" dummy variable is insignificant at the 0.10 level, indicating that there is no context effect in the valuation of the dredging only project. Respondents are willing to pay $95.13 for D when it is valued on its own, and $91.87 when it is valued first in an agenda offering D-DR after D. In the case of dredging with dam removal project, the coefficient on scenario 4 is significant at the 0.10 level, indicating that context effects are present in the valuation of the more inclusive project. WTP for D-DR is $72.14 when the good is valued alone (scenario 2) and $129.75 when it is valued first in an agenda (scenario 4), indicating that dredging with dam removal is valued more when it is offered to respondents within an agenda than when it is offered alone. The conclusion is that the context in which the good is presented in the CV scenario has a positive effect on the value of the more inclusive good (D-DR); whereas, it does not have any effect on the value of the less inclusive good (D).

Sequence results are shown in Table 9.4 for both D and D-DR. The coefficient on scenario 4 in the second column has a negative sign and is significant at the 0.05 level, indicating that D is valued less when it is offered

Table 9.4   Sequence effects

Variable	Coefficient	*t*-value	Coefficient	*t*-value
	D		D-DR	
Constant	1.570	1.53	2.343**	1.99
Parks	0.069	2.131	0.080**	2.39
Years in	−0.007	−1.167	−0.006	−0.87
Edu	0.183**	1.983	0.279***	2.90
Scenario 4	−0.468**	−2.111	−0.096	−0.43
Log (bid)	−0.467**	−2.272	−0.633***	−2.97
Log likelihood	−90.34		−87.33	
Sample size	150		148	

Notes:
**   Significant at the 0.5 level.
***   Significant at the .01 level.

second than when offered first within an agenda. This is reflected in WTP values for dredging only, $104.73 in scenario 3 and $40.79 in scenario 4. The presence of an order effect in valuing D is consistent with previous findings in the literature (Payne et al., 2000), which indicates that a particular resource is valued more when it is presented first than later in a sequence. The coefficient on scenario 4 is negative however insignificant, showing no order effect in the case of the more inclusive good (D-DR) as reflected in WTP amounts for that good – $183.16 in scenario 3 and $157.46 in scenario 4 – with the difference in WTP being insignificant at the .10 level. In fact, the negative sign on scenario 4 in the latter case indicates that D-DR might be valued more when it is offered after D as in scenario 3. This could be attributed to a possible composite nesting-sequence effect in valuing multiple-program agendas containing nested public goods: a more inclusive good is more likely to be valued more when presented after a less inclusive good (scenario 3) than when presented before (scenario 4). The opposite is also correct and conforms to the negative sequence result in the valuation of D. That is, D (the smaller good) is valued less when it is presented after D-DR (the more inclusive good) than when presented before D-DR in a sequence.

EQUITY ANALYSIS

Valuation of environmental regulations and policy changes is usually focused on the achievement of economic efficiency or potential Pareto improvement (PPI): a proposed change or policy is accepted if those who gain from carrying out a specific project or policy could, in principle, compensate those who lose so no one is worse off. Aggregate measures of value such as aggregate willingness to pay are common measures of economic efficiency. However, in reality, compensations by the gainers to the losers of a policy seldom take place and the disadvantaged must bear most if not all the cost of the adverse effects of the policy change or environmental degradation.

Furthermore, willingness to pay is largely dependent on the ability to pay and as such environmental resources are not shifted to those who only value them the most, but to those who value and can afford them as well (Gauna, 2002). One of the assumptions of neoclassical economic theory is constant marginal utility of money income across all individuals and groups in a society. This assumption has long been debated in the welfare economics literature and some economists (Blue and Tweeten, 1997; Hitzhusen, 2002) consider it to not be less subjective than other assumptions about marginal utility of money income. Constant marginal utility means that an additional dollar of benefits contributes equally to the well-being of individuals whether they are poor or wealthy. This assumption seems odd especially when considering some governmental policies such as the progressive income tax system, which taxes the rich at a higher rate of income than the poor, and thus implicitly assumes a higher marginal utility of income for the poor than for the rich. As such, several studies (for example, Ahmed, 1982) have tried to put different weights on the benefits accrued to different groups of individuals based on income, race, and social status. Blue and Tweeten (1997) went further and estimated marginal utilities for different classes of income by constructing a quality of life (QLI) index, a proxy measure of utility, using factor-weighted and simple-summation weighted aggregation of socio-psychological measures of well being. They found that income, age, and health were the variables having the greatest impact on QLI and that QLI was stable over time.

Previous studies (Timney, 2002) have indicated that environmental deterioration in minority and poor neighborhoods is often a result of social prejudices that existed when the environmental incident was introduced (for example, the construction of a new industry that emits its wastes into nearby rivers and streams). In another study, Hite (2000) using a hedonic price model to study the effects of proximity to landfills on real estate values in central Ohio found that minorities especially African-American households were unjustly exposed to landfills.

In the Mahoning River case, we study the distributional effects of river contamination and clean up including stated preference evaluation of environmental improvements. An examination of census data by townships shows a potential presence of environmental injustice in the river corridor prior to clean up; minorities and low-income groups are more exposed to the environmental bad (in this case, water pollution) compared to other groups in the population. Demographic comparisons indicate that, on average, townships inside the river corridor have more African Americans (15 percent vs 0.8 percent), are less educated (78 percent vs 89 percent have completed high school), and are poorer ($30 526 vs $47 249 of median household income) compared to townships outside the river corridor. This means that minorities and the disadvantaged might have disproportionately borne the social cost of river pollution that was originally caused by the steel mills a long time ago.

However, one might argue that if minorities and low incomes had prior knowledge about contamination in the river and chose to live along the river, environmental equity would not be an issue. This is because people would be trading contamination in the river for more housing benefits such as more bedrooms or lower property taxes or rents. A more critical question, raised by Dr Lauren Schroeder[1] is whether poor people and minorities had equivalent housing opportunities before choosing to live near the river or whether they had few choices. Do poor people live near the polluted Mahoning River because they have little choice or because the benefits outweigh the costs? Schroeder contends that "poor people and minorities, especially African Americans, live along the river despite the environmental degradation, not by choice, but by necessity." He also argues that historical segregation in housing in the area since the steel mills era still persists today and results in barriers discouraging movement of poor and minorities from environmentally impoverished areas along the river.

The analysis in this section proceeds by first classifying the contingent valuation sample into different groups based on demographic characteristics that are expected to be the most important demand shifters in the bid functions especially income, ethnicity, and education. To study distributional effects, CV models are estimated for different groups within each stratum (for example, black vs white and rich vs poor) and then tests are performed for differences in the log likelihood function and model coefficients. The testable hypothesis is that bid functions are not different between different classes of households. A rejection of the null hypothesis means that different classes of people value environmental improvements differently. This may not indicate evidence of environmental injustice. However, the incidence of these long-term river contamination impacts and the disproportionate distribution of minorities and poor households along the polluted river may provide evidence of environmental injustice.

Second, willingness to pay is estimated for each group and then compared to that of the opposite group in each classification. Third, the neoclassical assumption of equal marginal utility of income will be relaxed allowing for different measures of marginal utility to be assigned to different groups of individuals based on income, race, and/or exposure to the environmental disamenity. These measures are calculated using the quality of life index developed by Blue and Tweeten (1997) as well as the inverse of the progressive income tax ratio. The objective of this weighting mechanism is not to choose or recommend a specific weight or marginal utility measure for calculating benefits or costs; rather, the objective is to present decision makers with a sensitivity analysis of the economic viability of the restoration projects under different assumptions of marginal utility of income including the traditional assumption of equal marginal utility of income across all individuals or groups.

Since the contaminated segment of the Mahoning River (about 31 miles) is located in Mahoning and Trumbull counties, these counties are more affected by contamination in the river than other counties in the watershed. Examining census data by county, Table 9.5 shows that Mahoning and Trumbull counties have lower median household income and higher proportion of African Americans than other counties in the Mahoning River watershed, as well as in the whole watershed, which includes seven counties in northeast Ohio: Mahoning, Trumbull, Columbiana, Ashtabula, Geauga, Stark, and Portage. This might be an indication of environmental injustice, meaning that minorities and low-income groups in the watershed have been exposed to the contamination in the river more than the population at large.

In the analysis that follows, the term "inside MR corridor" is used to indicate counties inside the Lower Mahoning River corridor, namely, Mahoning and Trumbull counties, and the term "outside MR corridor" is used to indicate counties outside the Lower Mahoning River corridor, namely, Ashtabula, Geauga, Portage, Columbiana, and Stark counties. This classification is mainly based on closure or exposure to the contaminated segment of the river; that is, the lower segment located in Mahoning and Trumbull counties. Originally, stratification of the sample was intended to be based on race, education, and income. Education in the sample is positively correlated with income ($\rho = .34$), and negatively correlated with being black ($\rho = -.01$),

Table 9.5 Income and race comparisons by location

County	Median household income	% of African Americans
Mahoning	$35 248	15.9
Trumbull	$38 298	7.9
Other counties	$42 841	3.4
NE Ohio	$40 112	5.6

so education is already represented in the classification of households by location.

As for the race variable, African Americans were underrepresented in the sample, 2 percent in the whole sample and 4 percent in Mahoning and Trumbull counties compared to 6 percent and 12 percent, respectively, in the population. Thus, race could not be used as a basis for classification given the limited number of African Americans who responded to the survey. Alternatively, since income in the sample is negatively correlated with being African American ($\rho = -.1$) and since the intensity of African Americans is higher inside MR corridor, the classification of individuals based on location will serve as a proxy for the black minority in the analysis of distribution effects. Table 9.6 depicts the two classification schemes used throughout this analysis.

Table 9.7 compares the demographic profiles of different income and location subgroups in the sample. For the location stratification, it is clear that households in Mahoning and Trumbull counties have lower income levels, have more African Americans, own fewer boats, are slightly less

Table 9.6   Classification schemes

Classification			
Location		Income	
Inside river corridor	Outside river corridor	Poor	Rich
Lives in Mahoning or Trumbull counties	Lives in other counties	≤ $40 000	> $40 000

Table 9.7   Descriptive statistics by location and income categories

Variable	Classification			
	Location		Income	
	Inside river corridor	Outside river corridor	Poor	Rich
INCOME/1000	$44.67	$50.53	$25.43	$71.00
AGE	56.15	56.84	61.49	50.11
WHITE	94%	95%	94%	95%
BLACK	5%	1%	4%	2%
OWN_BOAT	12%	24%	13%	23%
DISTANCE	6.66	43.26	19.66	23.49
EDU	2.87	2.99	2.62	3.32

educated, and live closer to the river than households in other counties in the watershed. As for the income strata, average income is significantly different between the rich and the poor. In addition, the poor subgroup has more African Americans, owns fewer boats, and is less educated than the rich subgroup. However, the poor in general do not live significantly closer to the river than the rich as indicated by the distance to the river variable. It should be noted that the *DISTANCE* variable measures the shortest distance to the Mahoning River in general and not specifically to the contaminated segment. Distance to the contaminated segment could not be obtained from the current survey and might have been more useful in demonstrating environmental injustice.

Table 9.8 shows estimated parameter coefficients and calculated WTP values for different location categories (for a more detailed analysis of environmental justice by income and location consult Abdul-Mohsen, 2005).

An important outcome of any environmental valuation study, from a policy standpoint, is the comparison of the proposed project's costs and benefits in order to determine its economic viability. Usually, the benefits accrued to all individuals or households in the affected population are added up to estimate the total benefits or economic value of the project or the policy change. This approach of the simple summation of benefits assumes that the marginal utility of income (MUI) is constant across all individuals or groups in a society. In other words, it implies that a dollar of income contributes to well-being equally regardless of whether dollars are accrued by poor or rich individuals. However, this implicit assumption of constant MUI is in contradiction with the diminishing marginal utility theory, which postulates that as the consumption of a particular good increases, the utility of consuming an incremental unit of that good decreases. If we apply this theory to income, assuming that income is a good or used to buy goods, poor individuals should have higher marginal utility of income than rich individuals.

In the current study, we apply different MUIs or weights to different groups of individuals using two of the quality of life indices derived by Blue and Tweeten as well as our own assumptions derived from actual governmental policies, especially the progressive income tax code. Then, these estimates of MUI are used in weighting the benefits accrued to different groups of individuals, especially the disadvantaged, to see how the economic viability of the proposed projects for river restoration varies under different assumptions about MUI.

Table 9.9 shows the analyses of benefits and costs for the inside and outside MR corridor groups under different assumptions of marginal utility of income. In the traditional benefit–cost analysis by location of groups, in which MUI is assumed to be one for all groups, the benefit–cost (BC) ratio is 0.68 for the dredging only project and 0.48 for the dredging

Table 9.8   Probit model estimations by location

| Variable | Dredging only | | | | | |
| | Inside MR corridor | | Outside MR corridor | | Pooled data | |
	Coefficient	*t*-value	Coefficient	*t*-value	Coefficient	*t*-value
Constant	0.171	0.16	0.885	0.57	0.326	0.39
ECONOMY	0.330***	3.03	0.748***	3.70	0.452***	4.95
EDU	0.174*	1.79	−0.019	−0.14	0.111	1.41
INCOME/1000	0.004	0.82	0.018***	2.63	0.008**	2.10
VER3	−0.071	−0.26	0.276	0.70	0.010	0.05
VER4	−0.547**	−1.94	−0.269	−0.66	−0.456**	−2.03
Log (bid$_D$)	−0.419**	−1.98	−1.012***	−3.04	−0.573***	−3.33
Log likelihood	−82.97		−40.39		−128.38	
Sample size	138		89		227	
LR (d.f.)			10.04 (7)			
MD (WTP$_D$)	$142.80		$71.20		$100.30	
Adj. MD (WTP$_D$)	$132.80		$60.10		$90.70	

| Variable | Dredging with dam removal | | | | | |
| | Inside MR corridor | | Outside MR corridor | | Pooled data | |
	Coefficient	*t*-value	Coefficient	*t*-value	Coefficient	*t*-value
Constant	0.617	0.50	2.358	1.36	1.448	1.50
OWN BOAT	0.406	1.18	0.589	1.34	0.469*	1.83
INCOME/1000	0.010**	2.07	0.015**	2.05	0.011***	2.93
EDU	0.103	0.93	0.458***	2.85	0.200**	2.26
VER3	0.367	1.29	0.312	0.74	0.386*	1.69
VER4	0.129	0.40	0.701*	1.73	0.371	1.54
Log (bid$_{D-DR}$)	−0.334	−1.47	−0.964***	−3.07	−0.582***	−3.30
Log likelihood	−77.24		−39.18		−121.32	
Sample size	122		86		208	
LR (d.f.)			9.80 (7)			
MD (WTP$_{D-DR}$)	$67.20		$111.80		$89.40	
Adj. MD (WTP$_{D-DR}$)	$53.70		$105.00		$80.70	

Notes:
*   Significant at the 0.1 level.
**   Significant at the 0.05 level.
***   Significant at the 0.01 level.

Table 9.9   Benefit–cost analysis by location

	D		D-DR	
	Inside corridor	Outside corridor	Inside corridor	Outside corridor
Med WTP	$133	$60	$54	$105
No. of households	191 610	318 782	191 610	318 782
Total cost	$27 859 487	$38 140 513	$38 412 323	$52 587 677
Aggregate B–C analysis				
Med WTP	$91		$81	
ΣWTP	$46 445 672		$41 341 752	
Aggregate B/C	0.70		0.45	
B–C analysis by location groups				
ΣWTP	$25 445 808	$19 158 798	$10 289 457	$33 472 110
B/C	0.91	0.50	0.27	0.64
Aggregate B/C	0.68		0.48	
Weighted B–C analysis (quadratic QLI)				
MUI	1.07	1	1.07	1
Weighted ΣWTP	$27 227 015	$19 158 798	$11 009 719	$33 472 110
B/C	0.98	0.50	0.29	0.64
Aggregate B/C	0.70		0.49	
Weighted B–C analysis (square root QLI)				
MUI	1.11	1	1.11	1
Weighted ΣWTP	$28 244 847	$19 158 798	$11 421 297	$33 472 110
B/C	1.01	0.50	0.30	0.64
Aggregate B/C	0.72		0.49	
Weighted B–C analysis (progressive income tax code)				
MUI	1.67	1	1.67	1
Weighted ΣWTP	$42 494 499	$19 158 798	$17 183 393	$33 472 110
B/C	1.53	0.50	0.45	0.64
Aggregate B/C	0.93		0.56	

with dam removal project. Additionally, BC ratio for dredging only is higher for the disadvantaged group inside MR corridor than for the outside group. The opposite is true for the more inclusive project (D-DR). This indicates that the less expensive dredging only project is preferred more by the disadvantaged group than by the other group. However, with the constant marginal utility of income assumption, both projects are not economically viable.

When we apply MUI values obtained from the quality of life index quadratic function by Blue and Tweeten (1.07 for the inside group and 1 for the outside group) to the total benefits estimated for each group, both projects become more economically appealing. The BC ratio of the disadvantaged group is now 0.98 for dredging only and 0.29 for dredging with dam removal. The BC ratio of the outside group is still as before for both projects since we assumed that MUI for the advantaged is unity under any weighting scheme. The economic viability of any project is influenced by the weight placed on the benefits accrued to the targeted group in the population affected by the project or the environmental change. As such, the income distribution or equity criterion of utility could be embedded into the efficiency criterion in a more inclusive benefit–cost analysis, which includes the traditional efficiency based analysis as one alternative. When applying the weights obtained from the square root QLI function (1.11 for the inside MR group and 1 for the outside MR group), the BC ratio for the targeted group is slightly higher (1.01 for the dredging only project and 0.30 for the dredging with dam removal project), however, both projects are still not economically viable in aggregate.

Applying the weights obtained from the marginal income tax rates to the benefits accrued by different groups, the dredging only project is almost economically viable (BC = 0.93) in aggregate but the larger more expensive project (D-DR) is still not viable. When considering benefit cost analysis for the disadvantaged group, expected benefits are approximately one and half times the costs for the dredging only project, and are only half the costs for the dredging with dam removal project. As more weight is placed on the benefits accrued to the inside MR corridor group, the dredging only project becomes more economically viable to policy-makers while the more inclusive project is not viable under any assumption about marginal utility of income. This shows that low-income households inside the Mahoning River corridor that are predominantly poor and African American are more supportive of the dredging only project than households outside the river corridor. One reason could be the lower cost of the dredging only project compared to dredging with dam removal. Another possible reason might be that people inside the river corridor are not in favor of removing the dams because some of the dams have recreational uses or are still used by the steel industry for cooling purposes.

CONCLUSION AND IMPLICATIONS

In conclusion, there was no evidence of a universal scope effect in the valuation of Mahoning River restoration projects, although scope effects were significant among past users of the river. On the other hand, there was mixed evidence of context and order effects. Particularly, WTP for the dredging only program was affected by the order in which the program was offered within the agenda but not affected by the context or whether the program was valued on its own or within a larger package. Conversely, WTP for the more inclusive program (dredging with dam removal) was sensitive to the context variation but invariant to the order variation. Based on these results, the more important question is how valid the CV instrument is and consequently how relevant the value estimates obtained using this instrument are for policy analysis.

As for the scope results, different studies in the literature have reached different explanations as to why some CV surveys fail to pass the scope test. One explanation is that of Carson and Mitchell (1993; 1995), Smith (1993), and Carson et al. (2001) that insensitivity to scope is the result of poor design and implementation of the survey instrument in terms of explaining the survey clearly to the respondent, plausibility of delivering the public good in question, and realism of the payment vehicle. Brown and Duffield (1995) offered another explanation for part-whole bias based on the relationship between previous use of the resource and familiarity with other substitutes. They concluded that previous users of an environmental resource are more familiar with its substitutes and hence are more likely to perceive and value changes to the resource than non-users. Our scope results are more consistent with Brown and Duffield findings and recommend that sensitivity to scope could be dependent on the type of the good being valued (for example, scope versus scale valuations) and on the specific characteristics of the individual being surveyed (for example, user versus nonuser).

With respect to the mixed evidence of context and sequence effects in the current study, many resource economists have argued that context and sequence effects in CV studies are expected by economic theory. For example, Randall and Hoehn (1996, p. 378) state that "standard economic theory predicts that the value of a particular prospect will vary in systematic ways, depending on what additional prospects are offered prior to or simultaneously with it." These effects are usually induced by substitution effects and the budget constraint. Carson et al. (1998) show that the value of a particular public good should be smaller the later it is offered in a sequence of goods under the assumption that these goods are normal goods and substitutes for each other.

The economic explanation for these phenomena is that each new public good the individual obtains reduces his available income to spend on private goods and other public goods, and that substitutability among public goods makes each new good added to the package less desirable than when valued by the individual as the only change in the pool of public goods (Carson et al., 2001). However, the literature does not provide any prediction on the appropriate magnitudes of context and sequence effects that should be

expected in CV studies. As such, the immediate question is which WTP estimate for a particular public good should be used for policy analysis. Should
independent values obtained by valuing each good as the only change to the
status quo be used? Alternatively, should the value obtained for each good
within a package be used? And, if so, in what sequence? The obvious answer
to the first question is no; independent WTP estimates for public goods
should not be used as the only basis for policy analysis if context or
sequence effects are deemed significant, as is the case in the current study.
For the second and third questions, there is no clear answer since it would
be difficult for the researcher to define the only one context and only one
sequence in which the public good should be valued. Rather, several con-
texts and sequences are usually available to the researcher to choose from.
A possible statistical remedy for this situation is to include context and
sequence factors in the estimation stage of the bid functions using all available observations on the particular good and then compensate for context
and sequence effects, if any, in the calculation stage of WTP.

NOTE

1. Lauren Schroeder is an Emeritus Professor at Youngstown State University and a long-
    time resident of the Mahoning River area.

REFERENCES

Abdul-Mohsen, A. (2005), "Economic efficiency and income distribution evalu-
    ation of toxics and dam removal using contingent valuation," doctoral disserta-
    tion, The Ohio State University, Columbus, Ohio.
Ahmed, H. (1982), "Income distribution and project analysis in less developed
    counties: an Egyptian case study," Master's thesis, The Ohio State University,
    Columbus, Ohio.
Blue, E.N. and L. Tweeten (1997), "The estimation of marginal utility of income for
    application to agricultural policy analysis," *Agricultural Economics*, **16**, 155–69.
Brown, T.C. and J.W. Duffield (1995), "Testing part-whole valuation effects in con-
    tingent valuation of instream flow protection," *Water Resources Research*, **31** (9),
    2341–51.
Carson, R.T. and R.C. Mitchell (1989), "Using surveys to value public goods: the
    contingent valuation method," Washington, DC: Resources for the Future.
Carson, R.T. and R.C. Mitchell (1993), "The issue of scope in contingent valuation
    studies," *American Journal of Agricultural Economics*, **75**, 1263–67.
Carson, R.T. and R.C. Mitchell (1995), "Sequencing and nesting in contingent
    valuation," *Journal of Environmental Economics and Management*, **28**, 155–73.
Carson, R.T., N.E. Flores, and W.M. Hanemann (1998), "Sequencing and valuing
    public goods," *Journal of Environmental Economics and Management*, **36**, 314–23.

Carson, R.T., N.E. Flores, and N.F. Meade (2001), "Contingent valuation: controversies and evidence," *Environmental and Resource Economics*, **19**, 172–210.

Gauna, E. (2002), "An essay on environmental justice: the past, the present, and back to the future," *Natural Resources Journal*, **42** (4), 701–22.

Haab, T.C. and K.E. McConnell (2002), *Valuing Environmental and Natural Resources: The Econometrics of Non-market Valuation*, Cheltenham, UK and Northampton, MA: Edward Edgar.

Hite, D. (2000), "A random utility model of environmental equity," *Growth and Change*, **31**, 40–58.

Hitzhusen, F. (2002), "Context, concepts, and policy on poverty and inequality," in R. Lal, D. Hansen, N. Uphoff, and S. Slack (eds), *Food Security and Environmental Quality in the Developing World*, Washington, DC: Lewis Publishers, pp. 419–28.

Hoehn, J. and A. Randall (1989), "Too many proposals pass the benefit cost test," *American Economic Review*, **79**, 543–51.

Kahneman, D. and J. Knetsch (1992a), "Contingent valuation and the value of public goods: reply," *Journal of Environmental Economics and Management*, **22**, 90–4.

Kahneman, D. and J. Knetsch (1992b), "Valuing public goods: the purchase of moral satisfaction," *Journal of Environmental Economics and Management*, **22**, 57–70.

Loomis, J., M. Lockwood, and T. Delay (1993), "Some empirical evidence on embedding effects in contingent valuation of forest protection," *Journal of Environmental Economics and Management*, **24**, 45–55.

McFadden, D. (1974), "Conditional logit analysis of qualitative choice behavior," in P. Zarembka (ed.), *Frontiers in Econometrics*, New York: Academic Press, pp. 105–42.

Ohio Department of Health (ODH) (2001), *Ohio Sport Fishing Consumption Advisory: Ohio Department of Health Year 2001 Fishing Season*, Columbus, OH: Ohio Department of Health.

Randall, A. (1987), *Resource Economics: An Economic Approach to Natural Resources and Environmental Policy*, New York: John Wiley & Sons.

Randall, A. and J. Hoehn (1996), "Embedding in market demand systems," *Journal of Environmental Economics and Management*, **30**, 369–80.

Schroeder, L. (1998), "Benthic habitat restoration of the Lower Mahoning River: ecological implication, part of the reconnaissance phase of the US Army Corp of Engineers' project on the restoration of Benthic habitats in the Lower Mahoning River, Northeastern Ohio," Department of Biological Sciences, Youngstown State University, Youngstown, OH.

Smith, V.K. (1993), "Non-market evaluation of environmental resources: an interpretative appraisal," *Land Economics*, **69** (1), 1–26.

Testa, R.W. (1997), "The partitioning of polycyclic hydrocarbons in the Mahoning River bottom sediments," master's thesis, Engineering, Youngstown State University.

Timney, M. (2002), "Must policy making wait until all the data are in? An empirical look at environmental justice," *Public Administration Review*, **62** (4), 506–08.

US Army Corps of Engineers (USACE), Pittsburgh District (1999), "Mahoning River environmental dredging reconnaissance study, Trumbull and Mahoning counties, Ohio," May.

Whitehead, J., T. Haab, and J.-C. Huang (1998), "Part-whole bias in contingent valuation: will scope effects be detected with inexpensive survey methods?" *Southern Economic Journal*, **65** (1), 160–68.

10. An economic analysis of Lower Great Miami River segment improvements

Radha Ayalasomayajula, P. Wilner Jeanty, and Fred J. Hitzhusen

INTRODUCTION

The Great Miami River Watershed is located in the southwest region of Ohio. The Great Miami River is 155 miles in length, and its watershed includes all or part of 15 counties with the headwaters in Hardin and Auglaize counties and the mouth in the Ohio River in Hamilton County. Interstates 70 and 75, two of the nation's longest Interstate highway systems, intersect just north of Dayton. Dayton, with a population of 190 000, is the largest city within the watershed. Other major cities within the watershed exceeding 50 000 populations include Springfield, Hamilton, and Middletown. There are 2360 miles of rivers and streams in the Great Miami River Watershed. Water quality in and recreational access to the watershed's rivers and streams have been concerns over the last 20 years.

Evaluation of fish and macroinvertebrate community performance in streams and rivers draining the Great and Little Miami River Basins indicates that most streams meet basic aquatic-life-use criteria set by the Ohio Environmental Protection Agency (EPA) for warm water habitat. According to the Ohio EPA, the Lower Great Miami and Whitewater River Watershed is impaired primarily by nutrient enrichment and habitat alterations. Over 80 percent of the river miles are impaired by nutrient enrichment and 40 percent by other habitat alterations. Such severe river and stream impairments commonly result from human development, inadequate agricultural practices and land use changes in the surrounding area. Gravel mining is included in this category, and is not presented separately. Throughout its 155 mile length, the Great Miami flows over 20 dams. The plunge pools, eddies, and runs below these dams often hold significant concentrations of fish.

Land-use and waste-management practices influence the quality of water found in streams and aquifers in the Great and Little Miami River Basins. Land use is approximately 79 percent agriculture, 13 percent urban (residential, industrial, and commercial), and 7 percent forest. An estimated 2.8 million people live in the Great and Little Miami River Basins; major urban areas include Cincinnati and Dayton, Ohio. Fertilizers and pesticides associated with agricultural activity, discharges from municipal and industrial wastewater-treatment and thermoelectric plants, urban runoff, and disposal of solid and hazardous wastes contribute contaminants to surface water and ground water throughout the area. Following the Clean Water Act of 1972 national regulators shut down dirty industries and other easily identifiable, point-source polluters. Now they are focusing on less easily managed pollutants, including the sediment dredged up by gravel mines and runoff from developed areas and farm fields.

SAND AND GRAVEL MINING IN OHIO

Sand and gravel mining is Ohio's second largest (on a tonnage basis) mining industry, next to coal. In 1996, Ohio had 292 reporting sand and gravel mines operating in 64 counties. The US Army Corps of Engineers can control intentional landfill operations, but not those that stir up or drop sediment back into the river stream as a by-product of mining. Churning the water and changing the shape of the stream, gravel-mining companies are a primary environmental threat to rivers of the post-Clean Water Act age. From a development point of view, gravel mining provides some benefits. It provides raw construction material and jobs. Retired mines have become recreational reservoirs such as the Dayton Hydrobowl on the Mad River, just north of where it joins the Great Miami. Many mines operate not within the river, but on the banks or in an area sectioned off from the main flow by a dike.

Several scientists (Kondolf, 1997; Krunkilton, 1982; Nelson, 1993) argue that mining may stir up sediment contaminated by past industrial spills, spreading toxins downriver. Fine-grained sand and silt can impede fish and bugs, and clog water treatment plants. Mining lowers the riverbed and causes the river to flow faster and cut deeper. It creates deep pools that may attract fish, but affects their natural feeding and spawning patterns. Mining on riverbanks destroys the natural buffer zone of trees and plants. A retired mine leaves a hole extending deep into the ground over the pollution sensitive Great Miami Aquifer – the sole source of drinking water for more than 90 percent of southwestern Ohio residents. Its use must be carefully regulated to protect the aquifer. Gravel mines dot the length of the Great Miami

River, with a concentration in Hamilton County. There are several in Whitewater Township, which has no zoning authority and little opportunity for public control of land use policy.

Sand and gravel are sold by the ton (2000 pounds). As with all high-volume and low-value commodities, transportation is the dominant factor controlling the ultimate cost of sand and gravel delivered to a job site. Long-haul transportation costs by barge, freighter, or rail may be as little as one-eighth the cost of long-haul truck transport. Transportation costs in congested urban areas generally are three to four times the cost of open-highway transportation. As an example, the cost of a dump-truck load of sand and gravel mined on the south side of Columbus doubles by the time it is delivered to a job site 10 miles away on the north side of the city. In order to minimize aggregate transportation costs, it is essential that aggregate be produced as close as possible to urban centers where most aggregate is consumed. For this reason, forward-looking land-use planners and zoning officials are using geologic maps to designate selected areas within their jurisdictions for future aggregate-mining development. After mining, sand and gravel pits are among the least expensive mining sites to reclaim and commonly are converted into aesthetically landscaped golf courses and attractive building sites for new houses. Post-mining land values commonly exceed pre-mining values when compared to non-mined land because of terrain improvements and the creation of wetlands and lakes and ponds for boating, fishing, and swimming. However, the appreciation of property values of most mining occurs only after reclamation of the mines as parks and golf courses (www.ohiodnr.com/geosurvey/geo_fact/ geo_f19.html).

STUDY OBJECTIVES

The objective of the study was to perform a comprehensive inventory of existing economic conditions of the corridor such as property values, recreation and tourism, and estimate economic impacts of variations in water quality improvements and infrastructure from selected improvements to the community thus providing a rationale for investments in these improvements. The study estimates through empirical analysis the effect of the following improvements of river corridor attributes:

- installation of a bike trail along the river
- installation of more access points to the river
- regulation of gravel mining, operation and reclamation on the banks of the river.

METHODOLOGY

Methodologies to estimate the impact of property, community and environmental attributes on values of residential properties along the river, and the recreation and tourism value of the river are the hedonic pricing (HP) method and the benefit transfer (BT) method to determine the benefits and costs of buffer zones and new boating access points. Types of gravel mining regulation and reclamation from other states are summarized. Hedonic pricing and BT methods as well as information from interviewing local people and gravel mining officials were used to get rough estimates of impacts.

ECONOMIC ANALYSIS OF THE GREAT MIAMI BIKE TRAIL

In the present study, we are proposing a 28-mile bike trail starting at the Warren-Montgomery County line, extending south to the confluence of the Great Miami River and the Ohio River. The actual cost of the 28-mile bike trail would include land acquisition costs, construction costs, and maintenance costs. For simplicity purposes, we have included no land acquisition costs, since most land in the proposed bike trail site is owned by the Miami Conservancy District (MCD), or other governmental agencies, is idle and not put to any economic use.

The cost of constructing a bike trail is estimated based on a Dubuque, Iowa Study (see Table 10.1 for cost components) as follows. The cost of

Table 10.1   Cost of nonmotorized multiuse trails (single treadway)

Trail element	Unit	Price per unit	Element width	Units per mile	Trail cost per mile
Clearing and grubbing	Acre	$2000.00	14 ft	1.7	$3400
Grading	Mile	$3000.00		1	$3000
Granular sub-base	Sq ft	$0.40	12 ft	63 360	$25 344
Asphalt	Sq ft	$1.00	10 ft	52 800	$52 800
Seeding/mulching	Acre	$1.00	10 ft	0.5	$800
Other costs	10% of trail cost				$8534
Contingency	15% of trail cost				$122 802
Other costs per mile					$106 700
Maintenance cost					$5000 per year

constructing a bikeway 28 miles long in 2000 was $2.9 million approximately. The adjusted cost of the bikeway in the year 2003 is $3.2 million. Maintenance cost, discounted present value, for 25 years (expected lifetime of the bike trail) is $45 385. Total cost of the construction and maintenance of bike trail is about $3 million. This does not include the cost of purchasing rights-of-way and major bridge structures. This estimate is based on current work for similar trails in other parts of Ohio, as estimated by the MCD. It is anticipated that about 75 percent of the cost will be paid by federal and state sources. The rest will be shared among local public entities and private donors. Most of the proposed right-of-way is on property owned by public agencies including: the cities of Franklin, Middletown and Hamilton, as well as the Ohio Department of Transportation, Metro Parks of Butler County, and the Miami Conservancy District. A small portion is privately held.

BENEFIT TRANSFER RESULTS FROM MOORE AND SIDERELIS

The values used in the benefit transfer that follows were obtained from a 1995 study, published by Siderelis and Moore. The authors investigated net benefits of bicycling and walking on abandoned railroad beds that have been converted to a rail-trail for recreation purposes. A sample of three diverse rail-trails from across the US, in Iowa, Florida, and California were studied. Users were systematically surveyed and counted on each trail during a period of one year, and were sent follow-up mail surveys. In the present study, we used the results from the Iowa bike trail, since it is the closest match in demographic, trail landscape and income indicators to the Great Miami Trail. The study findings state that on average, users spend $9.21 per day as a result of their trail visit to the Heritage Trail in Iowa, $11.02 at St Marks' Trail in Florida, and $3.87 per person per day at the Lafayette Trail in California. The findings of the Iowa trail are applied in the present study, after inflating the $9.21 expenditure to current dollars for the year 2003, using a consumer price index inflator (see Tables 10.2 and 10.3). The users are charged a fee of $1 per visit to the Iowa trail. Yearly visits to the trails were about 135 000; 170 000; and 4 000 000 in the Iowa, Florida, and California trails respectively. Our study adopted the benefit cost method and applied the findings of expenditures from the Iowa trail, and then applied the single point estimates of average consumer surplus or willingness to pay (WTP) per activity day per person.

The second set of benefit transfer values used in this study is average consumer surplus values per activity day per person from the study conducted

Table 10.2   Benefits from the Great Miami Bike Trail

	Estimate benefits	Lower benefits by 25%	Lower benefits by 50%
Calculated yearly visits to the trail	135 000		
Average trip expenditure (\$ per person per day \$11.09 adjusted to current dollars)	\$11.09		
Total annual expenditures	\$1 497 150	\$1 122 862	\$748 575
Discounted expenditures in 25 years	\$11 285 938	\$8 464 453	\$5 642 969

Table 10.3   Benefit–cost ratio of bike trail

Benefits	Benefit–cost ratio			
	4% interest rate	6% interest rate	8% interest rate	10% interest rate
Actual	7.21	5.90	4.92	4.19
Lower by 25%	5.41	4.42	3.69	3.14
Lower by 50%	3.60	2.95	2.46	2.09

Table 10.4   Average consumer surplus values per activity day per person

Activity	Biking	Adjusted to year 2003
Mean of estimates	\$45.15	\$21.20
Lower bound	\$17.61	\$21.20
Upper bound	\$62.68	\$75.71
Mean for northeast region	\$34.11	\$42.27

Total number of visitors/users: 135 000
Total economic benefits (lower bound): 135 000 × 21.20 = \$2 863 350
Total average economic benefits (mean for northeast): 135 000 × 42.27 = \$5 706 450

by Siderelis and Moore (Table 10.4). Consumer surplus is a value of a recreation activity beyond what must be paid to enjoy it. The benefit transfer estimate of a management, or a policy-induced change in recreation is the average consumer surplus estimate for the average individual from the benefit transfer literature. The mean, and the range of estimates for biking are provided in Table 10.4.

Applying the mean of estimates to the usage, we obtain the recreational economic benefits provided by the bike trail. Taking the lower bound estimate, the net benefits are 2.8 million dollars, and taking the average for the northeastern region, the net benefits are about 5.7 million dollars, per year.

ECONOMIC IMPACT OF GRAVEL MINING

In order to fully comprehend the economic importance of gravel mining in the study area, some basic income and employment statistics were gathered from the Bureau of Economic Analysis (www.bea.gov). Butler, Hamilton, Franklin, Portage, and Stark counties lead the sales in gravel and sand in the state, accounting for 46 percent of the total gravel sales. Total value of gravel and sand sold in Ohio in the year 2000 was $252 435 626. Average price of one ton of gravel was $4.53. Annual average of 1288 employees worked on average of 181 days in the year 2000. Total wages of $73 126 187 were paid to 1893 employees (1288 in production and 605 in non-production), and the average annual wage was $38 360. Gravel mining does not provide any substantial income and employment opportunities in the two counties. At the same time, gravel mines have very low assessed land value, at $12 816 per acre, compared to $30 817 for residential properties. This significantly erodes the tax base of the counties. Besides, gravel mine operations are intensive road users for transportation of gravel, which puts an additional burden on the county and township roads.

The river flows through six counties: Logan, Shelby, Miami, Montgomery, Butler, and Hamilton. The first three were not included since gravel mining is not a serious issue there. Butler and Hamilton counties are comparable respecting gravel mining. Data were gathered regarding property parcels located in the townships along the river. There are 119 homes in the sample. This is approximately 25 percent of the population of homes. The townships not adjoining the river were dropped from the sample, since the main objective of this section of the study was to determine the effect of river gravel mining on property values. The value of the homes was recorded from the county auditors' offices. This is the market-assessed value of the property. The values for the year 2002 were taken for the study. Information on the structural characteristics was also available from the parcel cards from the auditors' offices. Data for other characteristics, such as distance to gravel mines, distance from the urban centers, were obtained from the maps from the County Engineers' offices.

The final hedonic price function for the model is expressed as: LnVal = $\beta + \beta_1$Eastside + β_2Distance to Gravel Mine + β_3Distance to Urban Center + β_4LnAcres + β_5Downstream + β_6LnAge + β_7StoryHeight + β_8Rooms

$+ \beta_9$Bedrooms $+ \beta_{10}$LnLiving Area $+ \beta_{11}$Air Condition $+ \beta_{12}$ Heating $+$ β_{13}Fireplace $+ \beta_{14}$Half Bath $+ \beta_{15}$Full Bath.

Structural characteristics of a house are described by: number of rooms, number of bathrooms, garage spaces, age, various utilities including water supply, sewer system, septic system, and electricity. Other things equal, we expect that an additional bedroom or bathroom represent an extra amenity. The lifespan or durability of a house is associated with age and or type of construction. Since a majority of the houses were of the same type of construction, we did not include this variable. In light of the historical significance of houses more than a century old, we attempted to define age as a nonlinear (inverse) variable in the model. Since the results were not conclusive, a log form was adopted. Distance to the three urban centers is intended to provide a measure of relative locational advantage. The functional form that performed the best was a log-linear mixed form. The assessed value of property (the dependent variable), total acreage of the parcel, total living area, and age of the house were specified in log form. Log-linear mixed form incorporates diminishing marginal utility. A linear model would not have been desirable because it assumes that implicit price is constant regardless of the quantity of the attribute. The model explains 49 percent (adjusted R2) of the variation in the data, 4 of the 15 estimated coefficients are significantly different from zero at the 1 percent significance level, and two at the 10 percent significance level respectively, as illustrated in Table 10.5.

The coefficients for living area, acreage and age are elasticities, interpreted as percentage change in the value of a property due to a 1 percent change in the quantity of that characteristic, other things remaining the same. The other coefficients represent relative change in the price due to a unit change in the respective variables. When multiplied by 100, they represent percentage change in price due to a one unit change in the corresponding variables. As the area of the property increases by 1 percent, the value of the property is expected to increase by approximately 0.35 percent. Similarly, as the total living area increases by 1 percent, the value of the property is expected to increase by 0.048 percent. As the age of the house increases by one year, the value of the house is expected to decrease by 0.22 percent. The value of the property is expected to decrease by 13 percent if the property is located on the east side of the river, an additional room will decrease value by 15 percent, which is unexpected, an additional bedroom will increase the value by 18 percent, and an additional bathroom by 9 percent and an additional half bath by 64 percent. On average, as distance to the gravel mine increases by one mile, the value of the property increases by 16.7 percent. The assessed market values of the residential properties were expressed in thousands of dollars, and the coefficient, 167.25 is multiplied by 1000 to get the scale specific coefficient. It is assumed that the impact is insignificant beyond the 1 mile limit.

Table 10.5   Hedonic model coefficient estimates

Variable	Parameter estimate	*t*-value
Intercept	12.7***	7.73
Eastside	−0.13	−0.71
Distance to gravel mine	167.26***	13.53
Distance to urban center	−23.38***	−4.87
Acreage (lot size)	0.34***	6.02
Downstream	0.01	0.08
Age	−0.22	−1.58
Story height	−0.29	−1.21
Number of rooms	−0.15*	−1.73
Number of bedrooms	0.18	1.33
Living area	0.05	0.18
Air conditioning	0.23	1.07
Heating	−0.22	−0.67
Fireplace	0.59***	2.74
Half bath	0.64*	1.87
Full bath	0.09	0.44

Notes:
*** Significant at the 1 percent level.
** significant at the 5 percent level.
* significant at the 10 percent level.

Total number of single family dwellings = 238.

Total number of houses in the corridor within one mile of a gravel mine = 172.

Total loss of residential property value proximity (one mile or less) due to gravel mines = 172 × 16 725 = $2 876 700 (2.8 million, approximately).

The total decrease of revenues annually to the local government due to decreased property value resulting from proximity to gravel mining is estimated at $119 153 and presented in Table 10.6.

ECONOMIC ANALYSIS OF PROPOSED ACCESS POINTS

In order for local and state governments to allocate funds efficiently in recreational waterway activities, they need to know how beneficial these activities are likely to be. Recreational boating for example has been

Table 10.6   Tax revenue implications of gravel mining

County	Tax millage	Coefficient est.	Number of houses in the area	Tax revenue ($)
Butler	41.37	16 725	64	44 282.5
Hamilton	41.45	16 725	108	74 871.1
Total				119 153.0

identified to provide not only a significant economic impact but also a wide range of social and psychological benefits. As a result, expanding boating opportunities by constructing new boat ramps where needed is expected to not only enhance the recreational options of a given region but also to boost the local economy. In this perspective, the Great Miami River remains a potential valuable natural asset for the counties it flows through. The economic potential of the river is due to the scenic beauty of its corridor and the quality of its water. The Great Miami River has water quality problems, but the water quality is better than the average river in Ohio. According to the National Park Service, this part of the river is qualified to be a National Wild and Scenic River. However, because access points are lacking, the river is inconvenient for most recreational users, making it a greatly undervalued and underused natural resource. Such underutilization creates rationale for improving the Great Miami River segments by increasing the number of access points. We define an access point as any area that borders the river and may be accessible by car. An access point could be positive, such as a bike path, park, or boat launch; or negative, a place used for illegal dumping; or potentially positive, an area that could be developed for community recreational use.

The purpose of this section is to determine the benefits and costs from the allocation of funds to construction of new access points in Butler and Hamilton counties, Ohio through an *ex ante* analysis of the potential behavior of Great Miami River users. An attempt to identify the benefits is the first step in valuing them. The potential benefits of improving the Great Miami River can be summarized as follows:

• increase in recreational opportunities
• increase in real estate value such as land and housing
• increase in employment in the production and service sectors
• tourism development
• increase in the government tax base
• increase in the surrounding population welfare.

The costs to bring these benefits into existence include building the new access points, making them operational, and maintaining them. Methodologically, it would be ideal to use survey-based methods such as contingent valuation or contingent choice to estimate the benefits. However, these methods would generally be expensive and more difficult to apply given the time and funds allotted for the study. Alternatively, the benefit transfer method appears to be more appropriate because it allows obtaining economic estimates for a particular study using secondary data and previous studies at other sites. In applying the benefit transfer method the first step is to identify existing studies or values that can be used for the transfer. The second step is to determine, based on relevant criteria, whether these values are transferable. The next step is to assess the reliability of the previous studies. Finally, using available and relevant information, the existing values need to be adjusted to better mirror the values for the policy site (Desvouges et al., 1992). We found no study that had looked specifically at how river users would change their behavior if new river access points were to be brought into existence. In order to quantify the benefits resulting from additional access points, the following data are required:

- total number of users, and increase in users, particularly boaters due to installation of access points
- average amount spent per user per trip to the river.

The analysis draws upon two studies, authored by Hitzhusen et al. (2000) and Silva et al. (1997), for benefit transfer. Hitzhusen et al. (2000) estimated the number of users and estimated benefits accruing from river use in the Muskingum River. Silva et al. (1997) analyzed the behavior of Ohio boaters at newly constructed ramps on Ohio rivers and lakes using a survey-based method. As a result, these studies provide a good basis for benefit transfer. As well established in the literature on the benefit transfer approach, using these figures for transfers requires their adaptation to the policy site characteristics (Rosenberger and Loomis, 2000). The lack of information on the Great Miami River policy site has motivated the need to collect some baseline data. The method used is similar to the Delphi technique in the sense that it involves collecting opinions of a group of 10 people knowledgeable about the river use. As the Delphi method is contingent upon the judgment of knowledgeable experts (Martino, 1970), the results of the survey rely heavily on the opinion and information released by the respondents.

The questionnaires contained two types of questions. The first set of questions address the respondents' own use of the river and the second set asks for the respondents' opinion about how other people use the river. The questions concern types of use, frequency of use, trip supplies, expenditure on trips, additional visitation in response to potential installation of new access points to the river, and inhibiting factors to increasing use. Based on the survey results and findings by other studies, new estimates are calculated. It is noteworthy that the outcomes of this survey do not establish strong and generalizable statistical evidence, they just report opinions of a small group of knowledgeable users of the river, and should be considered and interpreted as such. This study is not the first to attempt to estimate recreation demand when user counts are unknown even if the number of visits is estimated by adding gate counts, tickets, or direct observations. A study by Johnston and Tyrrell (2003) highlighted the problems inherent in lack of information on user counts and proposed an estimation method. However, since it is based on the known total number of visits, their method is not applicable here.

TYPES OF USE OF THE RIVER

Questionnaire respondents were asked to indicate their primary activity when taking trips to the river. Most of them point out that they use the river mostly for walking/jogging, boating, fishing, and wildlife viewing. When asked about what they see other people use the river for, almost all respondents point to walking/jogging and fishing. The respondents were also asked how often they use the river in a month during the spring to fall season. The answers vary according to whether the respondents live close to or far from the river or depending on whether they have easy or difficult access. Those who live close indicate that their use of the river ranges from 8–10 times to 12–15 times in a month, whereas those having limited access report to have used the river between one and two times to three to five times. Combining all respondents, the number of trips taken to the river averages five trips in a month. Since any outdoor activity is weather or temperature driven, these trips are typically taken from spring to fall with the peak use time in summer. For hunters, the peak use time would coincide with the duck/goose season.

Regarding the use of the river by users other than the respondents on a typical sunny weekday and weekend day, the number of trips taken varies according to locations and facilities available at each location. Respondents indicate that north of Dayton, or at the West Carrollton Pool, 50 visitors may be observed on a weekend day and very few on a weekday. However, in Miami County where walkways and bike trails are typically lacking one can see 10 to 20 users. At other locations where access to the river is much easier, the number of people may vary from hundreds to thousands.

TRIP EXPENSES

A specific question asks the respondents to estimate the amount of money they spend on average when taking trips to the river. Since most of them live close to the river, their trip costs appear to be relatively small compared to results of other studies. However, almost everyone has reported expenditures on food, gas, and fishing supplies. Those whose trip purpose is hunting as well as fishing spend some money on fishing and hunting licenses. The amount of money reported spent on purchases for a trip varies between $5 and $10. This figure, however, does not include canoe and boat rentals, which makes the estimate a low-bound estimate.

INCREASE IN RIVER USE

To address the issue of additional trips to the river due to an improvement in access, respondents were asked to indicate whether they and other users would increase their visitation if more access points become available. If the answer was affirmative, then they were asked by how much they would be willing to increase their use. As expected, those who have easy and close access to the river argue that they would be less likely to increase their use. Whereas, those who live further from the river and who have very limited access report that they would double their use if more access points become available. They seem to be relatively knowledgeable about the current access conditions of the river. They state that access to the river is a major problem specifically when it comes to fishing from canoes. Increasing trips of course depends on the type of access points provided and the need for each type at specific locations. For some respondents, road and parking access would imply increase in use. For others, an increase in ramps for small boats would enhance boating traffic. Apparently, given the current access conditions, provision of access points should primarily target two areas: fishing (access for small boats) and walkway and bike trail. Although the respondents were cautious in making an educated guess about additional use by other users, they all agreed that new access points mean new places, more variety and more choices. Consequently, if they are made available, people will use them, as they will make access easier.

In addition, the respondents were invited to identify some inhibiting factors that would restrain them from increasing their use even if more public access points are provided. Among others, poor aquatic habitat was mostly mentioned. For installing the access points, three locations were identified based on distance to major road, distance to food and water facilities, proposed bike path locations, distance to current access points and distance to clusters of gravel mines. Placing two access points in Butler County and one in Hamilton County were suggested. Access point 1 would be located in the Burnet Woods park and recreation area, on the east side of the river along Middletown Road. Access point 2 would be installed near to Avon Woods Outdoor Education Center, on the east side of the river, along Neilan Boulevard. Finally, access point 3 would be placed on the west side of the river near Haven Road.

ESTIMATED BENEFITS OF PROPOSED ACCESS POINTS

The purpose of conducting the survey was to adjust the estimated benefits calculated from an earlier study of the total visitation to the Muskingum River. It is evident from the survey results that visitation to the river is related to whether the respondents live distant from or close to the river. The total visitation reported averages five trips a month, implying an average use of about one time a week. The relative dependence of this outcome on the location of the respondents' residence calls for a conservative but reasonable assumption that people take trips to the river two times during two weekends in a month and devote the other two weekends to other activities. Based on the idea that outdoor recreation is seasonal, there is a need to account for seasonality effects. Consequently, annual average visitation per user is assumed to be 18 (2×9) trips.

Relying on the Delphi survey respondents for the total visitation estimate would be inappropriate since this estimate would not result from a truly random sample. Alternatively, the study by Hitzhusen et al. (2000) on the Muskingum River is used for benefit transfer. In this study, data on the annual river use were collected on a daily basis by lockmasters at each lock and maintained by Blue Rock State Park in Muskingum County. Between 1983 and 1997, total visitation to 10 locks and dams averages 190 000 annually. Although the population living in Butler and Hamilton counties is almost twice the population of the counties comprising the Muskingum River watershed, half of this number, that is, 95 000 visits is used as a conservative assumption. This is because the Muskingum River has more access points.

In order to estimate additional spending by river users assuming availability of new access points, we need to estimate increase in visitation to the river. The results of the survey are very informative but not sufficient to precisely estimate the increase in visitation, creating the motivation for applying benefit transfer. Instead of using four additional visits a year as reported by Silva et al. (1997), a conservative amount of three visits is used. However, to value visitation to the river, the conservative $10 from the Delphi survey is used as average expenditure per user and per trip, which is reasonable as compared to estimates of $13.50 for the northeast region (Region 9) provided by the US Forest Service. Increase in visitation is determined by drawing upon findings by Silva et al. (1997) that 26.1 percent of users would increase their use by three visitation days if more access points were installed.

The estimates indicate a total annual economic benefit of $743 850 for the entire region. Based on the Silva et al. (1997) study, $325 806 representing 43.8 percent would be spent locally. These estimates rely on a very strong assumption that the number of visits is equal to the number of visiting individuals as follows:

Annual estimated visitation to the river = 95 000 visits.
Annual estimated increase in visitation = 26.1 percent of visitors.
Increase visitation = 95 000 × 26.1 = 24 795.
Annual expenditures for increased visitation = 24 795 x 10 x 3 = $743 850.

The study by Sylva et al. provides estimates for a one-time capital outlay and maintenance and operating costs for one boat ramp. To estimate the costs of building the access points, these figures are adjusted upward by 50 percent to account for inflation and any other discrepancies such as unexpected additional costs. However, to avoid double counting, the mowing costs are taken into account in the Great Miami bikeway economic analysis. To easily compare the costs and benefits over time, we express both costs and benefits in present value terms. The adjusted costs and their discounted present value are depicted in Table 10.7.

Based on the estimated cost and benefits, benefit–cost ratios are computed as follows:

$$\frac{DPVB}{DVPC} = \frac{\sum_{i=1}^{T} \frac{Bt}{(1+i)^t}}{\sum_{i=1}^{T} \frac{Ot}{(1+i)^t} + K} \qquad (10.1)$$

Table 10.7   Costs of building the three access points

	Cost per access point ($) of visits	Cost for three point ($) of visits	DPV ($)
Annual maintenance and operation cost	4 425	13 275	120 497
Initial capital outlay	637 500	1 912 500	

where $DPVB$ = Discounted Present Value of Benefits, $DPVC$ = Discounted Present Value of Costs, T = Time Horizon (25 years), B_t = Benefit in Year t, O_t = Operations and Maintenance Cost in Year t, K = Initial Capital Outlay, i = Discount Rate.

Instead of being economic surplus or consumer's surplus, these estimates merely represent direct expenditures in the regional and local economies. As indicated in Figure 10.1, consumer's surplus is the surplus benefit (triangle P*PE) over and above the cost (rectangle OVEP). The area abVO represents local expenditures. The key assumption behind the demand curve is that as costs/prices increase, the number of visits falls. There exists a price/cost P* at which no more visits will be made. This is called the 'choke price'. On the other hand, when costs are zero, the number of visits will be the highest (VT). At any price higher than zero, the number of visits will drop, for example, at a positive price P visits will drop to V. From Figure 10.1, we know that at a cost P an individual would make V visits. However, the individual is willing to pay almost P* for the first visit and any amount between P* and P for the following trips (up to V). From that point onwards, the cost of a visit is higher than what the individual is willing to pay for the trip. Estimating the consumer's surplus for taking additional trips requires either the knowledge of the width and height of the triangle P*PE or an estimated demand function. Based on the total visitation estimates, the consumer's surplus can be estimated if the choke price is known.

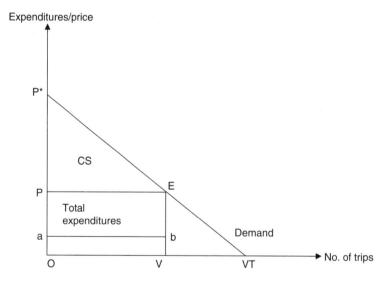

Figure 10.1   Consumer's surplus

Again, lack of information on the choke price requires using a study by Earnhart (2000) for benefit transfer. In this study, 310 survey respondents were asked to state the travel cost increase (in terms of access fee, travel time, and travel distance) needed to choke off demand for in-water recreation.

The responses identify each respondent's choke price. The results indicate an average demand-choking distance-related cost of $58 634, which we use as a choke price, since it is the largest demand-choking cost in the study by Earnhart. Assuming a linear demand curve, this results in a total annual consumer's surplus of $602 940, implying an annual per-trip consumer's surplus of $24, which is equivalent to $25.60 in 2003 dollars. This amount, which represents the annual per-trip economic benefit of installing new access points to the river, is consistent with findings by previous studies. For example, a study by Sommer (2001) found that large improvement in water quality results in an average increase in annual per-trip consumer's surplus of $29.23 for boaters.

The ideal way of conducting the analysis would be to estimate the change in consumer's surplus that would result from making new access points available. This type of analysis is presented in Figure 10.2 where V1–V0 represents additional trips and the area E0E1P**P* would be the change in consumer's surplus. Lack of information precludes such an analysis. This chapter only assesses the economic surplus of taking additional trips

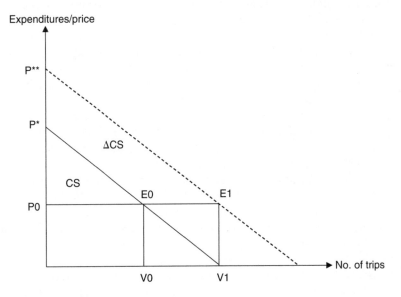

Figure 10.2   Change in consumer's surplus

assuming availability of new access points. Table 10.8 reports the discounted present value of benefits and costs and the corresponding benefit–cost ratios at the discount rates of 6 percent, 8 percent, and 10 percent. The benefit–cost ratios are nearly identical and are larger than unity, indicating that the benefits outweigh the costs. So, a sensitivity analysis was performed and the results are presented in Table 10.9. As depicted in Table 10.9, not all scenarios still yield a benefit–cost ratio that is greater than unity. For example, simply lowering the benefits by 75 percent results in benefit–cost ratios less than unity regardless of the level of the discount rate used. So does decreasing the annual benefits by 50 percent and increasing the costs by 50 percent when using a discount rate of 12 percent. These are poor expectations and perhaps based on unreasonably pessimistic assumptions. For more likely results, access for in-river recreation in the Great Miami is a potentially high paying investment.

SUMMARY AND CONCLUSIONS

The need for this research came from a request for economic valuation of benefits derived from a natural resource, the Great Miami River. Township trustees, Miami Conservancy District staff, citizens' action groups such as Friends of the Great Miami River and Rivers Unlimited wanted to explore possible solutions to enhance economic activity and recreation in the river corridor. One of the objectives of the study was to estimate the feasibility of buffer strip/zones along the river. Specifically, the goal was to determine the impacts of gravel mining on residential property values. If gravel mining affected property value, regulation of mining activity along the corridor would suggest a higher tax base and revenue for the region, besides enhancing the scenic beauty of the river.

One of the objectives of the study was also to determine economic impacts of expanding boating, fishing, and other instream recreation opportunities by constructing new boat ramps where needed. The purpose was not only to enhance the social capital of a given region but also to boost the local economy and increase recreational opportunities for river users.

The estimation of the costs and benefits of constructing a bike trail proved to be a challenge since we did not have a benchmark for estimating these figures. Besides, there was an ambiguity regarding the length and the location of the bike way, since some properties located adjacent to the river were privately owned residential, commercial, and industrial parcels. Therefore, benefit transfer values were simulated from the Heritage Trail, in Dubuque, Iowa, prepared by Siderelis and Moore (1995). The trail extends for 27 miles, and on average a person spends approximately $11.09

Table 10.8 Discounted benefits and costs of three access points

Estimated annual benefits	Costs estimates of three access points		DPV of benefits at 10%	DPV of benefits at 8%	DPV of benefits at 6%	DPV of costs at 10%	DPV of costs at 8%	DPV of costs at 6%
	Initial capital outlay	Annual maintenance and operations costs						
$743 850	$1 912 500	$13 275	6 751 926	7 940 599	9 508 635	2 032 997	2 054 211	2 082 194
Benefit–cost ratio			3.32	3.87	4.57			

Table 10.9 Sensitivity analysis

Scenarios	Estimated benefits ($)	DPV of benefits ($)		DPV of costs ($)		Benefit/ cost ratio	
		10%	12%	10%	12%	10%	12%
Lower the annual benefits by 25%	557 888	5 063 949	4 375 516	2 032 997	2 016 616	2.49	2.17
Lower the annual benefits by 50%	371 925	3 375 963	2 917 008	2 032 997	2 016 616	1.66	1.45
Lower benefits by 75%	185 963	1 687 986	1 458 508	2 032 997	2 016 616	0.83	0.72
Lower annual benefits by 50% and raise costs by 50%	371 925	3 375 963	2 917 008	3 049 496	3 024 924	1.11	0.96
Lower annual benefits by 75% and raise the costs by 50%	185 963	1 687 986	1 458 508	3 049 496	3 024 924	0.55	0.48

per trip on the bike trail. The aggregate benefits relevant to the local economy from the bike trail are estimated by multiplying the average amount spent by number of visitors per day. This study develops a methodology to estimate opportunity cost of acquiring land for the bikeway and buffer strips, and also develops methodology to estimate the total willingness to pay, not just expenditures for construction of a bike trail.

To estimate the impact of access points, again, the BT method was adopted. A study by Silva et al. (1997) which analyzed the behavior of Ohio boaters at newly constructed ramps using a survey-based method was used as the benchmark. The total annual visitation was estimated using benefit transfers from a study on the Muskingum River. The goal was to assess the economic benefits of installing new access points to the Great Miami River. Since applying the benefit transfer method requires adjusting the benefit estimates based on the policy site characteristics, the main problem encountered in conducting the analysis was finding baseline data on the use of the Great Miami River.

As a result, a preliminary survey was administered. Rather than detailed estimates on quantitative use of the river, the results of the survey give approximates of both quantitative and qualitative characteristics of the river use. For example, the type of activities for which people mostly use the river as well as some inhibiting factors to additional use contingent on more access points were identified. Based on benefit transfers from previous studies and the results from the preliminary survey, total estimated annual economic surplus of installing new access points were a reasonable amount of $602 940. The analysis relies heavily on a number of assumptions which when relaxed will yield different results. One such assumption is that only three access points will be installed. Using more access points in the calculation would change the benefit–cost ratios presented in the sensitivity analysis. Further refinement of the analysis can be made through a more comprehensive survey and more primary data collection and analysis of both benefits and costs.

To measure the effect of gravel mining on property values, a hedonic pricing method was used. The decrease in residential property value was estimated at $2 million resulting from proximity to gravel mining. This results in a tax revenue loss of more than $100 000 annually to the local governments.

REFERENCES

Desvouges,W.H., M.C. Naughton, and G.R. Parsons (1992), "Benefit transfer: conceptual problem in estimating water quality benefit using existing studies," *Water Resources Research*, **28**, 675–83.

Earnhart, D. (2000), "Using contingent behavior and contingent pricing analysis to improve the valuation of travel cost components," Department of Economics – University of Kansas.

Hitzhusen, F.J., S. Lowder, and R. Ayalasomayajula (2000), "Muskingum River economic valuation," Phase II Working Paper, Department of Agricultural, Environmental and Development Economics – The Ohio State University.

Johnston, R.J. and T.J. Tyrrell (2003), "Estimating recreational user counts," *American Journal of Agricultural Economics*, **85** (3), 554–68.

Kondolf, G.M. (1997), "Hungry water: effects of dams and gravel mining on river channels," *Environmental Management*, **21** (4), 533–51.

Krunkilton, R.L. (1982), "An overview of gravel mining in Missouri and fish and wildlife implications," *Wildlife Values of Gravel Pits*, St Paul, MN: University of Minnesota Agricultural Experiment Station, Miscellaneous Publication 17-1982, pp. 80–88.

Martino, J. (1970), "The precision of Delphi estimates," *Technological Forecasting and Social Change*, **1** (3), 293–9.

Nelson, E.L. (1993), "Instream sand and gravel mining," in C.F. Bryan and D.A. Rutherford (eds), *Impacts on Warmwater Streams: Guidelines for Evaluation*, Little Rock, AR: Southern Division – American Fisheries Society.

Rosenberger, R.S. and J.B. Loomis (2000), *Benefit Transfer of Outdoor Recreation Use Values: A Technical Document supporting the Forest Service Strategic Plan*, RMRS-GTR-72, Fort Collins, CO: USDA Forest Service, Rocky Mountain Research Station.

Siderelis, C. and R. Moore (1995), "Outdoor recreation net benefits of rail-trails," *Journal of Leisure Research*, **27** (4), 344–59.

Silva, K., K. Pisor, and F.J. Hitzhusen (1997), "An analysis of boaters at recently constructed ODNR boat ramps in Ohio," ESO 2389 ODNR Pilot Project, Department of Agricultural Economics – The Ohio State University.

Sommer, A. (2001), "Determining the value of improved water quality in the Hocking River Valley to Ohio boaters and fishers," thesis, Department of Agricultural, Environmental and Development Economics – The Ohio State University.

11. The Cuyahoga River Valley initiative: framing, codification, and preliminary economic analysis in an urban river corridor

Fred J. Hitzhusen, Sarah A. Kruse, Ashraf Abdul-Mohsen, Joana J. Ferreti-Meza, and Marc Hnytka

INTRODUCTION

As a capstone case for this book this chapter demonstrates the process of framing a set of critical issues in an urban river corridor, codifying supply and demand factors, outlining a research plan, and developing some preliminary hedonic and benefit transfer estimates to start the analysis and decision-making process. The framing, codification, and research phase subsets were developed under a seed grant from the Cleveland Foundation for the Cuyahoga County Planning Commission. The preliminary benefit transfer economic estimates were part of a class assignment for a course (AEDE 631) on benefit–cost analysis taught at The Ohio State University (OSU) by Professor Hitzhusen, autumn quarters 2004 and 2005 and the hedonic pricing estimates are from an MS thesis by Joana Ferreti-Meza.

The Cuyahoga River, located in northeast Ohio, is probably best known as "the river that caught on fire" and started a major environmental movement in the United States. Since that time, as a result of various clean-up and restoration efforts river function has improved and now provides both local citizens and tourists with more attractive amenities for recreation, relaxation, and enjoying the scenery. However, much remains to be done to restore and enhance the river.

The Cuyahoga Valley Initiative (CVI) is an ongoing effort to promote and improve the quality of both the river and the surrounding watershed as well as the services both provide to the local community. The purpose of this research plan is to address several options related to improving the river corridor and assess the economic potential of each. It involves the methods and analysis developed by OSU environmental economists, ecological engineers and aquatic biologists in an eight-year research program on river economics that has focused on rivers in Ohio, Michigan, and New York State.

We have worked closely with staff of the Cuyahoga County Planning Commission (CCPC) in developing this proposal and are particularly appreciative of the coordination and facilitation role played by Carol Thaler of that office. In addition, we have benefited from a careful reading of the report to CCPC by the Rocky Mountain Institute (RMI) and have had phone and e-mail contact with staff members of RMI. We have also reviewed information from the University of Vermont's Gund Institute for Ecological Economics and interacted with staff and board members of the Cuyahoga Valley National Park. The resulting river economics research proposal is developed in two phases (Figure 11.1), a baseline assessment of corridor economic value and economic analysis and rank of options for increasing economic well-being in the Cuyahoga Valley.

PHASE ONE: BASELINE ASSESSMENT OF CORRIDOR ECONOMIC VALUE

Time Frame

March 1, 2006 through December 31, 2006.

Objectives

The specific objectives of Phase 1 are:

1. Assessment of the current economic value of natural resource related amenities and infrastructure in the river corridor.
2. Assessment of preferences of a sample population for alternative options to enhance economic value in the river corridor.
3. Codification of primary demand and supply factors influencing river-related economic well-being.

Methods

1. Current economic value of corridor natural resource related amenities and infrastructure
This part of the study is concerned with assessing the economic value of current recreational and natural resource amenities that could be enjoyed by both local residents and visitors to the Cuyahoga River Valley (CRV)

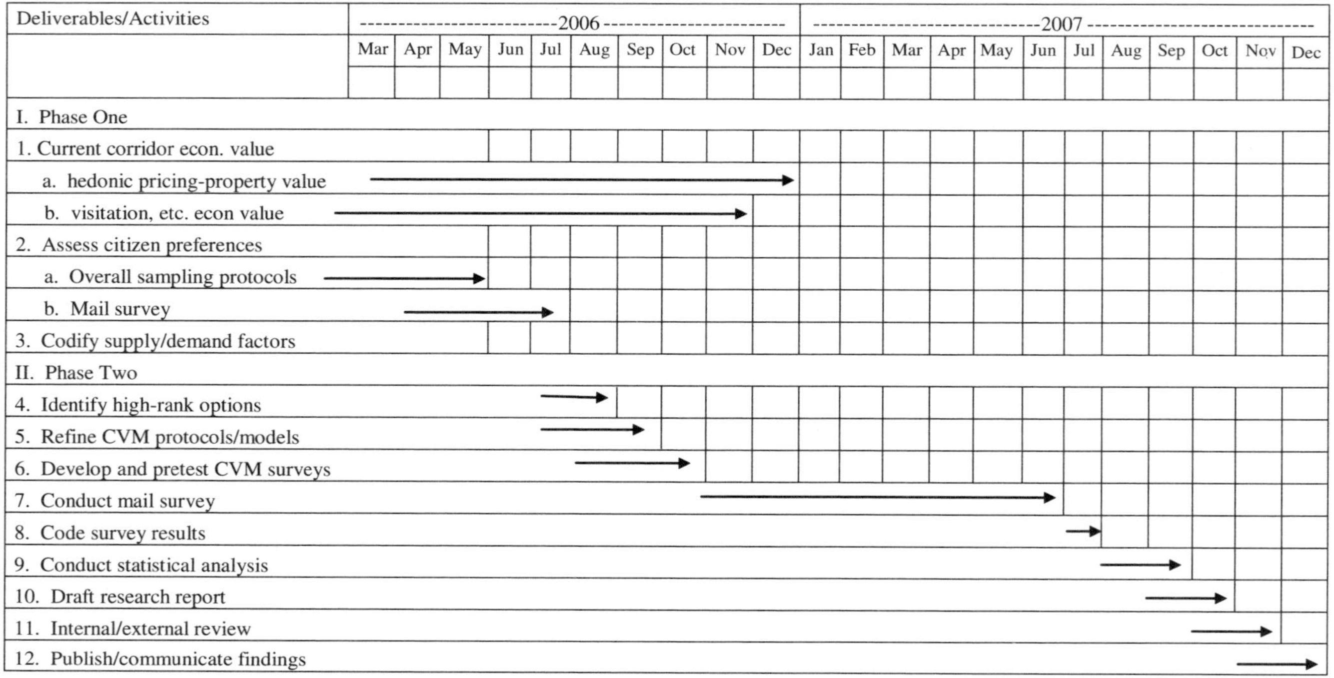

Deliverables/Activities	2006 Mar	Apr	May	Jun	Jul	Aug	Sep	Oct	Nov	Dec	2007 Jan	Feb	Mar	Apr	May	Jun	Jul	Aug	Sep	Oct	Nov	Dec
I. Phase One																						
1. Current corridor econ. value																						
a. hedonic pricing-property value										↑												
b. visitation, etc. econ value									↑													
2. Assess citizen preferences																						
a. Overall sampling protocols			↑																			
b. Mail survey					↑																	
3. Codify supply/demand factors																						
II. Phase Two																						
4. Identify high-rank options						↑																
5. Refine CVM protocols/models							↑															
6. Develop and pretest CVM surveys								↑														
7. Conduct mail survey																↑						
8. Code survey results																	↑					
9. Conduct statistical analysis																		↑				
10. Draft research report																			↑			
11. Internal/external review																					↑	
12. Publish/communicate findings																						↑

Figure 11.1   CVI river economics research time line

inside Cuyahoga County. Apart from the benefits provided by the Cuyahoga Valley National park and those already embedded in residential property values in the Valley, which will be estimated separately in Phase One of this study, these amenities might include, among others, current water-based recreational facilities on the Cuyahoga River such as available canoe liveries, boating and fishing docks, park and picnic facilities, current use of the towpath and scenic railway, and recreational visitations related to the steelmaking legacy (if any). Two valuation methods will be utilized to estimate current economic values in the river corridor depending on the type of values or benefits involved. These methods are benefit transfer and hedonic pricing.

A. Benefit transfer to estimate current visitation use value of the national park and the economic value of other amenities and infrastructure in the corridor   Given the multidimensional nature of the current amenities in the Cuyahoga River corridor, estimating an independent value for each of them would entail considerable cost and time. Alternatively, we will develop a benefit transfer (BT)[1] protocol to utilize benefits or values already estimated for similar river corridors (study sites) to estimate the current economic value of the Cuyahoga River corridor (policy site). Chosen study-site corridor(s) should be similar to CRV in both supply and demand side characteristics. In other words, site-specific and individual specific characteristics should be relatively similar between study and policy sites in order for the BT method to be viable and dependable. The static codification mentioned above would provide a way to identify these demand and supply characteristics for the Cuyahoga River Corridor and to explore similar river corridors which could be considered substitutes for the Cuyahoga.

Since only one third of the Cuyahoga Valley National Park (CVNP) is located in Cuyahoga County and given that CVNP is the only designated national park in Ohio, including the economic value of the park in the base-line benefit estimation for the CRV would underestimate the park's value. As such, this portion is focused on estimating the total use value of the Cuyahoga Valley National Park (CVNP) under the current water quality conditions of the Cuyahoga River which weaves through the park for 23 miles. The CVNP offers many recreational services to its visitors, such as, scenic train rides, historical sightseeing, nature walks, hiking, biking, picnicking, bird watching, golfing, fishing, and winter sports. The park is visited by about 3 million persons annually.

To estimate a total economic value for current use of the park (a base value), a second benefit transfer protocol is proposed. In this case, the policy site is the CVNP and the study sites are similar national parks or open natural spaces for which economic values have been estimated using any of the primary valuation methods such as travel cost and contingent valuation. In particular, average per-day or per-trip use values in the study sites will be used to estimate total use value at the policy site (CVNP). The main advantage of the benefit transfer method lies in avoiding the cost of doing original estimation of benefits in the policy site. This comes at a cost, however. Value estimates obtained using benefit transfer will be less accurate, in theory, than those obtained through primary data-collection methods (such as travel cost and contingent valuation methods). This trade-off between accuracy and cost is a function of two factors: the importance of the proposed policy change and the research budget (costs). In any case, benefit transfer could provide a benchmark for the value of the CVNP that could be used in a preliminary benefit cost analysis or as a starting point for a more comprehensive valuation task of the park and any proposed changes to its services.

B.   Hedonic pricing of amenity and infrastructure impacts on corridor residential property values   This section of Phase One assessment is twofold. The first part will use a mail survey to assess knowledge and awareness levels of riverfront residential property owners as they relate to current and future water quality of the Cuyahoga River, as well as knowledge of any remediation efforts currently underway, specifically the Cuyahoga River Remedial Action Plan (RAP). The goal of the RAP is to educate and work with local citizens and local officials to improve the river. If survey results determine that residential property owners have little knowledge of efforts of the RAP or current water quality conditions, then concern over housing values related to water quality is likely to be lower.

The second part of this section will assess the economic impacts of the water quality improvements by utilizing hedonic techniques (see Bejranonda et al., 1999; Dabrowska, 2004; Hitzhusen et al., 1997). Hedonic models have been widely used to examine the contribution of environmental quality to property prices. In other words, a house with an aesthetically pleasing view (that is, river or lake view) should sell for more than a house with similar structural characteristics located in a polluted or unattractive area. Hedonic pricing techniques allow this effect to be measured, holding other factors such as square footage and interior features (that is, number of bedrooms, number of baths) constant. The study will analyze the environmental characteristics of the Cuyahoga watershed, and its impacts on the property values of housing located near the river.

Using a small sample of properties, a preliminary model has been estimated including only the upper and lower sections of the river and results suggest that residential housing prices are significantly affected by water quality and the general amenity attributes of the river corridor. Separating the water quality and corridor amenity attributes will require some careful model specification and estimation including various measurements of water quality dimensions. The preliminary results indicate that improving water quality (or amenity attributes) would boost the value of properties in the Cuyahoga River area, giving property owners and elected officials a new reason to consider these factors when making decisions about land use and development issues. The preliminary study can be used as a basis for developing more detailed estimation of water quality impacts in the Lower Cuyahoga River Valley area.

The hedonic pricing model will segment the river (and related residential properties) into smaller segments in order to provide greater differentiation and explanatory power of the results. If sufficient variation in water quality exists and can be adequately quantified, useful policy outcomes can result. Survey results as proposed in the first part of this section will serve to substantiate any statistical relationship revealed in the hedonic study. If results confirm, as the rough estimates seem to indicate, that water quality and/or aesthetic factors are significantly related to property values, then information regarding the knowledge level of property owners would substantiate these results and make them more reliable for policy-makers.

2. Preferences for alternative options to enhance economic value in the river corridor

The purpose of the mail survey used in Phase One is to gather general data on demographics and the preferences of respondents for proposed improvements along the river corridor (that is, improving water quality, extending the towpath, and so on). Rank ordering of these preferences will facilitate the decision-making process in terms of assessing priorities before starting work on Phase Two of this project.

Initially, the sample area will be localized, focusing on the city of Cleveland and suburbs potentially affected (positively or negatively) by potential river corridor improvements. The primary mail survey sample frame would be a randomly selected subset of 1000 individuals living in the locations mentioned above. This number was chosen based on the need for at least 250 data points and the expectation of a 25 percent return rate after two mailings. Each survey packet will include a cover letter, survey, and pre-stamped return envelope. Approximately three weeks after the first mailing, a second survey packet will be sent to anyone who has not responded.

In the survey, individuals will be informed that a variety of river corridor improvements are being considered and the improvements will be roughly outlined and generally defined. Individuals will be asked to *rate* the priority of implementing each improvement using a five-point Likert scale, and will then be asked to *rank* the objectives in decreasing order of priority.

The potential river corridor improvements that will be included in the survey are as follows:

- non-point source pollution prevention
- green bulkheading
- erosion control strategies
- restrictions on landfills and filling of tributary valleys
- upgrading the sewer system in Cleveland to reduce sewage overflows
- stream daylighting
- creating Wetlands (particularly where tributaries merge with the Cuyahoga)
- scenic railroad extension
- towpath extension
- new parks at Canal Basin and on Whiskey Island
- Cuyahoga Valley Living Museum.

By asking individuals to both rate and rank their preferences, an assessment can be made of which objectives are a priority, and also the degree to which certain objectives are preferred over others. This information will be useful in determining whether the main objectives as determined by Cuyahoga County planners to be important for this study match the priorities of local citizens when considering improvements to the river corridor.

Results will also facilitate the priority of Phase Two objectives, and questions on basic demographics and recreational activity levels will be used to help create the static codification matrix (see section 3).

3. Codification of primary demand and supply factors influencing river-related economic well-being

This initial phase of the study would classify the Cuyahoga River based on the economic principles of supply and demand. Determining supply side factors includes identifying the hydrological, biological, and human-made infrastructure characteristics (that is, access points, parking, and picnic facilities) of the river in question. On the other hand, demand side factors require the identification of individual characteristics and demographic traits (that is, income, education, values, recreation levels) that influence the willingness to pay (WTP) of individuals for river-based amenities, that is, recreation, water quality, aesthetics (see Kruse, 2005).

The demand side codification allows for an analysis of how supply-side characteristics either positively or negatively affect individuals, which issues are most important to those individuals, and how much they are willing to pay for a change in the level of a particular river-related good or service. These demand-side characteristics are typically fairly consistent across sites with individual characteristics such as age, income, and distance from the river corridor affecting demand for the goods and services offered.

The codification of supply side factors allows for an assessment of the quality of the river ecosystem by examining how certain characteristics, either natural or human-made, have led to the current quality of the river. A second aspect of supply-side codification is the identification of river corridors that may serve as substitutes for the Cuyahoga. The existence of unique supply-side characteristics (that is, National Park, Lake Erie) or the possible creation of such goods and services (that is, towpath and scenic railway extensions) increases the likelihood that individuals will have a higher WTP for river-based amenities on the Cuyahoga River.

PHASE TWO: ECONOMIC ANALYSIS OF HIGH RANK OPTIONS

Time Frame

July 1, 2006 through December 31, 2007.

Objectives

The objectives of Phase Two are:

1. Identification of high rank options from planners and initial preference survey.
2. Development of methods for contingent valuation of willingness to pay.
3. Development of sampling and survey protocols for the CVM estimation.
4. Conduct of surveys, statistical analysis of factors related to WTP and development of policy implications.

Methods

This part of the study is concerned with valuing possible improvement in water quality in the river as it relates to the recreational use of the river and the flow of its natural services. It is also concerned with valuing other high rank options to enhance economic value in the river corridor such as proposed extensions of the towpath trail and scenic railway, establishing new parks and constructing a Cuyahoga Valley Living Museum. High rank options or alternatives will be determined by both the Cuyahoga County planners and local citizens through the primary preference survey.

1. Identification of high rank options
In general, options to enhance economic value in the Cuyahoga River
Corridor have been identified by the Cuyahoga County Planning staff and
can be classified into three subgroups depending on the outcome, as follows:

A.   Improving water quality in the Cuyahoga River   Water quality in the
Cuyahoga River is of great concern due to contamination from storm
water discharge, combined sewer overflows, and incompletely disinfected
wastewater from urban areas. As a result, water quality may pose a health
risk to people who might come into contact with the water and may limit
water-based recreational activities such as canoeing, swimming, and
wading. A number of measures have been proposed to improve water
quality in the river and enhance fish habitat. The following list by
Cuyahoga County planners summarizes some of the proposed measures:

- *Non-point pollution prevention measures.* Unhealthy waterways minimize the potential use of the river for recreation purposes. Measures
  can include minimizing use of fertilizers on residential lawns, re-
  establishing riparian buffers, construction techniques, site design,
  landscaping design, and so on.
- *Erosion control measures.* Erosion wears away the river bank, endan-
  gers the structural integrity of land, and may result in excess sedimentation which can choke natural habitats. Preventative measures
  include silt fencing around construction sites, preserving and replac-
  ing vegetation on hillsides and reducing unnaturally high peak flows
  in waterways due to runoff from impervious surfaces.
- *Restrictions on filling tributary valleys for development and landfills.*
  Most large tributary valleys to the Cuyahoga have been the site of
  landfills which narrow their width, remove natural vegetation, negatively impact the aesthetics, and impact the waterways that flow at
  their base. In order to address these issues ordinances such as riparian zone setbacks, hillside ordinances and planned unit development
  zones have been suggested in order to protect these natural features.
  In addition, greenway plans that identify these areas as community
  resources that should be protected can be developed in order to shape
  public policy toward the development of these areas.
- *Green bulkheading in the ship channel area of the flats.* Existing bulk-
  head design has resulted in an armoring of the river channel.
  Furthermore, bulkheading is not an optimal long term solution.
  Green bulkheading includes designs that incorporate habitat for fish
  and include vegetation which produces a more natural appearance.
  The Ohio EPA has developed a number of model designs and the

Cuyahoga RAP has received approval to receive wetlands mitigation funds for the creation of green bulkheads (the modification of existing bulkheads into green ones).

- *Wetlands re-creation in Cuyahoga County.* Development has resulted in the destruction of most wetlands in the county which serve as a natural filtering and flood control mechanism. Funds required to be paid by developments in Cuyahoga County for wetlands mitigation are often applied to sites outside of the county. One problem is a lack of approved wetland mitigation sites within the county.

- *Reducing sewage overflows into waterways in the area.* Older parts of Cuyahoga County (predominantly within the City of Cleveland) are serviced with combined sewers which spill raw sewage into area waterways in times of heavy rains when the sewers' capacity is exceeded. The North East Ohio Regional Sewer District (NEORSD) is implementing a policy of expanding the capacity of the sewer system via large tunnels and holding areas so that the number of times that sewage is released from overflows is reduced to three or four times annually.

- *Ship channel dredging policies.* The last 5 miles of the Cuyahoga River have been dredged from a natural depth of 3 to 6 feet to a depth of approximately 26 feet so that lake freighters can service the steel mills and building material companies. The increased depth has had an impact on water flow and oxygen levels of the river, adversely affecting its biological integrity. Aeration of the river and beneficial reuse of dredged material (which is currently disposed of in confined disposal facilities on the lakefront) constitute potential solutions.

- *Stream daylighting.* Many of the creeks that feed the Cuyahoga River have been buried or made part of the sewer system. "Daylighting" restores the natural drainage system using surface waterways by removing them from the pipes in which they were entombed. "Daylighting" still addresses flood control and storm water management objectives but also adds value by maximizing ecological and water quality benefits. It also begins to recognize stream corridors as potential amenities in site and urban design. The goal is to physically connect people to the natural systems in which they live. Then people can see and feel that nature is all around us; that it is a part of our daily lives.

B.   The ability for pedestrian and bicycle travel from the Flats through Cuyahoga County into Summit, Stark, and Tuscarawas Counties, and by train from the Cuyahoga Natural Park to Downtown Cleveland

- *Towpath trail extension.* The towpath has become a defining element in the Cuyahoga Valley landscape, especially after the establishment of the Cuyahoga Valley National Park in 1974. Plans have been completed for building the final segment of the towpath in Cuyahoga County from old Harvard Avenue to downtown Cleveland and the lakefront. The completion of this project will allow pedestrian and bicycle travel from the flats, completely through Cuyahoga County into Summit, Stark, and Tuscarawas Counties.

- *Scenic railway extension.* Plans are also underway to extend the scenic railway from its northern terminus at the gateway to the Cuyahoga Valley National Park all the way to downtown Cleveland. This will allow both visitors and residents to travel on a train through the CVNP to downtown Cleveland.

C. The ability to understand and appreciate Cleveland's heritage   The following projects are expected by Cuyahoga county planners to add economic value to the river corridor:

- *A new park at Canal Basin (along the Cuyahoga River in the flats, celebrating canal era).* At the historic terminus of the Ohio and Erie Canal, this Park will celebrate the early commercial history of northeast Ohio. During the height of the Canal's use from 1832 to 1850, Cleveland grew from a village of just over 1000 inhabitants to a city of 17 000. The construction of the Canal closed the circle of waterborne transportation, allowing goods to be cheaply transported from the eastern seaboard through the Erie Canal, across Lake Erie to Cleveland, down the Ohio and Erie Canal to the Ohio River, and down the Mississippi to New Orleans, effectively linking disparate parts of a fledgling nation together, and bringing Cleveland to prominence as an economic center. A new park would include public access to the river and interpretive displays and activities.
- *New park on Whiskey Island.* As one of the last remaining expanses of open land near downtown, Whiskey Island provides a unique opportunity to explore the history of the settlement of the Western Reserve, as well as a testament to the changes made to the Cuyahoga River over time. Lorenzo Carter, Cleveland's first permanent settler, built his family farm on the island. Irish immigrants who came to dig the Ohio and Erie Canal and re-channel the Cuyahoga River (including the opening of the present mouth of the river which forms the eastern boundary of Whiskey Island) settled here. The establishment of a park on Whiskey Island presents an opportunity to explore Cleveland's early history, understand the natural forces at work amid a highly urbanized area, illustrate the geographic and historic connection between the River and Lake Erie, and demonstrate how

sustainable techniques can be used to chart a course for Cleveland's future.

• *Cuyahoga Valley Living Museum.* This would be a series of experiences, packaged and promoted as self-guided and guided special tours through the valley. The living museum would educate visitors about the valley's past, allow visitors to experience industrial processes and participate in environmental restoration projects. The highlights of the living museum will include the steelmaking legacy, Rockefeller legacy and a new park at the site of the Cuyahoga River Fire.

2.   CVM methods

In order to value extensions of the towpath and the scenic railway, improvements of water quality in the Cuyahoga River and Cleveland's legacy options, the contingent valuation method (CVM) will be used to value the economic benefits of these high-rank options. Contingent valuation is a stated preference technique that has been used extensively in the literature to value nonmarketed public goods and environmental resources. The CVM is conducted by surveying a representative sample of residents in the valley and asking them directly to value the proposed extensions or enhancements. A properly designed CVM instrument (see Abdul-Mohsen, 2005; Irwin, 2001; Kruse, 2005) must accomplish the following tasks:

1.   Establish the baseline conditions or the status quo (Q) regarding the availability of the environmental resource and distribution of property rights over that resource.
2.   Describe the change in Q that would result from the proposed change in policy.
3.   Establish a contingent market, in which participants may, hypothetically, obtain the change in Q by paying a specified amount of money through a specified payment vehicle that is both relevant and familiar to respondents (for example, increases in taxes, good prices, and utility fees).
4.   Elicit participants maximum WTP for the proposed change in Q either directly through open-ended, bidding, or payment card formats, or indirectly through referenda.

In the Cuyahoga River Corridor case, the CVM questionnaire should first present the respondent with a clear description of the status quo of water quality, of the present location and use of the towpath and scenic railway and of current efforts to promote heritage. In the second part of the questionnaire, a contingent market will be constructed, in which the benefits of improving water quality in the river, of the extension of the railway and towpath and of showcasing history of area are presented to the respondents to value. The third part of the survey will include questions about different demographic and behavioral characteristics of the respondents such as income, age, education, race, and distance to the park. Questions about recreational activities at/on the river and at other substitute sites in the area will also be included since it is expected that past recreation on the river and past use of the current towpath and scenic railway will have a positive effect on WTP for the respective improvements. Nonusers might have value for enhancing water quality in the river in general but not for extensions of the towpath and scenic railway since the latter are more related to use of the park. It is also expected that users of substitute sites will be less supportive of improvements in the river corridor. However, this depends on the types of benefits or services provided by these sites in comparison to those provided by the Cuyahoga River Corridor including those provided by the national park.

One problem is how to value the various high-rank options to enhance economic value in the corridor in a cost-effective and credible way. One way is to include all the high-rank options in one scenario and each respondent will be asked to value these options consequentially. However, this might be a difficult task for the individual respondent to handle cognitively. Another, and maybe more appropriate way is to divide the list of proposed options into smaller sub-lists, which will be valued by independent samples of respondents. Each sub-list would include two or three options that are related in some aspect such as the outcome of the proposed options (that is, water quality improvement options, towpath and scenic railway options, and legacy options).

To insure that double counting of benefits of the different projects does not happen, appropriate surveying methods will be employed to avoid the overlapping of subsamples responding to the different valuation scenarios (see section 3). Since multiple CVM scenarios will be employed to value proposed improvements in the corridor, it is possible to use split sampling to examine the validity of the CVM estimates of willingness to pay. For example, extensions of the towpath and scenic railway could be valued using three scenarios: towpath extension, scenic railway extension, and towpath/scenic railway extension. The use of these three scenarios would allow testing for context, sequence, and scope effects in the CVM survey. This is important in order to validate the CVM results and to make sure that respondents understood the difference between these goods when answering the valuation question.

3.   Sampling and survey protocols

In order to value the different high rank options in a cost-effective manner, one comprehensive sample (2000–3000 data points) will be selected during

Phase One of the project. The sample area will be a 30-mile radius from a predetermined central point halfway between the lake front and the northern end of the national park (this appears to be in the general vicinity of where Kingsbury Run meets the Cuyahoga). This sample area was chosen because it is centered around the study area (the Cuyahoga River Corridor) but also includes part of neighboring counties whose residents are likely to benefit from the proposed improvements. The sample could be stratified to meet specific needs of the research. For example, a subsample of residents on or near the Cuyahoga River could be included to collect demographics that could be used in a second-stage estimation of the hedonic pricing model.

A problem that often occurs when multiple mail surveys are used is overlap between the surveys, meaning that individuals may receive surveys on more than one scenario. The objectives and methodology described in the sections above do call for the use of multiple mail surveys, and so in an effort to avoid overlap, sample sizes for all surveys will be estimated at the beginning of Phase One and combined. A random sample will then be drawn to cover the number of data points necessary for all surveys. By doing this, each survey will be sent to a random sample of the population without risking overlap.

This appears to be a proper solution for the overlap problem in that the sample area for each of the proposed mail surveys (that is, water quality improvements, extensions of the towpath and scenic railway, and so on) all appear to affect a roughly similar population. If it is found later that these populations are less similar than the initial assessment implies, then the notion of overlap may not be an issue, and different samples for each survey will simply be drawn from the respective affected population.

PRELIMINARY BENEFIT TRANSFER AND HEDONIC ANALYSES

Towpath Trail Extension

In order to determine the expected benefits for the trail extension, we will use the method of benefit transfer. This will allow us to use an existing study to get a reasonable estimate of the benefits for the towpath trail extension. The focus of the current benefit–cost analysis is the recent proposal to extend the multiuse trail from its current terminus at Harvard Avenue all the way to downtown Cleveland and the lakefront. The distance would be approximately 5 miles and would consist of a paved 10-foot wide path, and a 50-foot swath that would provide an area for environmental improvements, landscape improvements, and, where needed, buffers and safety measures for adjacent property owners.[2] The Cuyahoga County Planning Commission (CCPC) stated that they want the trail to fit in with the existing uses of the land that it would occupy. By doing so, the local landowners and residents will hopefully be more receptive to the project.

The CCPC estimates that land acquisition, funding sources, and design work will take three to six years before construction could take place.[3] Construction could take up to five years. Projects like multiuse trails have relatively high upfront capital costs and relatively long, low cost lives. For these reasons a benefit–cost study should have a time horizon of at least 15 to 20 years. The physical boundaries will first and foremost be the 5-mile long, 50-foot path that will be constructed. As far as the impacts go, the study will primarily look at the impact of the Greater Cleveland area as well as its effects on the utility of individuals who utilize the Cuyahoga Valley National Park.

The primary gainers who were identified as deriving the most benefit from the project are as follows. The first group of gainers is defined as the residents of Cleveland and the surrounding metropolitan area, especially those within close proximity to the extension or any existing part of the trail. Local businesses such as restaurants and shops located in close proximity to the trail will also benefit from the increased activity created by the trail.[4] Finally, the major focus of the project are those individuals who visit the Cuyahoga Valley National Park. Park visitors will now be able to ride, jog, rollerblade, or walk from the national park straight into the heart of Cleveland where they can benefit from complementary activities such as the Rock and Roll Hall of Fame, the Great Lake Science Center, or a whole host of other cultural and entertainment opportunities.[5]

The project also has the potential to cause other parties or individuals to lose utility. One group that could be worse off as a result of the project would be the taxpayers not using the trail. If other funding is not available, the money will have to be taken from public funds accumulated through taxation. Another group that might lose utility as a result of the project are those who own the land where the proposed trail will pass through. If the project takes place, some landowners could be forced into selling their land through the use of eminent domain if they are not willing to sell to the city.

The CCPC has developed preliminary estimates for the cost of the project based on previous projects. They estimate the cost for the 5-mile trail with 50-foot easement to be between $24.5 and $47.8 million. This includes land acquisition, construction, and any additional trail or easement amenities.[6] This amount may seem large and variable for this type of project, but the area where the project is taking place is in an urban area where land prices and construction costs may be higher and more uncertain than in suburban or rural areas.

To get a preliminary estimate of the monetary value of the benefits prior to conducting further, potentially costly studies, visitation data on the existing trail can be used to estimate the increased visits that the new trail section will generate. This method has some inherent, potentially flawed assumptions, but can provide a low-bound estimate for the value of the trail extension. The current length of the trail is around 60 miles and accounts for over 2 million visits per year. This equates to an average of 33 333 visits per mile of trail. Thus, it would seem reasonable to assume that an additional 5 miles of trail would contribute at least an additional 166 665 visits annually since it would connect lake front Cleveland with the national park. An additional factor is the higher density of the surrounding urban area of the proposed extension as opposed to the suburban and rural area surrounding the existing trail.

By using a benefit transfer method to calculate the value of a visit to a multiuse trail and multiplying that by the estimated additional visits generated by the trail addition, a low-bound estimate for the annual value of the trail is obtained. A study looking at another trail in Ohio: Ohio's Little Miami Scenic Trail found that visitors spent an average of $13.54 per visit on food, beverages, and transportation to the trail.[7] Using this number the Ohio and Erie Canal Towpath Trail extension would be valued at $2 256 644 annually. With an average estimated outlay of $36 million and annual maintenance costs of $250 000, it would take about 18 years for the benefits to equal costs.

Water Quality and Housing Values

An MS thesis by Joana Ferreti-Meza (2006) developed and applied a hedonic pricing model to analyze the impact of water quality and other factors along the Lower Cuyahoga River on residential property values located near the river. Four versions of the hedonic model were estimated.

The Northern Ohio Data and Information Service (NODIS), the Maxine Goodman Levin College of Urban Affairs and the Cleveland State University [24] provided the Cuyahoga County Auditor's database tables and the geospatial layers of the parcels, and other descriptive characteristics for this hedonic study. The Arc View software was used to consistently match the data from the water quality stations of the Total Maximum Daily Loads (TMDL) for the Lower Cuyahoga River [27] to each property or parcel_id information. The geographic information system (GIS) software was also employed to match the data from the US Census Bureau. Finally, the software allowed creating distance variables from each parcel such as the distance from the parcel to the river or to Cleveland downtown which is considered the main business center in Cuyahoga County. The final database consisted of 2131 properties sold during 2004 and within a 1-mile radius from the closest water quality station.

The four models consistently reported evidence of the importance of water quality on property values along the segments of the Cuyahoga River within Cuyahoga County. Although the amounts that people are willing to pay for additional units of physical elements (that is, extra buildings, having heater, or living where the white population prevails) are generally greater than water quality impacts, when the effect of a cleaner river is extended to the properties along polluted segments of the Cuyahoga River the amount increases to millions of dollars. For instance, in Model 1 the implicit price of having a fireplace is $28 698 while the implicit price of a one unit increase on IBI or ICI2 is $1735 and $6278 respectively. However as previously stated, when the implicit price on the one unit improvement on water quality is multiplied by the 53 760 parcels the amounts increase to $76 million and $262 million respectively for the IBI and ICI2 indicators provided by the Ohio EPA.

EPILOGUE

Future funding of this proposed initiative is uncertain, but it is intended to give a detailed example of the development of a set of proposed river upgrades and the methods for economic analysis of them.

NOTES

1. Benefit transfer is a secondary valuation method that transfers consumer surplus values already estimated for similar site(s) (study site) to the site of interest (policy site) for which data for primary valuation are not available (see Rosenberger and Loomis, 2000; French and Hitzhusen, 2001; and Ayalasomayajula et al., 2003).
2. http://planning.co.cuyahoga.oh.us/towpath/.
3. http://planning.co.cuyahoga.oh.us/towpath/.
4. www.americantrails.org/resources/economics/Little MiamiEcon.doc.
5. www.cleveland.com/entertainment/.
6. http://planning.co.cuyahoga.oh.us/towpath/.
7. www.trailsandgreenways.org/resources/benefits/topics/tgc_economic.pdf.

REFERENCES

Abdul-Mohsen, A. (2005), "Economic efficiency and income distribution evaluation of toxics and dam removal using contingent valuation," PhD dissertation, AEDE Department, The Ohio State University.

Ayalasomayajula, R., F.J. Hitzhusen and P.W. Jeanty (2003), "Sustaining a river: an economic impact study of Lower Great Miami River segment improvements," research report, Rivers Unlimited.

Bejranonda, S., F. Hitzhusen and D. Hite (1999), "Agricultural sedimentation impacts on lakeside property values," *Agricultural and Resource Economics Review*, October, **28** (2), 208–18.

Dabrowska, K. (2004), "A hedonic evaluation of environmental disamenities: the case of a contaminated river corridor and a landfill," MS thesis, AEDE Department, The Ohio State University.

Ferreti-Meza, J. (2006), "Water quality and property value on the Lower Cuyahoga River: a hedonic analysis," MS thesis, AEDE, The Ohio State University.

French, D.D. and F.J. Hitzhusen (2001), "Status of benefit transfer in the United States and Canada-Commout," *Canadian Journal of Agricultural Econics*, **49**, 259–61.

Hitzhusen, F., A. Abdul-Mohsen, and S. Kruse (2004), "Toward improved economic analysis using contingent valuation: some methodological considerations applied to river toxics and dam removal," selected paper, AAEA Annual Meeting, Denver, CO, July 3.

Hitzhusen, F.J., L. Friedman, K. Sylva, and D. Hite (1997), "Hedonic price and travel cost estimation of stripmine impacts on lake-based property and recreation values," ESO 2376, AEDE, The Ohio State University, November.

Hitzhusen, F.J., S. Lowder, and R. Ayalasomayajula (2000), *Muskingum River Economic Valuation*, Phase II Working Paper, AEDE Department, The Ohio State University.

Irvin, S.K. (2001), "Estimating economic benefits to society from river and stream protection," MS thesis, The Ohio State University.

Kruse, S. (2005), "Toward improved economic analysis of dam removal: some CVM considerations applied to the Ballville Dam, Fremont, OH," PhD dissertation, AEDE Department, The Ohio State University.

Rosenberger, R. and J.B. Loomis. (2000), *Benefit Transfer of Outdoor Recreation Use Values*, Fort Collins, CO: US Department of Agriculture, Forest Service.

12. Overview, key findings, and approaches including benefit transfer for generalization of research results

Fred J. Hitzhusen and Sarah A. Kruse

OVERVIEW

This book has reported on a large, eight-year research program at The Ohio State University to develop methods and estimates of the benefits and costs of various water quality, infrastructure, scenic, and historic river corridor impacts and improvements as a guide to economic analysis and public policy on river and related watershed restoration. The research focuses on evaluation of rivers in the Great Lakes region of the United States and involves a team of environmental economists, an ecological engineer and two aquatic biologists. When the various corridor impact or improvement benefits broadly conceived are expressed in a common economic metric and compared to their full economic costs, one has a basis for assessing river corridors in an economic development, welfare economic and public policy context.

The earliest civilizations were developed along rivers for the rich farmland along their banks and easy transportation. Irrigation of farm lands and water powered industry were followed by large dams and locks for irrigation, residential and industrial water supply, recreation boating and fishing, hydroelectric power and barge transportation of products. Rivers today have the potential to play an important role in the development of an economically depressed region by providing water supply, transportation, waste assimilation, and a wide array of recreation and tourism activities. Rivers as a source of waste disposal are increasingly in conflict with water supply, recreation and tourism and major intra and inter-country conflicts exist over the use rights to large river systems. Thus, the river corridor system or basin appears to be an important, but relatively underutilized focus for economic analysis and public policy.

Treatment costs, hedonic pricing, contingent valuation, benefit transfer and capture estimation, aquatic biology, and hydrodynamic-ecologic simulation models and methods have been developed to value impacts on river corridors. Impacts include such items as household waste, pesticides, industrial toxics, gravel mining and agricultural run-off as well as improvements such as household waste treatment, dredging of toxics, zoning, greenways, dam removals, dam and lock upgrades, bike trails, towpaths, ramps and other recreational infrastructure. Previous chapters have introduced some important innovations for codification of river supply and demand factors, testing for scope, context and sequence effects in contingent valuation model (CVM) mail surveys, benefit transfer including calibration of transfer functions and capture including linking of first stage hedonic pricing and property tax revenue models, structured elicitation groups for assessing constructed vs. static preferences, distribution impacts and equity weighting for contaminated river segments and integration of economic, ecologic, and aquatic models for assessing dam removal.

KEY FINDINGS FROM ECONOMIC ANALYSES/CASES

Chapter 3 reports on an attempt to determine willingness to pay for additional protection of Ohio surface waters which by definition include streams, rivers, creeks, ditches, lakes, reservoirs, ponds, marshes, wetlands, or other waterways. The CVM results reported in Chapter 3 demonstrate that Ohio adult citizen consumers place a relatively high value on the protection of all surface waters in the state. For example, based on aggregation of individual preferences adult Ohioans place a mean value per person of $10.52 and an aggregate value of $89 million to protect 20 percent of available pollutant assimilative capacity in all of the states surface waters. For an additional 20 percent of protection the willingness to pay (WTP) is $59 million and at 70 percent the WTP approaches zero, so diminishing returns are observed for additional protection of assimilative capacity.

In contrast to the more macro approach of Chapter 3, Chapters 4–11 are designed to focus on assessing the economics in ecological context of various water quality and infrastructure improvements in eight representative rivers/cases in the Great Lakes region of the United States.

Chapter 4 reports on an explicit attempt to integrate environmental economic, ecological engineering and aquatic biology models in assessing the impacts from the proposed removal of the *high-head* Ballville Dam in the Sandusky River in northcentral Ohio. Utilization of hydrodynamic and fish migration modeling made it possible to construct more realistic scenarios for the CVM willingness to pay analysis. In addition, an open-ended (OE) WTP question was compared to a dichotomous choice (DC) question in two sub-samples of the survey. The Turnbull low-bound estimate of social benefits for a 30-mile radius area around the dam is over $12 million which exceeds the estimated cost of removing the dam. Some additional class-room based experimental economic analyses were done to compare the CVM stated preference and a constructed preference/focus group approach for determining WTP for the Ballville Dam removal.

Chapter 5 is similar in focus to Chapter 4 with the exception that it reports on an economic assessment of a proposed removal of the Fort Covington *low-head* dam on the Salmon River in upstate New York. In addition, the Salmon River drains into the St Lawrence Seaway (which links Lake Ontario with the Atlantic Ocean) while the Sandusky River drains into Lake Erie. The CVM analysis suggests that removal of the Fort Covington dam would result in benefits far exceeding costs – even the conservative, lower-bound estimate of WTP resulted in benefits four times greater than the costs. Furthermore, nonuse values were more important than use values and greater benefits were evident outside of the area most affected by the dam removal. This raises some important distributions issues.

Chapter 6 reports on an economic assessment of four major infrastructure and water quality improvements in the Muskingum River corridor in southeastern Ohio. The proposed improvements include: (1) increased water quality through improved household septic waste treatment, (2) extending a bike trail/greenway along the river, (3) repair of historic locks and dams on the river, and (4) zoning and subdivision restrictions in three counties of the river corridor. Hedonic pricing, CVM, benefit transfer, and benefit capture techniques were employed to determine the social benefits and costs of each of the major improvements. The benefit–cost ratio results show the bike trail/greenway ranked first (6.49) followed by zoning (5.39), lock and dam upgrades (1.51), and household septic upgrades (1.44). Benefit capture results linked increased residential property values to increased property tax revenues for local government and schools, and identified key variables explaining variation in the CVM, WTP values. The latter could be used to increase funding and support for future river restoration efforts.

Chapter 7 develops an economic analysis of how boaters and anglers value improvements in water quality in the Hocking River Valley in southeastern Ohio, a region heavily impacted by acid coal mine drainage. Revealed and stated preference techniques are combined to estimate how these two groups value recreation trips under baseline conditions, and how individuals may respond to proposed changes in water quality. The results indicate that the majority of the benefits in the sample accrue to anglers, and that there are likely to be large differences in how boaters and anglers respond to changes in water quality. At the margin, per-trip gains in consumer surplus for anglers are largest for small changes in water quality, while per-trip values remain relatively constant for both small and large changes in water quality for boaters. The results also indicate that substitution with alternative sites may be relatively small because the alternative site in our study region is a complement in demand. Further, less than 50 percent of the respondents in our sample indicate that they would take fewer trips elsewhere if water quality improves in the study area, suggesting that much of the increase in value will not be offset by reductions in value elsewhere.

Chapter 8 investigates the impact of farming practices and pesticide use on drinking water treatment costs for 11 communities located in the Maumee River basin in northwestern Ohio. Farming practices and pesticide use are sources of nonpoint surface water pollution in intensely farmed watersheds. Besides having ecological impacts, farming practices may have direct economic effects on communities. Using multivariate statistical analysis, it was determined that a 1 percent reduction in the pesticide application rate in the Maumee River basin would result in a $3600 decrease in water treatment costs among all 11 communities in the study. Other findings are that urban land uses increase turbidity by a larger amount than agricultural land uses, suggesting that controlling urban runoff may also lead to decreased drinking water treatment costs.

Chapter 9 evaluates the economic efficiency and equity impacts of a proposed project to dredge toxics and remove dams in order to restore the contaminated lower Mahoning River in northeast Ohio. This research has both theoretical and empirical implications for the use of CVM to value public goods and environmental resources. A contingent valuation model was utilized to estimate WTP for the various recreational, health and ecological benefits of restoring the Mahoning River including the use of split sampling to test for scope, sequence, and context effects. An equity issue is addressed by examining whether poor and minority households in the area have been unjustly exposed to contamination in the river and therefore, whether the use of a different weighting scheme for different demographic groups (that is, by income, race, and so on) would be justified. Efficiency results indicate the sensitivity to scope is dependent on the type of good being valued and on the characteristics of the respondents especially with respect to past use of the resource. Equity results show people of color disproportionately impacted by the river toxics and benefit–cost evidence stronger when the constant marginal utility of money income assumption is relaxed.

Chapter 10 deals with economic assessment of water quality impacts from in-stream gravel mining and with infrastructure improvements for recreational access to the Lower Great Miami River in southwest Ohio. A baseline assessment of river recreational values and a benefit transfer analysis of adding a 28-mile bike trail and three access points are combined with a hedonic pricing assessment of the impact of in-stream gravel mining in the river. The discounted present value (DPV) of the proposed bike trail benefits were roughly double the DPV of costs. For the three recreational/boating access points the benefit–cost ratios ranged from 3.32 to 4.57 and in the sensitivity analysis they exceeded 1.0 in most cases. The hedonic pricing results showed a $2 million decrease in residential property values from proximity to in-stream gravel mining. This in turn translated into a $119 000 annual loss in property tax revenues to the local governments.

Chapter 11 involved framing, codification and some preliminary economic analysis of several initiatives to upgrade the Cuyahoga River in northern Ohio. The intent of this chapter was to demonstrate these processes in producing a proposal for economic analysis of selected improvements in an urban river corridor. Specific components included codifying supply and demand factors for this river, outlining a research plan for key improvements and developing some preliminary hedonic and benefit transfer estimates to start the analysis and decision-making process.

With the exception of dredging of toxics from the Mahoning River, fully subsidized septic upgrades, and the impact on drinking water treatment costs of farming practices and pesticide use in the Maumee River Basin, the benefit–cost results are quite robust. In other words, most of our analyses of various water quality and infrastructure improvements in the eight case study rivers show relatively large net benefits to society. The eight case study rivers were chosen to be representative of rivers in the Great Lakes region of the US. However, further evidence would be helpful in determining both the representativeness of this sample of rivers and how well the results can be generalized. The next section attempts to provide some of this evidence.

TOWARD GENERALIZATION OF RESULTS

One way to start the process of generalizing the foregoing research results would be to inventory the major rivers in the Great Lakes area or related drainage basins and compare them to the eight case study rivers in this book. Some key supply side factors such as river length, flow, water quality and selected infrastructure as well as demand-side factors such as income and education of the surrounding population could be utilized in the comparisons. The map in Figure 12.1 names and locates the main rivers in the Lake Erie Drainage Basin. Similar inventories also could be done in other Great Lakes and regions of the United States, Canada, or Europe where similar conditions prevail.

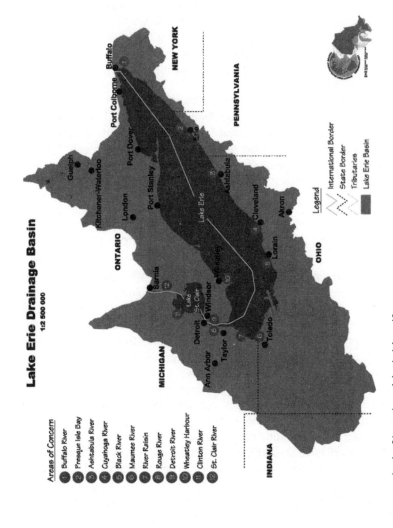

Source: www.epa.gov/region2/water/greatlakes/eriebas.gif.

Figure 12.1   Lake Erie Drainage Basin

Another alternative would be to identify major rivers in the Great Lakes region or other areas that have serious water quality or other problems. These rivers could then be paired with one or more of the eight rivers studied in this research. The US Environmental Protection Agency has used a similar strategy in their Areas of Concern (AOC) designation to target clean up of the most polluted areas in the Great Lakes regions of the United States and Canada. A total of 25 rivers in the Great Lakes region have been given this designation including two in the Lake Erie Basin, the Maumee and the Cuyahoga which were included as case studies in this book. See Figure 12.1 and Table 12.1 for location and characteristics of these Lake Erie Basin rivers.

A more detailed approach to generalization of results would be to propose specific benefit transfers from the case study rivers analyzed in this book to other rivers of concern. Benefit transfer is "easier said than done" and getting highly accurate and reliable results can be extremely difficult. The following section illustrates some of the difficulties when attempting to utilize benefit transfer to generalize research results on the Ballville Dam removal (Chapter 4) and two other dam removals in the Great Lakes Region.

BENEFIT TRANSFER AND DAM REMOVAL

It is generally agreed that primary research that involves data collection, is a "first-best" strategy when performing a cost–benefit analysis because it facilitates the gathering of statistical information that is relevant and specific to the action or resource being evaluated; however, there are occasions where primary research may not be a viable option due to (1) budget constraints, (2) time limitations, and/or (3) because the resource impacts are expected to be low or insignificant. In all three cases, not accounting for the economic value of the action or resource, but giving it a zero value in the analysis, would be a "worst-best" scenario. When primary research is not an option, but an evaluation of the proposed change is necessary, then benefit transfer is a commonly proposed "second-best" strategy.

Benefit transfer is defined as the adaptation and use of economic information derived from a specific site(s) under certain resource and policy conditions to a site with similar resources and conditions (Rosenberger and Loomis, 2001). Typically, the site with the original data is called the "study" site, while the site to which the data is transferred is called the "policy" site. While this methodology tends to be less costly than primary data collection in terms of both money and time, it may be valid and reliable only under certain conditions, and even when these conditions are satisfied there may be additional limitations associated with the application of benefit transfer.

The Great Lakes Protection Fund is interested in exploring the relevance of benefit-transfer for dam removal policy for a variety of reasons, including the growing national trend of dam removal and the high costs of primary data collection.

Conditions for Performing Benefit Transfer

Rosenberger and Loomis (2001) list several necessary conditions that must be satisfied in order to perform an effective and efficient benefit transfer. First, the context of the policy site needs to be thoroughly defined both by the extent and magnitude of the expected resource change, as well as the extent and magnitude of the population that will be affected by the impacts. It is also necessary to identify the type of measurement to be used, the kinds of values to be measured as well as the degree of certainty the researcher has in the data to be transferred.

Secondly, the study site must meet certain conditions critical for benefit transfer. Without quality study site data, there is little or no chance for a successful benefit transfer. It is important that the original study, or studies, use sound economic methods and the correct empirical techniques. The study must also contain statistical information on the relationship between the benefits and the demographic and physical characteristics of the site.

Finally, correspondence between study and policy sites should exhibit a sufficient level of similarity in terms of the nature of the environmental change, the market for the environmental commodity and the demographic characteristics of the affected population. It is also important that the quality and types of recreational activities between the two sites do not vary greatly in terms of such things as intensity, duration, and skill requirements.

It is the case that most primary research was not done with the idea of future benefit transfer applications in mind. Because of that, it is not always possible to meet the above conditions using original data and it is important that the cost of performing benefit transfers with incomplete information be accounted for by the researcher.

Potential Limitations of Benefit Transfer

The first group of factors that potentially limits the reliability and validity of benefit transfers relates to the general quality of the original study. Benefit transfer estimates can be no more reliable than the study site estimates on which they were based, and a key assumption in benefit transfer is that the data from the study site correctly estimate the true values for the environmental good in question. The quality of the benefit transfer process

Table 12.1 *River characteristics*

Site name	Drainage area (total/Mi^2)	River length (Mi)	Water quality	Average streamflow (cubic feet/sec)	Average discharge (cubic feet/sec)	Land use			Population
						Agriculture	Urban[a]	Forest[b]	
Buffalo River	487	–	Impaired				Mainly urban		21 633
Ashtabula River	137		Good**	488 (at will.)	324 (at will.)	Mainly agricultural and wooded			
Cuyahoga River	813	100	Fair**	1404 (at Indep)	866 (at Indep)	Forest > urban > agriculture*			
Black River	467	109	Fair/Poor**		377	Mostly agricultural**			
Maumee River (IN)		25				Mostly agricultural*			
Maumee River (OH)		105	Poor*			Mostly agricultural*			
River Raisin (MI)	132	40	Impaired			Mostly agricultural and forest*			

Rouge River (MI)	438	125	Impaired	> 50%	> 50 miles	1.5 million
Detroit River (MI)	810	32	Impaired	Mainly urban		
Clinton River (MI)	760	80	Impaired	Forest > urban > agriculture*		
St Clair River (MI)		40	Impaired	Mainly agricultural		

Notes:

The above data without * are based on EPA website data at www.epa.gov/grtlakes/aoc/index.html.

The data marked with * are based on source from www.heidelberg.edu/offices/wql/Unit_Area_Loads.pdf.

The data marked with ** are based on source from http://www.glc.org/basin/pubs/projects/oh_CREPWatQual_pubs01.pdf.

[a] Includes residential and industrial/commercial/transportation.

[b] Includes Anderson Classes: mixed forest, deciduous forest, evergreen forest and woody wetlands.

The data containing streamflow and discharge are based on USGS gaging station and some of them are updated to 2004, some of them never updated.

Below are detailed breakdown of water status according to EPA data 2002 at:

1. http://iaspub.epa.gov/tmdl/w305b_report_v2.huc?p_huc=04090001&p_state=MI.

2. http://oaspub.epa.gov/waters/w305b_report_v2.state?p_state=OH#total_assessed_waters.

is directly related to the quality of the original study. As Rosenberger and Loomis (2001) note, this is the "garbage-in, garbage-out" factor.

A second limitation is the availability of existing studies. The availability of original valuation studies that match the context of a specific policy site may be limited because of variation in site characteristics or available substitutes and, as noted previously, even if a sufficiently similar study site is found, most primary research was not designed for benefit transfer purposes.

A third group of potentially limiting factors is related to methodological issues. Differences across study sites in research methods and statistical analysis can lead to large differences in the values estimated. Variation in research methods, such as what questions are asked, how the questions are asked, and how environmental impacts are measured can affect estimates, and similarly, model misspecification or the choice of functional form can affect the statistical analysis.

Accounting for the availability of substitute goods is important when estimating the value of a proposed resource change. Failure to collect study site data on the availability of substitutes and the prices of substitutes can limit the completeness of the original data. It is important for the researcher to also be aware of the types of values measured in the original study – use versus nonuse, and apply the values appropriately in the benefit transfer application.

Fourth, the level of similarity between the study site and the policy site is an important factor when determining the efficiency and effectiveness of benefit transfer. Variation in the characteristics of the two sites, such as site location, site quality or difference in quality changes, can all affect the estimated values. It may also be the case that either the study site or policy site has a unique characteristic(s) (that is, endangered species, historical landmark) not found in the other site.

Finally, there is the issue of data stability over time. Original studies were done at various points in time, and if relevant differences exist between then and now they may not be measurable or identifiable. All of the factors listed above have the potential to lead to error or bias in the method. One of the main objectives of a benefit transfer is to minimize the mean square error between the "true" value and the transferred value of impacts at the policy site. A potential problem is that the "true" values are only approximations derived from data at the study site, and are therefore subject to error themselves. A number of recent studies have tested the convergent validity and reliability of various benefit transfer methods (for example, Loomis et al., 1995; Rosenberger and Loomis, 2001). The general indication of these studies has been that benefit transfer cannot replace original research, especially when the costs of being wrong are high, such as in court case evidence (Rosenberger and Loomis, 2001).

Types of Benefit Transfer Methods

When conducting benefit transfer, there are three broadly defined approaches: (1) value transfer and (2) expert judgment and (3) function transfer (Bergstrom and De Civita, 1999). Value transfers involve the transfer of a single (point) estimate from the study site, or a measure of central tendency of the estimates from several study sites, such as mean or median value. An example of a value transfer would be estimating the total benefits of fishing at the policy site to be the product of the estimated value per fishing day at the study site and the total number of fishing days at the policy site (Vincent et al., 1986).

Expert judgment methods use an expert opinion or judgment process to estimate total benefits at the policy site. For example, the policy site benefits could be estimated as the product of an expert judgment value of fishing value per day at the study site and the number of fishing days at the policy site. Finally, function transfers involve either the transfer of a benefit or demand function from the study site, or a meta-regression analysis which involves several study sites. The functions are then fitted to the characteristics of the specific policy site and the adopted function is used to predict a benefit estimate for the policy site. Again using fishing as an example, the total benefits at the policy site might be estimated using a demand function derived from study site recreational data.

Procedure

The first step of the benefit transfer procedure (Figure 12.2) is to identify the policy site context, or in other words, define and quantify the resource(s) that will be affected by the proposed policy. This includes not only defining the various economic benefits associated with the change, but also the provisions and quality levels of those benefits (Fischhoff and Furby, 1988). Some examples include assessing the extent of the expected impacts on site or resource attributes, such as water quality, aquatic habitat, and fish spawning levels. Socioeconomic characteristics of the affected population such as age, income, and recreation participation levels may also need to be determined. The last part of the initial step is to identify the resource commodity, the market for the resource, and the nature of the change. These characteristics must exhibit sufficient similarity between the study and policy site in order to perform an efficient benefit transfer (Rosenberger and Loomis, 2001).

The second step involves a thorough search of the literature for relevant study sites. This can be done using traditional search procedures such as reviewing journal articles, citations, books, and government reports, or by

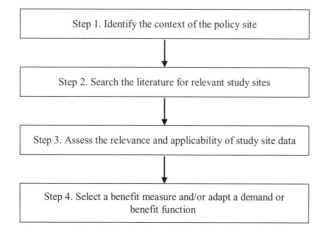

Source: Taken from Rosenberger and Loomis (2001).

Figure 12.2 Procedure for performing a benefit transfer

using electronic research databases such as the Environmental Valuation Reference Inventory (EVRI) or the Social Science Citation Index. While the number and variety of valuation studies continues to increase, it does not necessarily mean that finding a quality study site is easy. Boyle and Bergstrom (1992) note that "while a large number of valuation studies have been conducted, the number of study sites actually relevant to a particular issue may be limited." This may be due to a variety of factors, such as the uniqueness of the site-specific characteristics of either the study site or policy site, or to differences in the methodology used for each study.

The third step is to assess the relevance and applicability of study site data selected for the benefit transfer. Values from potential study sites need to be examined to determine whether or not they are suitable for transfer. In order to objectively evaluate potential study site values, Boyle and Bergstrom (1992) suggest the following idealized technical criteria: (1) the nonmarket commodity valued at the study site must be identical to the nonmarket commodity to be valued at the policy site; (2) the populations affected by the nonmarket commodity at both sites have identical characteristics; and (3) the assignment of property rights at both sites must lead to the same theoretical appropriate welfare measure.

Independent of equivalence between study site and policy site characteristics, the quality of the original study must also be evaluated in terms of its theoretical construction, data collection procedures, statistical application, and application of nonmarket values. In cases where site characteristics, socio-demographic characteristics, and/or the nature of the proposed policy are not identical between study site and policy site it may be necessary to systematically adjust study site values and/or use supplemental data. Benefit transfer values may also be improved through the collection of primary data on the key site and socio-demographic characteristics at the policy site. Such information may assist in determining the feasibility of a benefit transfer and improve the necessary adjustments of policy site values.

The final step in the process involves the selection of a benefit measure and/or demand or benefit function. As discussed previously, this could be a value transfer, such as a point estimate or average value, or a function transfer, such as a demand/benefit function or meta-analysis benefit function.

For several reasons the issue of dam removal is one that appears ideal for benefit transfer application. First, a growing number of dams are being considered for removal. There are now over 76 000 dams listed on the National Registry, and an estimated 2 million dams of smaller size. Over 50 percent of the dams officially accounted for in the United States will be up for license renewal in the next decade (Liggett, 2002) and 80 percent will have exceeded their typical life expectancy by the year 2020. A shift in changing social values has also prompted owners of small dams and/or dams no longer used for economic purposes to reconsider the maintenance/removal issue.

In many cases, the issue of dam removal involves assessing the impacts dam removal would have on a variety of nonmarket goods and services (for example, ecology of the watershed, local riparian species, public recreation). Collecting primary data for each specific dam would be expensive and time intensive, and budget and/or time constraints may mean that primary data collection is not always a viable option. Even with sufficient finances, primary data collection may not be justified because the expected resource impacts of removing the dam are low or insignificant, especially in the case of low-head dams or dams that have already been breached. All of this suggests that the use of a method other than traditional primary data collection, such as benefit transfer, would be advantageous.

As discussed in the section on benefit transfer procedures, there are a number of key characteristics that must be identified at both the study site and policy site. In order for the benefit transfer to be efficient there needs to be sufficient similarity between study site and policy site for each of these characteristics (see Table 12.2).

KEY CHARACTERISTICS TO IDENTIFY

In order to examine the level of similarity among proposed dam removal sites, key characteristics (as suggested above) for three different proposed

Table 12.2   Characteristics that require identification at both study and policy sites

---

(1) The resource affected by the proposed policy
(2) The extent of the expected site or resource impacts
(3) The population affected (extent and magnitude)
(4) Socio-demographic characteristics of the affected population
(5) Site characteristics
(6) The commodity, market, and nature of the change

---

dam removal sites were identified and put into a matrix (see Table 12.3). The three dams are all part of a study being done at The Ohio State University and are all located in the Great Lakes Watershed. Each dam was initially chosen for the study (1) because it was being considered for removal, and (2) because an initial assessment of all three dams suggested that they were sufficiently similar for comparison. In other words, these dams were chosen with the expectation that they would be sufficiently similar for a benefit transfer application.

All three dams were built in the early 1900s to be used as a source of hydropower and are of relatively similar dimensions (height and length). But there are few additional similarities. Only one of the dams is still used to produce hydroelectricity while of the other two, the reservoir behind one serves as a city's water supply and the other is not being used at all. One dam is listed on the National Register of Historic Places, while another dam is located on a designated Scenic River, which would inevitably be improved by its removal. Recreation on all three rivers consists mainly of boating, fishing, and swimming, but the levels of all three types of recreation vary greatly, as does the variety of fish available for sport fishing.

While education level, race, and age distribution are all similar between the three communities located closest to the dams, population density and per capita income vary significantly, and the community with the lowest per capita income faces losing \$220 000 annually in tax revenue from Consumer's Energy (owner of the dam) if the dam is removed.

Finally, a comparison of the advantages and disadvantages of removing each dam demonstrates the effects removal would have on the river, the environment, and the local community. Removing all three dams would improve natural fish movements by increasing the length of free-flowing river and improving water quality; however, the removal of the Croton Dam would mean the loss of a National Historic Place, the loss of hydropower, the loss of a reservoir for recreation and the loss of almost \$250 000 in tax revenue annually for the local community. On the other

Table 12.3 Comparison of key characteristics for three dams

BT conditions Resource Proposed change	Study site Ballville Dam Dam removal	Policy site 1 Sturgeon Dam Dam removal	Policy site 2 Croton Dam Dam removal
Advantages	1. Improve fish spawning habitat through increasing length of free-flowing river and improving water quality 2. Provide additional recreational land and recreational opportunities 3. Scenic river restoration/ preservation 4. Increase potential for commerce during fish spawning runs	1. Improve natural fish movements through increasing length of free-flowing river and improved water quality 2. Renew habitat for smallmouth bass, cool-water forage fish and aquatic plant and insect communities 3. Creation of relatively rare seasonally flooded wetlands and deciduous floodplain forest 4. Public access to previously submerged steep-walled rock canyon with waterfalls and rapids 5. Increase recreational opportunities 6. Economic savings for Wis. Electric	1. Improve natural fish movements through increasing length of free-flowing river and improved water quality
Disadvantages	1. Loss of Fremont water supply 2. Lost "lake" atmosphere for property owners 3. Lost "lake" atmosphere for recreation	1. 248 acres of lake habitat lost 2. Loss of portage and boat launches as well as lake based recreation 3. Loss of $25 000 in tax revenue annually	1. Loss of hydropower 2. Loss of National Historic Place 3. Loss of lake area for recreation 4. Loss of $22 000 in tax revenue annually

Table 12.3 (continued)

	Study site	Policy site 1	Policy site 2
BT conditions Resource **Proposed change**	Ballville Dam Dam removal	Sturgeon Dam Dam removal	Croton Dam Dam removal
	4. Increased soil erosion potential along river 5. Short-term impacts relative to existing sediment removal and transport	4. Short-term impacts relative to existing sediment stabilization and transport downstream	
Bearer of cost	Unknown (public)	Wisconsin Electric (private)	Unknown
Project status	No decision to remove has been made	First stage of removal is completed	No decision to remove has been made
Time line	Cannot remove before 2014	In the process of being removed	Cannot remove before 2034
Cultural norms **Site characteristics**	Mid-western United States Built in 1911	Mid-western United States Built in 1924	Mid-western United States Built in 1907
Length	121.9 m	66.1 m	233 m
Maximum height	10.5 m	16.2 m	12.2 m
Classification	High hazard	High hazard	High hazard
Uses	City water supply	Hydroelectric power (no longer used)	Industry, processing, extraction and hydroelectric energy
Proximity to major population	2.4 km from Fremont, OH (pop. 17 648)	2.8 km from Loretto, MI	14.48 km from Newaygo, MI (pop. 1670)

	Sandusky River	Sturgeon River	Muskegon River
Sediment behind the dam	At least partially contaminated	Not contaminated	Not contaminated
River name	Sandusky River	Sturgeon River	Muskegon River
River/dam classification	Scenic river since 1970	–	National Register of Historic Places
Water quality	Poor in the spring	Meets MDEQ standards	Meets MDEQ standards
Endangered species	Bald eagles	Bald eagles, Osprey	Karner blue butterfly
Current recreational uses	Fishing, canoeing	Boating, canoeing	Fishing, boating, picnicking, swimming
After removal recreational uses	Fishing, canoeing	Kayaking, canoeing, fishing, hiking	Unknown
Potential for soil erosion	None	None	Unknown
Demographics	Sandusky County, Ohio	Dickinson County, Michigan	Newaygo County, Michigan
Land area	409 sq. miles	766 sq. miles	842 sq. miles
Population per square mile	151.0	35.8	56.8
Population	61 673 (2001)	27 291 (2001)	49 013 (2002)
Per capita income	$23 315 (1999)	$23 402 (1999)	$16 976 (1999)
Education	82.1% high school graduates, 11.9% with bachelor's degree or higher	88.8% high school graduates, 16.7% with bachelor's degree or higher	78.7% high school graduates, 11.4% with bachelor's degree or higher
Age distribution	26.2% under 18, 14.5% over 65 (2000)	25.1% under 18, 18.1% over 65 (2000)	29.1% under 18, 12.8% over 65 (2000)
Primary employment	Manufacturing, trade, services and government	Government, manufacturing, construction and retail	Manufacturing, retail trade, education, health, social services

hand, the removal of the Sturgeon Dam led to economic savings for Wisconsin Electric, created a relatively rare seasonally flooded wetlands and deciduous floodplain forest, and gave public access to a previously submerged steep-walled rock canyon with waterfalls and rapids.

ASSESSING THE QUALITY AND APPLICABILITY OF ORIGINAL DAM REMOVAL STUDIES

There are several ways to assess the quality of an original study. First, the internal validity of the study can be examined. In other words, the study must include sufficient information to assess both validity and reliability of the results. This refers to such things as reporting the estimated WTP function, the statistical techniques used, the definition of variables included in the model, and any data manipulation (Brouwer, 2000).

Another way to assess the quality of an original study is by looking at the external validity of the study. According to Brouwer (2000), unlike the travel cost or hedonic pricing methods, contingent valuation allows for such an assessment through the survey format itself, that is, via response rates, protest bids, and stated reasons for WTP by respondents. Reporting of these results is not always standard practice, but perhaps should be as such information may be important in determining whether or not a particular study is suitable for benefit transfer.

The issues of availability of quality original studies, and the applicability of these studies to the policy site are closely related to the idea of site similarity. While the number of dams, especially low-head dams, being removed is increasing, there are still only a limited number of valuation studies that deal with willingness to pay for dam removal. Using four completed studies on dam removal, Table 12.4 illustrates the differences not only in basic dam/site characteristics, but also in survey design, implementation and analysis.

In almost every category listed for comparison, dissimilarities were found. Basic geography and dam location varied as studies were conducted in the Pacific Northwest, and the Northeast. The heights of the dams being considered for removal ranged from 64 m to a mere 5.2 m. In most cases the major concern was assessing WTP to improve fish populations and spawning habitat, though some studies also looked at recreational opportunities, improved water quality and river restoration, though in each study the major species of fish affected was different.

Another major area of difference was the extent of impact dam removal would have. The Elwha and Glines Canyon dams removal was expected to have a national impact due to the expected ecological improvements, the four species of fish involved (salmon and steelhead) and the proximity of

Table 12.4   Comparison of key elements in past dam removal studies

	Edwards Dam (Boyle et al., 1991)	Newport No. 11 Dam (Gilbert et al., 1996)	Elwha and Glines Canyon Dams (Loomis, 1996)
Proposed change	Dam removal	Dam removal	Dam removal
Location	Maine	Vermont	Washington
Dam height	7.3 m	5.2 m	33 m and 64 m
Species affected	9 species of migratory fish	Salmon	Salmon/steelhead
Extent of impact	Local/regional	Regional	National
Method	Contingent valuation	Contingent valuation	Contingent valuation
Sample	Maine residents and non-residents with fishing licenses	County and state	County, state and national
Sample size	n/a	n/a	600, 900, 1000
Response rate	n/a	n/a	77%, 68%, 55%
Survey type	n/a	Telephone	Mail
Values measured	Use (anglers only)	Use and nonuse	Use and nonuse
WTP question	n/a	OE	DC
WTP estimate	n/a	Mean: $67, $52	Mean: $59, $73, $68
Benefits estimate	$36–48 million (recreational anglers only)	$390 000 (county residents only)	$94–138 million annual (local) $3.5–6.3 billion annual (nat'l)
Time frame	n/a	n/a	10 years

	4 Snake River Dams (Loomis, 2002)	Ballville Dam (Kruse, 2004)	Fort Covington Dam (Warren, 2004)
Proposed change	Dam removal	Dam removal	Dam removal
Location	Washington	Ohio	New York
Dam height	30 m for all	10.5 m	3 m
Species affected	Chinook salmon	Walleye	Walleye and Eastern sand darter
Extent of impact	Regional	Local/regional	Local

Table 12.4   (continued)

	4 Snake River Dams (Loomis, 2002)	Ballville Dam (Kruse, 2004)	Fort Covington Dam (Warren, 2004)
Method	Travel cost method	Contingent valuation	Contingent valuation
Sample	Boat ramp visitors and Pacific NW/ California households	County and 30-mile radius	City and county
Sample size	10 000	724, 250	300, 300
Response rate	43.5%	35%, 21%	43%, 23.5%
Survey type	Mail	Mail and SEG	Mail
Values measured	Use (recreational)	Use and nonuse	Use and nonuse
WTP question	–	DC and OE	DC
WTP estimate	–	Mean: $43, $44	Mean: $30, $71
Benefits estimate	$193–311 million annual (recreational values only)	$1 206 246 (county) $17 442 523 (30-mile)	$167 876 (city) $722 628 (county)
Time frame	100 years	NPV	NPV

the dams to Olympic National Park. On the other hand, the removal of the Edwards Dam is expected to only have a local impact based on the size of the dam, the significance of the river, and the expected ecological improvements of dam removal.

Three of the four studies used contingent valuation (CV) methodology, but only two of the four chose to measure both use and nonuse values. Of the two that chose to measure only use values, one measured all recreational values while the other only estimated the value of dam removal to recreational anglers. Survey samples varied from licensed anglers and boat ramp visitors, to a random stratified sample consisting of county, state, and national strata.

Benefits were aggregated across different populations in each study as well. Two of the studies estimated the benefits of dam removal to recreational users and anglers, while the other two aggregated both use and nonuse values across local and/or national populations. The stream of benefits for one study was estimated for a 100-year time frame, while another used a 10-year time frame.

CONCLUSION

Standardizing the methodology used in dam removal studies would not only allow for comparison between completed studies, but also allow for an assessment of the applicability of studies for benefit transfer. Guidelines should include such things as basic methods for completing a contingent valuation study on dam removal (that is, sample frame, area to sample), examples of surveys and cover letters that relate specifically to dam removal, and a sample format of how to correctly report data. Providing a detailed summary of a CV survey is important for two reasons: (1) it allows the research to be critiqued by others, and (2) it provides an open example from which other researchers can learn. Every CV study should clearly report such items as the sample population, the sampling frame, the sample size, nonresponse rate and components, and item nonresponse for important questions.

The comparison of dams in the previous section provides convincing evidence that dam removal not only involves a large number of key variables, but also that these variables are likely to differ significantly between removal scenarios. One question still unanswered is whether this variation significantly affects WTP for dam removal, and if so, which attributes or indicators are more influential.

Many difficulties have been encountered in this detailed attempt to generalize findings from our dam removal case through benefit transfer methods. One might ask if similar difficulties would be likely in the other specific river water quality and infrastructure changes or improvements evaluated in this research effort. For example, riverine greenways and trails appear to be less complex in their outputs and benefits than dam removal, and dam removal outputs/benefits may be less complex than those from dredging of toxics or protecting endangered aquatic species. The answer to this question is unclear without further efforts at codifying, particularly the various nonmarket costs and benefits flowing from river and other natural resource degradation and restoration efforts. This codification effort would appear to be a worthy next step in the evolution of natural resource and environmental economic analysis. One might view it as a hopefully less complex and costly counterpart to the human genome mapping effort, currently underway at several university and private research labs.

REFERENCES

Bergstrom, J.C. and P. De Civita (1999), "Status of benefits transfer in the United States and Canada: a review," *Canadian Journal of Agricultural Economics*, **47**, 79–87.

Boyle, K.J. and J.C. Bergstrom (1992), "Benefit transfer studies: myths, pragmatism, and idealism," *Water Resources Research*, **28** (3), 657–63.

Boyle, K.J., M.F. Teisl, and S.D. Reiling (1991), *Economic Benefits Accruing to Sport Fisheries on the Lower Kennebec River from the Provision of Fish Passage at Edwards Dam or from the Removal of Edwards Dam*, prepared for the Maine Department of Marine Resources, Augusta, Maine.

Brouwer, R. (2000), "Environmental value transfer: state of the art and future prospects," *Ecological Economics*, **32**, 137–52.

Fischhoff, B. and L. Furby (1988), "Measuring values: a conceptual framework for interpreting transactions with special reference to contingent valuation of visibility," *Journal of Risk and Uncertainty*, **1**, 147–84.

Gilbert, A.H., L.G. Frymier, and K. Dolan (1996), *The Clyde River Valuation Study: A Research Report on the Value of Dam Removal and Landlocked Salmon Restoration on the Clyde River to Vermont State Residents*, prepared for the Vermont Natural Resources Council, Montpelier, Vermont.

Kruse, S. (2005), "Creating an interdisciplinary framework for economic valuation: a CVM application to dam removal," PhD dissertation, AED Economics Department, The Ohio State University, Columbus, Ohio.

Liggett, J.A. (2002), "What is hydraulic engineering?" *Journal of American Society Civil Engineers*, **128**, 1–10.

Loomis, J.B. (1996), "Measuring the economic benefits of removing dams and restoring the Elwha River: results of a contingent valuation survey," *Water Resources Research*, **32** (2), 441–7.

Loomis, J.B. (2002), "Quantifying recreation use values from removing dams and restoring free-flowing rivers: a contingent behavior travel cost demand model for the Lower Snake River," *Water Resources Research*, **38** (6), 21–8.

Loomis, J.B., B. Roach, F. Ward and R. Ready (1995), "Testing the transferability of recreation demand models across regions: a study of Corps of Engineers reservoirs," *Water Resources Research*, **31** (3), 721–30.

Rosenberger, R. and J.B. Loomis (2001), *Benefit Transfer of Outdoor Recreation Use Values*, Fort Collins, CO: US Dept. of Agriculture, Forest Service.

Vincent, M.K., D. Mosher and W.J. Hansen (1986), *National Economic Development Procedures Manual: Recreation. Volume I: Recreation Use and Benefit Estimation Techniques*, IWR Report 86-R-4. Fort Belvoir, VA: Water Resources Support Center, Institute for Water Resources, US Army Corps of Engineers.

Warren, D.W. (2004), "An estimation of the economic benefits of low-head dam removal," MS thesis, AED Economics Department, The Ohio State University, Columbus, Ohio.

Index